Lodging in Britain's Monasteries

Eileen Barish

All Hallows Convent, page 25

Inexpensive Accommodations
Remarkable Historic Buildings
Legendary Locations

Lodging in Britain's Monasteries
by Eileen Barish

Anacapa Press
7320 East Sixth Avenue, Scottsdale, AZ 85253
Tel: (800) 638-3637
www.monasteriesofbritain.com

ISBN #1-884465-28-5
Library of Congress Control Number: 2008912117
Printed and bound in the United States of America

Also by Eileen Barish

Lodging in Italy's Monasteries
www.monasteriesofitaly.com

Lodging in Spain's Monasteries
www.monasteriesofspain.com

Lodging in France's Monasteries
www.monasteriesoffrance.com

While due care has been exercised in the compilation of this directory, we are not responsible for errors or omissions. Information changes and we are sorry for any inconvenience that might occur. Inclusion in this guide does not constitute endorsement or recommendation by the author or publisher. It is intended as a guide to assist in providing information to the public and the listings are offered as an aid to travelers.

SPECIAL SALES

Copies of this book are available at special discounts when purchased in bulk for fund-raising and educational use as well as for premiums and special sales promotions. Custom editions and book excerpts can also be produced to specification. For details, call 1-800-638-3637.

Claret Center, page 18

Acknowledgements

Launde Abbey, page 58

This book would not have been possible without the diligent efforts of Francesca Pasquini, our research manager and colleague. From the onset, her determination and thoroughness was apparent in every stage of the project. Not only did she carefully document the research data accumulated from hundreds of interviews, but she filled her reports with insight into Britain, its customs, traditions, geography, linguistics and enchanting peculiarities. Thank you Francesca. Understanding the consuming nature of research, we are grateful to Dario Pasquini for his patience.

Since nothing in life is possible without love and encouragement, I am eternally grateful to Harvey, my number one champion. And to Nona, Kenny, Chris and especially to Katie for always believing.   Eileen Barish

Credits

Author — Eileen Barish
Publisher and Managing Editor — Harvey Barish
Senior Researcher — Francesca Pasquini
Cover Design — Tom Blanck
Book Layout — Boothe Heffington

∞

The author and publisher are greatly indebted to the people and organizations that so generously supplied the photos for this book. First and foremost we would like to thank the monasteries, convents and retreats that provided the photos used to illustrate their institutions. We are also grateful to the local and regional tourist bureaus throughout Britain.

Chester House, page 82

How To Use This Guide

This book is an introduction to Britain's monasteries, convents and retreat houses that extend hospitality to guests. It is organized as follows:

Section One: Monasteries offering hospitality to all

These establishments welcome everyone regardless of religion, with or without a spiritual purpose. Listings in Section One describe the monastery, its setting, history, architecture, artwork, products made by the order, folklore and surrounding tourist sites. It provides all the information needed to make an informed lodging decision and the wherewithal to reserve a room including:

Accommodations

Type and number of rooms, indicating private (en-suite) or shared baths.

Amenities

Meals and facilities available to guests.

Cost of lodging

Lodging and meal rates are approximate. Some rates are quoted on a per person basis while others are per room. When no rate is given, the monastery or convent either requests only a donation or reserves the right to determine the rate when reservations are made, depending on the number of people, number of meals and time of the year.

Directions

Directions to each location are provided by car and public transportation.

Contact

Information includes the person in charge of hospitality, address, telephone, fax and where available, website and email address. An example follows.

Contact person	The Warden
Name of Monastery	Launde Abbey
Address	East Norton
City, Zone, Country	Leicestershire, LE7 9XB, England, UK
Tel/Fax	0044 (0) 1572 717454
Website	www.launde.org.uk
Email address	laundeabbey@leicester.anglican.org

Section Two: Monasteries offering hospitality for spiritual endeavors.

These establishments welcome guests specifically for retreat, vocation or other spiritual purposes. Listings in Section Two include the basic contact information necessary to make a reservation.

Table of Contents

Section One:
Monasteries offering hospitality to all

Table of Contents

Table of Contents

Section Two:
Monasteries offering hospitality for spiritual endeavors

Caldey Abbey, page 330

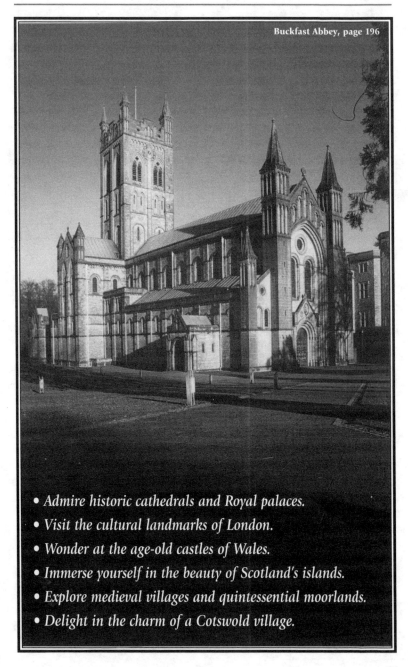

Buckfast Abbey, page 196

- *Admire historic cathedrals and Royal palaces.*
- *Visit the cultural landmarks of London.*
- *Wonder at the age-old castles of Wales.*
- *Immerse yourself in the beauty of Scotland's islands.*
- *Explore medieval villages and quintessential moorlands.*
- *Delight in the charm of a Cotswold village.*

Introduction

Spend a night or a week at a monastery and come away filled with the essence of Britain, its history, art, architecture and local traditions

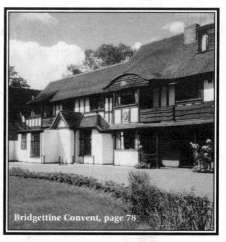

Bridgettine Convent, page 78

Awaken each morning in a charming hamlet, coastal village or bustling town. Mingle with the locals at the daily market. Stroll the medieval quarters and cobblestone streets of a quaint enclave. Have the quintessential English cup of tea or a foamy pint of ale at the corner pub. Admire idiosyncratic timber-framed houses and royal castles, thatched roof or grey stone cottages and Tudor mansions, as enchanting today as they were hundreds of years ago. Walk through ancient moorlands and heaths that are so much a part of Britain's landscape.

Open to all, regardless of religious denomination, lodging at monasteries, convents and retreat houses is a unique experience, a new approach to travel that Britons and other Europeans have been enjoying for decades, sometimes centuries. Whether you're seeking the sophistication of a city, the quaintness of the countryside or the simplicity of a tiny coastal village, each of the monasteries, convents and retreat houses described in this guide represents a singular experience, one that will linger long after you've returned home. They each share many welcoming attributes such as cleanliness, graciousness, beauty, safety and a divine sense of serenity.

But perhaps the most remarkable aspect of this niche travel experience is the very low cost of accommodations and meals. Rates range from a voluntary

Introduction

donation to an average of about £35 per night. Most include a full English breakfast and many serve lunch and dinner for a few additional pounds.

Monasteries, convents and retreat houses form an integral part of Britian's history and heritage and are emblematic of the diverse culture to be experienced. More than just lodging particulars, *Lodging in Britain's Monasteries* provides history-laced vignettes offering insight into the little known villages and places unspoiled by tourism; information not readily found in other guidebooks. In addition to extensive research into the small towns and villages of Britain, the customs, folklore, cultural landmarks, heritage and unusual geographical highlights of the regions are also covered.

Minsteracres Monastery and Retreat House, page 96

Monastic orders, including the associated diocese within the regions covered, have traditionally offered hospitality to travelers. This book introduces you to a remarkable travel resource and to a centuries-old custom that allows you to immerse yourself in another time and place; an unhurried venue, one of serenity and tranquility. Staying at a monastery or retreat house is a rewarding experience but it is important to remember that these destinations are not hotels or B&Bs and should be regarded accordingly.

Whether you're planning a trip to Britain or simply enjoy armchair travel, you will be enlightened and entertained by this guide.

Introduction

The monasteries, convents and retreat houses described in Section One offer hospitality to all without religious obligation.

The information necessary to plan a trip is included: contact person, address, telephone, fax, email address and website, amenities and a description of accommodations and rates. With this book you can make reservations over the Internet, by email, snail mail, fax or telephone. When calling or faxing, be certain to take into account any time difference in order to avoid waking someone in the middle of the night. For those institutions that offer email portals, we suggest emailing your requests.

Section Two is a listing of monasteries, convents and retreat houses that offer hospitality to guests who would like to participate in the religious life or simply experience a time of spiritual retreat and renewal. Pertinent contact information is provided.

Aylesford Priory, "The Friars", page 136

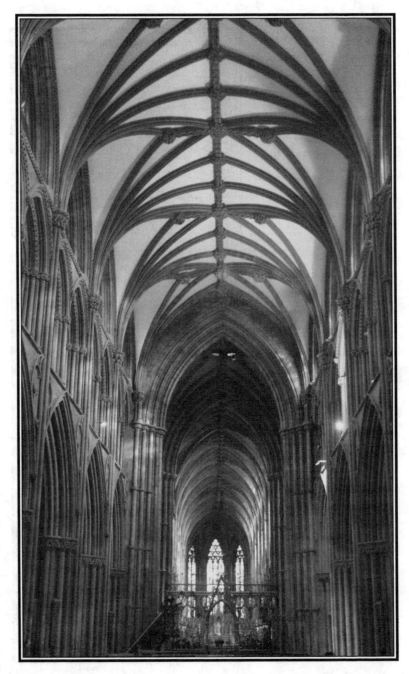

Section One

Monasteries Offering Hospitality to All

Regions of Britain

To assist readers in planning their trip, we have divided the listings into the regions of Britain indicated on the map above. These are the traditonal regions used by most of British tourist bureaus.

**EAST OF
ENGLAND**

Claret Centre
Claretian Missionaries

Region: East of England	County: Cambridgeshire	City: Buckden Towers

The Claretian Missionaries is a Roman Catholic order founded by Saint Anthony Claret, a Catalonian priest from Vic, Spain. The Claret Centre is in Buckden Towers in a magnificent setting formed by a 15th century palace and Victorian additions. It is secluded from the outside world by 15 acres of lovingly tended grounds and gardens.

Over the centuries Buckden (otherwise spelled Bugden) has been home to the Bishops of Lincoln. This, combined with its location on the Great North Road (which connected London to the north at the time of the Conquest), greatly increased the importance of the village. Buckden Palace is midway between London and Lincoln and has seen many royal visitors. The most famous is probably Queen Katherine of Aragon who was imprisoned in the palace from 1533 to 1534 by Henry VIII after the annulment of their marriage. In 1534 she was moved to Kimbolton Castle where she lived until her death in 1536.

Buckden Towers' nine-hundred-year history has been documented since the *Domesday Book of 1086*, a chronicle that registered the wealth of the country and thereby established the amount of revenue due to William I.

Church of St. Hugh

The modern church of St. Hugh takes its name from Hugh de Avalon, bishop from 1186 to 1200. He built a new house on the site to replace the original wooden structure. The works were completed by Robert Grosseteste, bishop from 1235 until 1253. It was during that time that the Great Hall was added to the complex.

Unfortunately a fire in 1291 destroyed most of the buildings. The new structures were completed between 1480 and 1514 by Bishops John Russell (whose arms appear on the inner gatehouse) and William Smith. Over the ensuing centuries, the fortune of Buckden Palace alternated between prosperity and decadence due to various political vicissitudes as well as the high cost of maintaining such a large property. In the 18th century the palace became popular with visitors but in the 19th century, its importance decreased and it was decided to demolish half of the main buildings and sell the materials and furnishings.

In 1974 the Claret Centre began offering hospitality for conferences and spiritual retreats. In 1988 responding to the appeal of the brothers, the house and property were completely restored. The moat was excavated and the gardens extensively embellished and developed. Today the Centre offers hospitality to individuals and groups for holidays, spiritual retreats and conferences. In addition to spiritual direction, a number of courses are offered as well.

Cambridgeshire is about an hour north of London in East Anglia. Situated on the River Cam, its most famous city is Cambridge, home of the university bearing the same name, a university that has dominated the town since the early 13th century. Smaller than Oxford but just as pretty and with a university equally revered, Cambridge is an enchanting tumble of ornate gateways and cobbled streets thronged with students. Each of the university buildings

Cambridge

has something special to recommend it. Trinity College, the largest college, boasts a massive court and hall. Henry VIII founded it in 1546 and its impressive gateway is a paragon of Tudor style; its library built by Sir Christopher Wren.

Built of white Yorkshire limestone, King's College is one of the finest buildings in Cambridge, a masterpiece of Late-Gothic architecture. King Henry VI laid the foundation stone in 1446 and dedicated it to the Virgin Mary. The fan-vaulted ceiling of King's College Chapel represents one of the finest examples of Perpendicular Gothic architecture in England. The ceiling is supported by 22 buttresses and was built by master stonemason John Wastell. This late medieval gem took 70 years to build. The stained glass windows are embellished with Tudor coats of arms and relate the story of Mary, Jesus and the Apostles. As first stipulated by Henry VI, daily services continue to be conducted by the world-famous choir.

Art lovers will appreciate the Fitzwilliam Museum whose galleries are festooned with works by masterly painters such as Gainsborough, Stubbs, Cezanne and Picasso.

For a good overview of the university, walk along The Backs where the lawns of six of the oldest colleges lead down to the River Cam. Outdoor enthusiasts might consider renting a punt, a flat-bottomed boat propelled by a long pole. Punting is enjoyed by students and visitors alike and punts can be hired from boatyards along the river.

Cambridgeshire itself is split into two very different landscapes; to the south are rolling chalk hills to the north the Fens. Drained in the 17th century the Fens represent a unique and distinctive area. Crisscrossed by waterways they offer incredible views and impressive sunsets and are home to some of Britain's most important nature reserves.

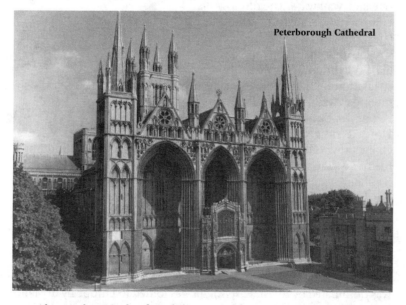

Peterborough Cathedral

Almost due north of Buckden, Peterborough was given cathedral status by Henry VIII in 1541. Formerly it had been one of the great Benedictine abbey churches but that ended with the Dissolution. Its wondrous Norman cathedral has a towering west front, one of the most impressive feats of medieval architecture in Britain and a unique painted nave ceiling. It shelters the tomb of Katherine of Aragon and was also the former burial place of Mary Queen of Scots.

East of Peterborough and considered the "Capital of the Fens," Wisbech is a lovely market town on the River Nene. Full of character and history, its heritage dates to 664 when it was first mentioned in a charter of the Saxon King Wulphere. The town is best known for its beautiful Georgian terraces of graceful architecture that flank the river. The most famous house on the banks of the river is Peckover House. Built in the 1720s, it is an important example of domestic architecture of the period and now belongs to the National Trust. It has fine paneled rooms and an outstanding Victorian garden.

Another town of the Fens is Spalding, famous as the center of the country's flower industry. Set on the River Welland, it possesses an attractive waterfront of grand Georgian terraces and pretty tree-edged riverside walkways. The old town is compact and easy to navigate. The Crescent has an appealing curved street with a charming mix of Georgian, Victorian and contemporary structures. Set in five acres of lush grounds, Ayscoughfee Hall Museum is one of the best in the region. Housed in a 15th century mer-

Spalding

chant's town house, the museum relates the story of the building's history. Models and interactive displays are used to bring Ayscoughfee's 500-year journey to life. The museum also explores the story of the South Lincolnshire Fens and the lives of its people from earliest times to the present.

The Fens is a tableau of dramatic skies, sweeping vistas that stretch for miles and wide-open landscapes. Long before the Romans invaded Britain there were over 2,500 square miles of Fens. This vast, flat landscape has a long and fascinating history. 10,000 years ago the land was dominated by forest. East Anglia was joined to Europe by dry land and her rivers were tributaries of the Rhine. As the Ice Age came to an end, the forest was flooded and the trees died and fell to form the rich peat soils that are cultivated today. Crisscrossed with peaceful waterways and cycling trails, the terrain is dotted with church spires and clusters of villages. There are many events held each year celebrating the history and heritage of this singular land including The Spalding Flower Parade, the Wisbech Rose Fair, the King's Lynn Festivals and Boston's Party in the Park.

Between Peterborough and Spalding is the market town of Crowland. Founded by St. Guthlac, a Benedictine monk born in 667 AD, he lived very simply and provided spiritual guidance for those who sought him out including King Ethelbald. After his death in 714 AD, the king built Crowland Abbey in his memory. The impressive remains of the medieval church are notable for their statues and a dogtooth Norman arch.

Accommodations (The Inner Gatehouse)

There are various types of accommodations. The Inner Gatehouse built in 1480 and then restored, is the home of the Claretian Missionaries and contains four self-catering apartments:

St. Michael: 4 beds in 2 double rooms with shower, toilet, kitchen and dining area.

St. David: 2 beds in 1 double room with bath/shower and toilet; kitchen with microwave cooker.

All Saints: 3 beds in a triple room with bath/shower and toilet; kitchen with microwave cooker.

St. Jude: 1 twin room with bath/shower and toilet; kitchen with microwave cooker.

Amenities

Meals are usually not supplied. Special requests can be made to the resident chef and paid separately. Towels and linens are supplied. Guests have access to the extensive grounds of the house.

Accommodations (The Great Tower)

The Great Tower: Built in 1480 it was turned into a seminary in the 1950s by the Claretians, then into a youth center in the 1970s and recently restored. There are two floors with 40 beds in two dormitories, each with 20 beds. Each floor has bathroom facilities plus accommodations for 2 leaders per floor.

Amenities

All meals can be supplied on request. There is also a fully equipped kitchen and dining room. Towels and linens are not provided. The King's Room can be used as a lounge, meeting room, dance hall and for medieval banquets.

Accommodations (The Main House)

The Main House: A fine 19th century Victorian building, the facilities are suitable for individuals and small groups. There are 15 twin rooms, some with private baths.

ENGLAND

Amenities

All meals can be provided with the lodging. There is a resident chef and it is possible to have B&B, half board or full board. Towels and linens are provided. There is a wide range of well-equipped meeting and conference facilities.

Cost per person/per night

Cost per person ranges between £12.50 (per night in a dorm) and £45 (full board in a twin room), depending on the type of accommodation and number of meals included. Price per apartment per night: £30 – £70 depending on the apartment and day of the week.

Special rules

Pets are not allowed. The house closes at 10:30 PM but arrangements can be made for later returns.

Directions

By car: From London take A1 north and exit at Buckden Towers. The Centre is located on High Street, just off A1, 2 miles south of the junction between A1 and A14.

By train: Take a train from London King's Cross to either Huntingdon or St. Neots and then a taxi to Buckden.

Contact

The Claret Centre
The Towers
High St
Buckden
St. Neots
Cambs. PE19 5TA
England, UK
Tel: 0044 (0)1480 810344
(Office hours are 9 - 5 Monday to Friday local time)
Website: www.buckden-towers.org.uk
Email: claret_centre@claret.org.uk

Region: East of England   County: Norfolk   City: Ditchingham

All Hallows Convent

Community of All Hallows Sisters

The Community of All Hallows is an Anglican order operating under the jurisdiction of the Church of England. Founded by Lavinia Crosse in 1855, it remains the largest Anglican community in England.

The work of the sisters focuses on hospitality and spiritual direction in its retreat and conference centers. The community also manages a guesthouse in Norwich. "It is a very open community," said Christine, secretary of the convent, "very much involved with social and spiritual activities." The community of sisters resides in one of the original 19th century brick buildings, whereas two of the three retreat houses dates to the 1960s.

All Hallows occupies a beautiful 47-acre site on the outskirts of the village of Ditchingham, near the historic town of Bungay, a vibrant and charming market town in a loop of the River Waveney. The town is steeped in history and is home to the remains of a Norman castle, Saxon church, Roman well and Benedictine priory.

The remains of the Norman castle, built by the Bigods in 1165, is offset by massive gatehouse towers, a bridge pit and curtain walls. The inner bailey, a pleasant grassed area, commands fine views across the Waveney Valley.

East Anglia, including Norfolk, is a region of flat, fertile farmlands stretching along a low coast bordering the North Sea and the Wash. A series of connected lakes, known as the Broads, occupies the eastern portion of the county and provides sanctuary for many forms of wildlife. The area is peppered with windmills, churches and medieval barns and is particularly appealing to nature enthusiasts drawn to its seal colonies and bird preserves. Throughout the region are distinctive cottages: pink-washed examples in Suffolk, flint cottages in Norfolk and thatched roofs everywhere attest to the captivating singularity of the landscape. The Berney Arms Windmill is the tallest in Norfolk. Built around 1870, the structure has seven floors. It was still in use as a windmill until 1951 and is now a tourist attraction.

Heading southwest of Ditchingham and the convent are numerous towns that perpetuate a rich historical heritage. Harleston is a traditional South Norfolk town that began as an ancient marketplace and stage post for travelers between London and Norwich. A market is still held every Wednesday. The town's history is mirrored in the Georgian buildings and other landmarks including the Italianate clock tower. In an alleyway off Broad Street is the mysterious Harleston Stone, an enigmatic block of granite that has inspired many local legends.

The appealing market town of Bury St. Edmunds is the burial place of King Edmund, last king of East Anglia. Killed by the Danes in the mid 9th century, his shrine became a pilgrimage site and the core of a new Benedictine monastery, now quaint ruins in the beautiful Abbey Gardens behind the cathedral. It is still easy to imagine the once impressive 11th century structure whose architecture included five massive gate towers. The best preserved ruins of the abbey are the two gateways that front onto the main street. Built in the first half of the 12th century, the taller tower, a massive and beautiful edifice highlighted by gargoyles, is of Norman provenance. The shorter gate provided access to the great court and the abbot's palace. Two octagonal turrets originally capped the upper story of the gate. During the Middle Ages the abbey was one of the most powerful of medieval Europe and noted for its illuminated manuscripts, one of which, the *Bury Bible*, is now in the keeping of Corpus Christi College in Cambridge. Among six of the richest Benedictine houses in England, it was one of only seven abbeys granted freedom from Episcopal domination. In 1214 English barons struggling against King John took an oath in the abbey to compel him to accept their demands. The result was the *Magna Carta*, the most famous document of British constitutional history.

Bury St. Edmunds prides itself on its storied history, atmospheric ruins and handsome Georgian architecture. Moyses Hall was built by a Jewish merchant in the 12th century and is believed to be the oldest surviving dwelling house in East Anglia. Today it shelters displays of Bronze Age archaeological finds, medieval artifacts and a diary of a 13th century monk. St. Mary's Church, ca. 15th century, is famous for its hammer-beam ceiling and contains the tomb of Mary Tudor, sister of Henry VIII. Queen Victoria had a stained glass window fitted into the church to commemorate Mary's interment. For a glimpse into the past, visit the churchyard of St. Mary's and peruse the intriguing burial tombs.

Continuing southwest from Bury St. Edmunds is the pretty little town of Saffron Walden. Set in a beautiful milieu, its name originates from the saffron harvested from the yellow crocuses that bloom in profusion throughout the area. This ancient town conserves a cluster of gabled and timber-framed buildings and a large Saxon cemetery. Some of the town's old houses showcase examples of pargeting, decorative patterned plastering. The finest example of this unusual decorative style can be seen in the Sun Inn. On Castle Hill stands the largest turf-cut maze in Britain.

Nearly due south of Bury St. Edmunds lies Ipswich, one of England's oldest towns. Its museum preserves replicas of the silverworks from the Roman Mildenhall Treasure and the Sutton Hoo Treasure, an ornately decorated purse lid believed to date to the 7th century. A gallery devoted to the town's origins includes Saxon weapons, jewelry and other artifacts.

Ipswich's history is reflected in parts of the ancient road that still exist as well as the earth ramparts that circle the town center. More than likely built by Vikings, the ramparts were meant to prevent re-capture of the town by the English but the Vikings' attempts to protect themselves proved unsuccessful.

Around 1380 Chaucer satirized the merchants of Ipswich in the *Canterbury Tales*. Cardinal Wolsey was born in Ipswich and became one of Henry VIII's closet advisors. Wolsey founded a college in Ipswich in 1528 and remains one of the town's noted native sons.

The Ancient House is accentuated by a particularly fine example of pargeting. It depicts scenes from the "four continents" of the world. When the hall was built in 1670, Australia was yet to be known as a single continent by Europeans.

Many celebrated artists and writers have lived and worked in Ipswich including Thomas Gainsborough and Charles Dickens who used the town as a setting for scenes in *The Pickwick Papers*. The hotel where he stayed was made famous in one of his chapters wherein he vividly described the hotel's meandering corridors and stairs.

Heading south along the coast from Ditchingham, Aldeburgh old fort is a charming seaside town where fishermen still draw their boats up onto the shore and sell their haul on the beach. The town survived as a fishing village until the 19th century when it became a popular seaside resort. Much of its distinctive and whimsical architecture derives from this period. It is internationally famous for the Aldeburgh Festival begun by Benjamin Britten and takes place in June each year. On Aldeburgh Beach stands an unusual sculpture, *The Scallop*, dedicated to Britten who often walked along the beach in the afternoons. Created from stainless steel by Suffolk-based artist Maggi Hambling, it stands four meters high and was unveiled in November 2003. The piece is comprised of two interlocking scallop shells, each broken, the

The Scallop

upright shell bearing the words: "I hear those voices that will not be drowned," taken from Britten's opera *Peter Grimes*. The sculpture is meant to be enjoyed both visually and tactilely and people are encouraged to sit on it and watch the sea. Another draw of the town is the historic timber-framed Moot Hall that has been used for council meetings for over 400 years and houses the local museum.

Region: East of England   County: Norfolk   City: Ditchingham

Saint Gabriel's Conference Center

Accommodations

Saint Gabriel's Conference Center: The center can host up to 120 guests and be hired by parish and ecumenical groups, churches, charities, schools and businesses. There are single, twin and family rooms. All 85 bedrooms have their own washbasin, and 40 rooms have private baths. Two singles are suited for disabled guests and there are wheelchair lifts to make the whole venue accessible. St. Gabriel's is a full-board venue for day or residential stays. Smaller groups (minimum 10-12) can be hosted together with other groups. For further information and reservations, contact the Warden by telephone at 0044 (0) 1986 892133, by post at St. Gabriel's Conference Centre, Ditchingham, Bungay, Suffolk, NR35 2DZ, or email - saint.gabriels@btinternet.com.

Region: East of England   County: Norfolk   City: Ditchingham

ST. MARY'S LODGE: A self-catering quiet house, it is ideal for personal retreats and guests seeking solitude and silence. It has its own chapel and two art rooms with basic material provided. For reservations, contact the Guest Sister by letter or telephone at 0044 (0) 1986 892731.

ALL HALLOWS HOUSE: The house has its own spacious garden and summerhouse and is within easy reach of the Convent Chapel. It has 2 double and 4 single rooms on the first floor and a single room on the ground floor. The two bathrooms and three toilets of the house are shared but each room has its own washbasin. There are two sitting rooms. Guests are not provided with breakfast and dinner but there is a dining room and a large kitchen that guest may use. If desired, lunch can be taken with the sisters (in silence). For reservations, contact the Guest Sister by letter or telephone 0044 (0) 1986 892840 or email: allhallowshouse@UK2.net.

HOLY CROSS: The guest wing of the original convent, it has preserved the charm of the ancient structure. It may be booked by individuals and small groups. There are 11 single rooms on the first and second floors of the house. There are two sitting rooms available for guest use. Breakfast and dinner are provided in the dining room. If desired, lunch can be taken with the sisters (in silence). For reservations contact the Guest Sister by letter or telephone at 0044 (0) 1986 894092.

Amenities
There are tennis courts, a playing field and in the summer months, an open-air swimming pool. Linens are provided but guests are required to provide their own towel and soap. The sisters can fulfill special dietary requirements or guests may bring their own food.

Cost per person/per night
Voluntary contribution. Suggested cost per person for full board is approximately £35.

Directions
NOTE: The convent is isolated. Guests wishing to visit the surrounding area should arrive by car. In other cases, the best accommodation is the guesthouse in Norwich (see page #36), well connected by public transportation.

By car: From London take A12. South of Ipswich (Copdock) turn left onto A14 (Bury St. Edmunds). After approximately 7 miles take A140 (Norwich). Approximately 15 miles further (Scole) take A143 (Great Yarmouth) and continue to the outskirts of Bungay. Staying on A143 turn left at second roundabout B1332 (Norwich). Approximately 1.5 miles further, turn right at sign-posted All Hallows Convent (Belsey Bridge Road).

By train: There are two ways to get to All Hallows from London.
1) London Liverpool Street to Ipswich and then take the local train to Beccles. From Beccles take a taxi to All Hallows.
2) London Liverpool Street to Norwich and then a bus from Norwich to Bungay. Take either #58 which leaves Norwich from St. Stephens Street, stand C at 25 past and 5 to every hour until 6:25 PM (Mon-Sat); or #588 which leaves Norwich from St. Stephens Street, stand C at 20 to every hour until 5:40 PM (Mon-Sat). The journey takes approximately an hour. Ask the driver to let you know when to get off in Ditchingham (at top of Belsey Bridge Road or Drapers Lane). It is about a ten-minute walk to the convent down a single country lane.

Contact

To make a reservation at any of the guesthouses, contact the Guest Sister of each house directly by telephone or email as provided above or write to:

> The Guest Sister at (relevant house)
> All Hallows Convent, Ditchingham
> Bungay, Suffolk NR 35 2DT
> England, UK
> Telephone – see above for each house.

For general information, contact the Convent Secretary at the above address, telephone at 0044 (0) 1986 892749 or by using the link on the website.

Website: www.all-hallows.org

Email: (For general information only.)

allhallowsconvent@btitinternet.com or info@all-hallows.org

Bishop Woodford House
Diocese of Ely

Bishop Woodford House is the retreat house of the Diocese of Ely and is situated on the grounds of the former Bishop Woodford College. Both the house and the college are named after James Russell Woodford, the eminent Victorian Bishop of Ely, founder of the college. After almost a century of theological training, the college closed in 1964. Since 1973 the Bishop Woodford House has offered hospitality to individuals and groups for holidays, retreats, conferences and meetings – either self organized or organized by the House.

Woodford House is a modern building that is only a ten-minute walk from the Ely Cathedral. The House is encompassed by a colorful garden, an oasis of peace and tranquility. The chapel is a Victorian structure and was previously settled in another part of the city but dismantled and rebuilt by Bishop Woodford House.

Norman nave

The early life of Ely began with a monastery and town situated on an island in the midst of a vast expanse of marshland in the center of the Fens. Named for the eels that swam in the shallow waters, the town is dominated by its enormous Norman cathedral that rises dramatically above the countryside. Most likely founded by St. Etherelda in the year 673, the present building dates from 1083. When its tower collapsed in the early 14th century, a Lantern Tower, an elaborate octagonal structure surmounted by a timber vault carrying an octagonal lantern, replaced it. Fortunately 63-foot massive oak beams resting on stone pillars support the 400 tons of wood and lead.

Norman cathedral

The cathedral displays rare beauty and is imbued with a strong sense of serenity. It is a historical treasure trove; the majestic Norman nave is 208′ long, its ceiling elaborately painted in the 19th century by artists le Strange and Perry. In the 13th century the choir was rebuilt to provide a more worthy setting for the shrine to St. Etherelda. The Lady Chapel was added to the north transept in the 14th century. The Norman crossing tower is unique in medieval English church architecture and is the cathedral's most characteristic feature. The exterior decoration to the north wall of the nave displays fine 12th century carving. Of the cloister, now destroyed, three 12th century doorways remain. These are thought to be among the finest examples of surviving Norman architecture. There are two chantry chapels to the east end of the cathedral. Both are from the 16th century and present fine carving; one is dedicated to Bishop Alcock, the other, distinguished by early Renaissance motifs, is in honor of Bishop West. The Porta is a 14th century gatehouse and the main entrance to the Benedictine Priory and 13th century St. Mary's Church.

Ely boasts an illustrious history and is the place where Hereward the Wake held out against William the Conqueror. The city has several attractive Georgian properties as well as excellent examples of early timber-framed buildings. One of England's oldest schools, King's School, was founded in the city in AD 970. Edward the Confessor entered the school in 1010 and presented the town with a charter on his ascension to the throne.

Forming a triangle to the northwest of Ely are the towns of Chatteris, March and Whittlesea. In Neolithic times, Chatteris would have been a seaside town but today this busy little place is fifty miles from the nearest beach. The town grew up around the Abbey of St. Mary, ca. 1010. There is little sign of the abbey today but the town has an attractive church, a museum and many listed buildings dating from the 16th century.

March lies at the center of a network of railways linking the Fens to the surrounding counties and is most famous for its medieval church, St. Wendreda. Lying at the end of Church Street, the edifice is distinguished by a double hammer-beam roof with 120 carved angels spreading their wings. The River Nene winds its way through the town center where it passes an elaborate fountain and pretty gardens. A town trail and charming riverside walks are the best ways to take in the high spots and learn a little of the local legends. A handsome arched bridge spans the river beneath which slow moving boats vie for position with graceful swans and ducks. The March Museum relates the story of the town and has fascinating displays of life during the 19th and early 20th centuries. The grounds of the museum shelter a reconstructed Fenland cottage with an outside privy.

Whittlesea has an interesting maze of streets with architecture spanning several centuries. There are timber-framed houses with thatched roofs, examples of mellow buff local brick structures and even a few stone houses. Whittlesea is mentioned in the *Domesday Book of 1086.*

The entire region is rich in archaeological remains as evidenced by the Flag and Fen Bronze Age Centre and Heritage Museum. Whittlesea still celebrates the old agricultural custom of Straw Bear Dancing in early January. At that time the bear (a man in a straw costume), is accompanied by his keeper and followed by more than 200 dancers and musicians in colorful costumes. Although more common at one time, this is now the only place in Britain to see such a sight.

**Whittlesea
Straw Bear Festival**

Accommodations

32 beds in 14 standard singles, 10 en-suite singles and 4 en-suite twins.

Region: East of England   County: Cambridgeshire   City: Ely

Amenities

All meals are supplied. B&B, half board or full board available. Towels and linens are provided. There are two large and two small meeting rooms, a chapel, small library, bookshop, a licensed bar and gardens.

Cost per person/per night

Standard tariff £58 for full board; private bath supplement £5.50 per night.
Bed & Breakfast £28, half board £44.50, bed only £22.50.
Extra meals per person: breakfast £5.00; lunch £12.50; dinner/Sunday lunch £14.00.
Special discounts for groups outside the UK. A deposit is necessary to secure the reservation.

Directions

By car: From London take M11 to Cambridge and at Ely take the A10. At the roundabout, where the A10 bypasses Ely to the left, continue straight across following signs for Ely Town Centre. At the outskirts of the town there is a gas station on the left. Immediately after this, turn right onto Barton Road. Follow the road past the Cathedral Car Park on the left and shortly afterwards turn right into the car park for Bishop Woodford House.
By train: Take a train from London Liverpool Street or King's Cross to Ely. Come out of the station and turn left along the road. Continue straight across the roundabout and up the hill. At the roundabout at the top of the hill turn left onto Barton Road. The House is about 200 meters further on the left. It takes about 10 minutes to walk or 5 minutes in a taxi.

Contact

The Warden
Bishop Woodford House
Retreat & Conference Centre
Barton Road, Ely
Cambridgeshire CB7 4DX
England, UK
Tel: 0044 (0)1353 663039
Fax: 0044 (0)1353 665305
Website: www.bwh.org.uk
Email: bwh@ely.anglican.org

All Hallows House
Community of All Hallows Sisters

All Hallows House is situated in the center of Norwich, next to Saint Julian, the guesthouse. This oasis of peace in the middle of a busy city is managed by All Hallows Sisters, a lively community actively involved in offering hospitality and social services. The House in Norwich was built in the fifties at the time of the major reconstruction of the medieval church of St. Julian. There is a pretty green setting that overlooks the garden of the church. "No one would think there is a garden here," said Sister Pamela. "It is like being one side in the city and one side in the country and this is a bonus."

The Anglo-Saxon church of Saint Julian was erected about 1,000 years ago along the River Wensum at a time when Norwich was the second most important city of England. The church was dedicated to Julian the Hospitaller.

In the 14th and early 15th century, a woman from Norwich chose to live her life as an anchoress (hermit) in a small room by the church. During this time she had a series of visions of the Passion of Christ and the Love of God. From then on she was known as Dame or Lady Julian and offered advice and comfort to all those who came to her window.

Some twenty years later Julian began to write about the meaning of her visions. The outcome of these insights on God's love was a book called *The Revelations of Divine Love*. The book was written at a time when personal thinking in religious matters was at significant risk of

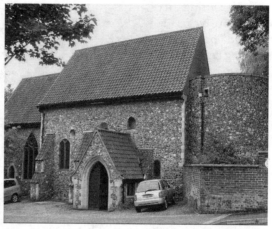

being considered heretical and this made Julian's work quite remarkable, especially considering she was the first woman to write a book in English. Julian's thinking was ahead of her time, her vision of spirituality and God's love was optimistic and regarded God as a benevolent Father and Mother. Her work, published and distributed throughout the world, is still regarded as a classic in the canon of Western spirituality.

The church is a charming stone building. The north side has survived almost intact despite the bombings that took place during WWII and contains two Anglo-Saxon windows found during the reconstruction. During this time, Julian's cell was rebuilt above some of the original foundations unearthed in the early 20th century. The reredos, made in 1931 in Oberammergau, miraculously survived the bombing.

A Norman doorway from another nearby church opens into Julian's cell, a simply decorated room with a memorial stone and a small stained glass window. The entrance to All Hallows House is almost opposite Dragon Hall; a Grade 1 listed building dating to 1430 and one of the most important historic buildings of Norwich.

Norwich is the most complete medieval city in Britain. A delightful jumble of lanes and alleys, it is a place that possesses a rare blend of historic interest and modern sophistication. It is comprised of an intricate network of winding streets and over 1,500 historic buildings; from the splendor of the Norman cathedral and castle to charming Elm Hill with its timber-framed houses.

The city is dominated by the gleaming white cathedral which claims the largest cloisters in England and the second largest spire in the country. Built over 900 years ago, it took more than two hundred years to complete. An iconic building it is much beloved by the citizenry. During its first 450 years it formed part of a thriving Benedictine monastery serving the needs of the monks, pilgrims and scholars as well as the people of Norfolk.

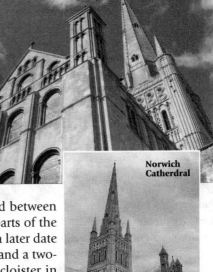

Norwich Catherdral

A vast building, the structure of the cathedral is primarily in the Norman style having been constructed between the late 11th century. Other parts of the cathedral were completed at a later date including the spire, ca. 1465 and a two-story cloister, the only such cloister in England.

The cathedral is comprised of flint and mortar faced with limestone brought in from Caen. Standing at 315' the cathedral's spire is the second tallest in England and dominates the skyline; only the spire of Salisbury Cathedral is higher. Like Salisbury and Ely, the cathedral lacks a ring of bells – the only three English cathedrals to do so. One of the best views of the cathedral's spire can be had from St. James' Hill on Mousehold Heath. The roof bosses of the vault number over 1,000 and each is adorned with a theological image. A roof boss is a carved picture in stone that relates a story. They are practical as well as decorative. A stone roof boss is a keystone that actually holds the stone ribs of the ceiling in place. The nave vault presents the history of the world from creation; the cloister includes a series showing the life of Christ and the Apocalypse. The cathedral grounds contain a number of interesting buildings from the 15th through the 19th centuries.

The castle was built by the Normans as a Royal Palace 900 years ago and is one of the finest Norman secular buildings in Europe. Used as a prison from the 14th century, it became a museum in 1894. It is packed with treasures including collections of fine art, archaeology and natural history. Some of the exhibits are of national importance including the world's largest collection of ceramic teapots. Norwich Castle is an 11th century earthwork motte and bailey fortress founded by King William I. Early in the 12th century King Henry I added a huge ornate keep and the enormous motte. In the early 13th century drum towers and a gatehouse were also added with a drawbridge and stone bridge spanning the dry ditch. In 1824 Anthony Salvin restored the interior of the keep and refaced its exterior, reproducing the original blank arcading.

Below the castle is the recently refurbished market, the largest open-air market in the country with stalls selling a wide range of goods. The market is open six days a week.

The important cobbled street of Elm Hill is one of the oldest in Norwich and a leap back in time. Largely rebuilt after the great fire of 1507, it still retains its Tudor character. As an aside, there are more Tudor houses in Elm Hill than in the City of London.

Strangers Hall is one of the oldest buildings in Norwich and houses a museum of English domestic life that dipicts how people lived from Tudor to Victorian times. There is a warren of passages, staircases and interlinked rooms including one made completely from paper. The Royal Norfolk Regimental Museum features a superb dragon crown-post roof.

Norwich Market

Along the Riverside Walk are two interesting buildings. Pulls Ferry is a 14th century arch named after a ferryman that marks the start of an ancient canal to the cathedral. The canal was used to ferry stone as close to the construction site as possible. Cow Tower is a medieval brick defensive lookout built at the end of the 12th century at a strategic bend in the river.

The long history of the nearby market town of Wymondham is reflected in the unusual timber-framed market cross building. Another striking structure is the ancient Wymondham Abbey that dates from Norman times. 2007 marked the 900th anniversary of the foundation of the abbey by William d'Albini. The railway station is a Grade II listed building and the starting point for the Mid-Norfolk Railway.

Accommodations
3 double and 3 single rooms with shared baths. Each room has a sink with hot and cold water and facilities for making hot drinks. Both men and women are welcome.

Amenities
Towels and linens are supplied. Breakfast and dinner are supplied during the week. On Sunday lunch is supplied with a light snack in the evening. There are two sitting rooms, a garden and chapel. Parking is available.

Cost per person/per night
Voluntary contribution (about £35 per night per person). The full cost to the Community for one person's 24-hour stay is £35.00. Guests are invited to make a realistic donation towards covering this and a minimum of £27 is suggested. According to the Guest Sister, "We know it may not always be possible to contribute this amount. In case of need please discuss your circumstances with me."

Special rules
To avoid disturbing those who are in retreat, silence should be observed as much as possible, from Compline, the last service of the night, until breakfast.

Directions
By car: From London take M11. At junction 9 exit M11 and take A11 towards Newmarket and Norwich. At junction 38 follow the signs to Thetford and Norwich and continue through six roundabouts. Take the 4th exit to Newmarket Rd. Continue on A11 and after the

second roundabout take the third exit to Queens Rd. Turn left on Finkelgate, then left again on Ber Street, right on Thorn Lane and finally right again on Rouen Road.

By train: Take a train from London Liverpool Street to Norwich and then walk (10 minutes) or take a taxi to All Hallows House.

Contact

Guest Sister
All Hallows House
Rouen Road
Norwich, NR1 1QT
England, UK
Tel: 0044 (0)1603 624738
Email: sister@friendsofjulian.org.
Website: www.friendsofjulian.org.uk or www.all-hallows.org

Monastery of Christ Our Saviour

Monks of the Olivetan Congregation

The monastery is in Turvey, a small welcoming village of Bedfordshire between Bedford and Milton Keynes. Turvey Monastery was founded in 1980 by a group of monks coming from Cock-

fosters Monastery (North London) led by Dom Edmund Jones. Their aim was to occupy some of the smaller buildings of a large property called Turvey "Abbey" (although it had never been a religious institution before). The monks were to share liturgy with a group of nuns of the same congregation who arrived the ensuing year and occupied the former residential house and a larger portion of the property (see page #370).

The two independent communities live separately but worship together and share some of the work. The monks lead a simple life focusing on hospitality and ecumenical work. Since their arrival an extension has been added to the original buildings to house the Turvey Centre for Group Therapy. A non-religious organization, it provides certified training courses in group therapy for professional psychotherapists as well as a place where analysts can practice their profession and provide psychotherapy services.

ENGLAND

The village history begins, like many English villages, with a probable Roman settlement. In the Middle Ages a knight of William the Conqueror was granted landship of Turvey. His family continued to be lords of Turvey for many centuries. At the end of the 18th century, two members of the Higgins family purchased the village. Their successors, rebuilt the village from about 1847 onwards.

The village houses are all in limestone and have preserved the integrity of the local traditional architecture. Turvey House is a neo-classical structure set in handsome parkland bordering the River Great Ouse at the entrance to the village. The principal rooms contain a fine collection of 18th and 19th century English and continental furniture and accoutrements. There is also a walled garden on the property. The entire area is characterized by beautiful countryside.

Bedford

Nearby, the historic county town of Bedford is a lively, cosmopolitan place with a rich history and heritage. Built upon the banks of the River Great Ouse, it claims one of the finest riverside settings in England. It was an important center for trade and settlement in the Saxon period. In 1066, a motte and bailey castle was built in the town and remained there until its destruction in 1224. The Castle Mound is one of the most prominent remnants of Bedford's medieval castle and one of the oldest visible elements of Bedford's historic fabric. A timber-framed building has been erected atop the mound, affording a commanding view over the river.

Bedford is a thriving market town with its original charter dating

Bedford

back more than 800 years. The town hosts a market on Wednesdays and Saturdays and farmer's markets are held once a month. The Bedford Museum contains collections of national importance and reveals Bedfordshire's past from prehistoric times to the foundations of Bedford as the market town it is today.

The Cecil Higgins Art Gallery shelters the splendid collection of Cecil Higgins and includes many of the greatest names in art including Turner, Gainsborough, Picasso and Matisse in addition to ceramics, glass, lace and silver.

A trip into the Bedfordshire countryside rewards visitors with beautiful scenery, charming villages, markets and traditional village fairs. Elstow is a quaint village with a row of Tudor cottages from the 17th century. It is famous as the home of John Bunyan who was imprisoned because he refused to give up preaching and submit to the power of the state. The Abbey Church of St. Helena and St. Mary is the truncated remnant of a larger monastic church overlooking Elstow Green and Moot Hall, a Tudor timber-framed market house dating back to the 15th century. The church preserves two stained glass windows connected to Bunyan; one depicts scenes from the *Pilgrim's Progress*, the other the *Holy Wars*.

Abbey Church of St. Helena and St. Mary

Elstow Abbey was founded in 1078 by the niece of William the Conqueror. It became one of the richest of the Benedictine nunneries In its heyday, the fourteenth century, the building was twice its present size. The end of the abbey came in 1539 as part of the Dissolution of the Monasteries. By the time of Elizabeth I, the church itself had been reduced to its present dimensions. It is defined by six Norman arches, reminders of the abbey's long history of Christian worship.

Potton is an ancient market town. In 1783 a fire destroyed half the town in twenty minutes and the Market Square and many of the surrounding roads were rebuilt at that time but some fine examples of Georgian architecture remain. Not far from the town and standing on a little hill is St. Mary's Church ca. 13th century. The interior harbors a striking stained glass window erected in 1994 to commemorate the 900th anniversary of the church.

Old Warden is among Bedfordshire's most beautiful villages. Much of it was rebuilt in the 18th and 19th centuries as a model estate village with ornate cottages. Just outside the village stand the remains of Warden Abbey founded in 1135. After the Dissolution it was largely demolished except for a red brick wing with wonderful chimney stacks.

The entire estate village of Southill is a Conservation Area. A pleasant mix of largely 18th and 19th century cottages and farms, the parish church of All Saints dates from the 14th century.

Biggleswade is also an ancient market town and is the largest town in East Bedfordshire. At one time the Great North Road passed through the center of town. Biggleswade's Market Square holds a weekly market whose roots can be traced to the 12th century.

Accommodations
10 single rooms, some of which can become double. 3 rooms have a private bath. Both men and women are welcome.

Amenities
Towels and linens are provided. All meals can be provided on request. The monks usually provide breakfast and dinner; lunch only for groups but arrangements can be made for all types of combinations including self-catering. There are two large sitting rooms and a library. Simple self-catering facilities are also available for guest use.

Cost per person/per night
No fixed charge but the suggested contributions are, half board £30, full board £35.

Special Rules
After 7:30 PM and until 9:00 AM the monks observe "great silence." During this time they avoid speaking and invite guests to join in the practice.

Directions
By car: From London take M1 and exit at junction 14. Take A509 via Olney to join A428. Follow the signs to Bedford on A428. Turvey Abbey is the first group of buildings on the left approaching Turvey. The Monks' Guesthouse entrance is from Jack's Lane.

By train/bus: Get off at Bedford (London St. Pancras – Leicester and Sheffield line) and take a bus to Turvey. Get off at the first stop in Turvey. The bus line, Bedford-Nottingham, runs hourly during the week but less frequently during weekends. It does not run in the evening hours.

Region: East of England	County: Bedfordshsire	City: Turvey

Contact

Brother John via email or phone. A letter of confirmation via ordinary mail is necessary to secure booking.

Monastery of Christ Our Saviour
Turvey
Bedford MK43 8DH
England, UK
Tel: 0044 (0) 1234 881211
Fax: 0044 (0) 1234 888952
Website: www.turveyabbey.org.uk - the website belongs to the nuns, click on Monastery Christ Our Saviour for the monks.
Email: turveymonks@yahoo.co.uk

Region: East of England   County: Norfolk   City: Walsingham

Our Lady of Walsingham

Marist Fathers, Diocese of East Anglia

The shrine of Our Lady of Walsingham is in Little Walsingham, one of the two conjoined factions that form the village of Walsingham (Little and Great Walsingham), surrounded by the beautiful countryside of Norfolk, near the eastern coast of England. Walsingham has been a place of pilgrimage since medieval times when travel to Rome and Compostella was virtually impossible. Founded in 1061 and until the Reformation, Our Lady of Walsingham was considered among the most important religious sites in all of Christendom. The original shrine was destroyed at the Reformation. Many years passed until the Slipper Chapel, a 14th century wayside chapel was restored and pilgrimage to Walsingham began once more.

In 1934 the English bishops named the Slipper Chapel the Roman Catholic Shrine of Our Lady. Thousands of people have visited

the shrine – some from a spiritual need for the atmosphere of peace that seems to emanate from the chapels, some for aesthetic reasons. Others are merely drawn to the shrine and pleasantness of the town.

Little Walsingham lies hidden deep in a secluded corner of Norfolk, approachable only by narrow, winding lanes flanked by high, thick hedgerows unchanged from the days when traffic went on foot or by horseback. The town's streets reveal medieval timber-framed, jetted structures, a ruined abbey, a Friday marketplace ringed with Georgian public houses and the Common Place with its surrounding shops.

Walsingham has a long and prestigious history. Once known as the Nazareth of England, it ranked alongside Rome and Jerusalem in importance as a place of pilgrimage. It was visited by all of England's Kings and Queens, starting with Henry III in 1226 up to and including Henry the VIII who visited twice, in 1486 as a Prince and in 1511 as King, the last reigning monarch to visit. Twenty years after his visit, the abbey fell to the Reformation and today lies in ruins.

The Chapel of Reconciliation is a new edifice built in 1980 to replace an open-air altar and accommodate the increasing number of visitors. The style of the structure is reminiscent of a typical Norfolk barn. Additionally it was designed to enhance acoustics.

The Fourteen Stations of the Cross at Walsingham have a special history. In 1948, as a reply to the invitation of Pope Pius XII to express penance and pray for peace after WWII, 400 men divided into 14 groups started from 14 different cities throughout Britain and carried the 14 crosses to Walsingham (each for about 200 miles).

The Anglican Shrine occupies an island site in the village of Little Walsingham. Close to the ruins of the original medieval priory (destroyed in 1538), the present day shrine was gradually created from derelict farm buildings and cottages. Within the Shrine Church is the "Holy House" a replica of the house in Nazareth. Above the altar is the niche where the statue of Our Lady of Walsingham sits amidst candles and votive lights.

Walsingham is in East Anglia, a realm of fishing villages, beaches, ancient market towns and peaceful inland waterways. To the south of Walsingham is the delightful old market town of Swaffham. Considered the best-preserved Georgian town in East Anglia, its triangular shaped marketplace is enriched with handsome Georgian buildings such as the Assembly Rooms and an 18th century Butter Cross that still hosts a popular market every Saturday. The 15th century Church of St. Peter and St. Paul is one of the finest in the region. It has a double hammerbeam roof and memorial to the famous Pedlar of Swaffham. The local history museum preserves collections from the Stone Age to modern times.

Swaffham Market

Nearby Binham Priory was built by Pierre de Valoines a nephew of William the Conqueror. Its position is wondrous, set on a rolling landscape beneath soft Norfolk skies. Glimpsing the relics of the former building, preserved around the existing church, evokes an image of what this once great priory must have looked like all those centuries a go.

Evidence supports the fact that the impressive west front was built in the early 13th century with its displays of arcading small columns and dogtooth ornament. The unusually large window with its geometric tracery was probably added at a later date. Its nave arcade has richly adorned arches with zigzag and billet moldings. It is easy to recognize the changes from Norman style to Early English. The treasures of the priory include an impressive Perpendicular seven-sacrament font and the remains of the Rood screen.

A few miles from Walsingham is enchanting Wells-Next-The-Sea with old houses, shops and pubs lining the maze of narrow streets leading to the quayside. The harbor has a long maritime history as a port and is home to its own fishing fleet. One of the joys of this inviting town is to stroll along the harbor watching fishing boats land and pleasure craft sail by.

Outdoor enthusiasts will appreciate the nearby Norfolk Broads, a nature reserve combining miles of lakes, rivers, marshes, birds, butterflies, wildlife and intriguingly tangled woods that is best explored by boat (rentals and guided boat trips are available). The area is also home to Pedlars Way, built by the Romans through the territory of fearsome rebel queen Boudicca after the emperor's legions eventually crushed her armies. It's a delightful venue of flint villages, 1,000-year old churches and amazing sea views.

Southwest of Walsingham is King's Lynn, a typical English town on the east bank of the River Great Ouse. Over the years the town has been known variously as Bishop's Lynn and Lynn Regis and occasionally re-

King's Lynn

ferred to by locals as simply Lynn, the Celtic word for lake. The third largest settlement in Norfolk, it is home to Sandringham House, the Norfolk residence of the British Royal Family. The Neo-Elizabethan house can be visited when the Royal Family is not in residence. Its vast park is endowed with glorious old trees. The museum shelters hunting trophies and vintage cars belonging to the Royal Family.

It is believed that there has been some habitation at King's Lynn for well over a thousand years but it wasn't until St. Margaret's Church was founded in 1101 that the town began appearing on records. The church features massive west towers that impart the air of a cathedral. The west front contains two extraordinary brasses, probably of Flemish workmanship. The 14th century pieces represent a vintage scene and a peacock feast.

By the 14th century the town was the third port of England. It retains two medieval buildings, once warehouses of the Hanseatic League, in use between the 15th and 17th centuries. They are the only remaining structures of the Hanseatic League in England. The league was an alliance of trading guilds that established and maintained a trade monopoly over the Baltic Sea and most of Northern Europe for a time in the Late Middle Ages and early modern period, between the 13th and 17th centuries.

When Henry VIII dissolved the monasteries in 1538, the town and manor became royal property. As a result, the town was renamed King's Lynn and Lynn Regis, however, it was King's Lynn that stuck. The town's 17th century Customs House was built in Palladian style and designed by local architect Henry Bell. In the area around King Street are several handsome Tudor and Georgian houses.

The King's Lynn Festival, held every July, is East Anglia's most important cultural gathering. The festival offers concerts and recitals of music from medieval ballads to opera. For rock and roll enthusiasts, the concert is preceded by a free R&R concert.

Accommodations

Elmham House provides the accommodations. A Georgian structure, it was formerly Walsingham Grammar School, founded in the 17th century. There are several single and double rooms, some with shared baths (standard), some with private baths (en-suite). All are equipped with basins with hot and cold water.

Region: East of England	County: Norfolk	City: Walsingham

Amenities

Linens are supplied in both types of accommodations. Towels are supplied only in en-suite rooms. All meals can be provided by previous arrangement. Pets are not allowed.

Cost per person/per night

Tariffs include VAT and breakfast.
En-suite rooms £27 (no reduction for children).
Standard £19 (adults), £9.50 (children).
Lunch/dinner £6.60, packed lunch £3.80.
Note: Check the website for current rates.

Directions

By car: From London and the south, leave the M11 at junction 9 (Newmarket, Norwich). Take the A11 towards Newmarket (this merges with the A14). After 6 miles follow the sign A11 (Thetford, Norwich). At Barton Mills roundabout, take the A1065 (2nd exit) through Brandon and Swaffham. In Swaffham turn right at the mini roundabout through the Market Square sign-posted Cromer, Fakenham (A18). Bypass Fakenham to King's Lynn-Fakenham Road (A148). Cross over the roundabout, turn left after 300 yards onto B1105, sign-posted Walsingham. Once on the B1105 follow the signs for Little Walsingham and the Shrine.

By train: There are no trains to Walsingham. The nearest train stations are Norwich and King's Lynn (about 27 miles from Walsingham). Buses run regularly from both stations to Walsingham via Fakenham.

By bus: London, Norwich and King's Lynn are regularly connected to Fakenham. Once there take a local bus to Walsingham.

Contact

Pilgrim Bureau
Friday Market Place
Little Walsingham
Norfork NR22 6DB
England, UK
Tel: 0044 (0) 1328 820217
Fax: 0044 (0) 1328 821087
Website: www.walsingham.org.uk
Email: elmhamhouse@walsingham.org.uk

**EAST
MIDLANDS**

Region: East Midlands   County: Derbyshire   City: Derby

Convent of the Holy Name

Sisters of the Community of the Holy Name

The convent is the motherhouse of the Order of the Holy Name whose foundation dates back to 1865 when the first two sisters were professed in the Parish of St. Peter's Vauxhall, London. The founders were inspired by the Catholic and Evangelical movements. In 1887 the community established the motherhouse in Malvern Link and a number of "Mission Houses" in various areas of England.

The sisters of the motherhouse moved to Derby in 1990 and took up residence in a former private mansion enveloped by extensive and beautiful grounds, the ideal location for a quiet relaxing stay. There are about twenty-five sisters actively involved in social work in many venues in the city.

The convent is in Oakwood, on the outskirts of Derby, famous for being the place where the British Industrial Revolution began with the first factories and spinning mills.

Derby sits on the edge of the Peak District National Park, a protected area with a remarkable sense of space and solitude, a place of diverse landscapes exuding an aura of history. The Romans who built a fort, Derventio, first settled Derby. When the Anglo-Saxons arrived, they renamed the fort Little Chester, as it is still known today. Derby began to develop as a manufacturing center at the end of the 17th century. The Derby Cathedral was built during the reign of Henry VIII and remains a characteristic landmark and the town's most impressive building. Its heritage can be traced to the 10th century but the tower was built during the reign of Henry VIII and is second only to the Boston Stump as the tallest church tower in England. Completed about

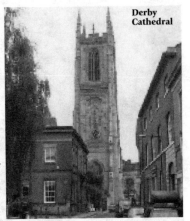

Derby Cathedral

1530, it was incorporated into the present building in 1725 when the medieval church was largely demolished. The tower is 212' to the top of the pinnacles and there are 189 steps to the roof. It is open on certain days throughout the year and by special arrangement.

The church was largely rebuilt by James Gibbs in the early 18th century with many of its original treasures retained. They include superb tombs and monuments, especially to the "much married" Bess of Hardwick, Countess of Shrewsbury. Its prized possession is the intricate wrought iron screen, the work of Robert Bakewell. The entrance gates to the cathedral are also from Bakewell. They were made by him for a private house and gifted to the cathedral in 1958. The Derby Museum and Art Gallery houses a wide range of important and attractive exhibits covering porcelain, paintings, archaeology, history and geology. There is also an assemblage of paintings by the celebrated 18th century Derby artist Joseph Wright.

At the center of Derby lies historic St. Peter's Church whose roots began in Norman times. The church of today dates mainly from the

14th century. St. Mary's Roman Catholic Church has been a place of Christian worship for over 800 years. It displays a 117' tower designed by Pugin in 1838 that was once topped with a statue of the Blessed Virgin. Another feature of the town is St. Mary's Chapel on St. Mary's Bridge over the River Derwent. This dates from the 14th century and is one of the few surviving bridge chapels in the country.

St. Mary's Chapel on St. Mary's Bridge

Apart from being blessed with historic churches and grand houses, there is also interesting domestic architecture in Derby, some dating back to the Georgian period. The gracious black and white timber-framed Dolphin Inn is a former coaching inn said to have been a favorite of highwaymen and is believed to be haunted.

Kedleston Hall, home of the Curzon family for almost 900 years, features some of the finest surviving Adam interiors in England. The estate's sumptuous staterooms reveal a fabulous collection of painting and furniture. Its principal architectural feature is the great marble hall with twenty pink alabaster pillars. There is also furniture by Chippendale and other leading cabinetmakers of the day. The exterior of the south front is outstanding; its center is in the form of a Roman triumphal arch and the curving dome and staircase showcase Adams' genius.

To the south of Derby and nestled amid ancient parkland is the Baroque mansion of Calke Abbey. With interiors largely unaltered since the late 1800s, the structure preserves a comprehensive natural history treasure, underground tunnels, a secret garden and a restored Orangery.

Swarkestone is an easy drive from the convent. This small village grew up on the receded banks of the River Trent. It is spanned by a graceful multi-arched bridge built in the 14th century and restored at the beginning of the 19th. There is a legend surrounding the bridge – it was supposedly built by sisters who had watched their lovers die while attempting to cross the old wooden ford on horseback.

Swarkestone is also noted for its beautiful church. The interior reveals ancient treasures such as 16th and 17th century commemoratives to members of the Hartpur family. A relic of the Hartpur estate can be seen in a meadow above the village. Known as the Hartpur Summer House, it is all that was left of the estate after the family took up residence at Calke Abbey.

Not far from Derby, the late 17th century Sudbury Hall has a lavish interior that was featured in the BBC drama *Pride and Prejudice*. It preserves one of the grandest long galleries and staircases in England. Next to Sudbury Hall are the Museum of Childhood and a reconstructed Victorian schoolroom and nursery with an interesting array of old toys and games.

North of Derby and lying in a deep gorge is the town of Matlock. Originally a string of small settlements, it wasn't until the discovery of medicinal springs in Matlock Bath that the area became a popular attraction in the 18th century. Towering limestone cliffs, meandering riverside paths and ancient woodlands form part of the five historic parks that link Matlock and Matlock Baths. Enjoy a summer concert in Hall Leys Park, spot wildflowers on the slopes of High Tor or marvel at tufa rock and bubbling thermal spring water in Derwent Gardens. There is a ferry link across the river to "Lovers Walk" and peaceful riverside strolls.

Northeast of Matlock is the red brick market town of Chesterfield, best known for the unusual church spire of its 14th century church. Although the spire started out straight, it is nearly ten inches out of line and leans a bit further every year. It gives the impression that it could fall down in the next strong gale but having stood for over 600 years, that seems quite unlikely.

Accommodations
The cottage on the convent's grounds has 7 beds in single rooms with shared baths. Both men and women are welcome.

Amenities
All meals are provided with the lodging. Guests may eat with the sisters or prepare their own meals in the kitchen at their disposal. Towels and linens are supplied. There is a sitting room.

Cost per person/per night
Voluntary contribution.

Special rules
Hospitality is offered only from Tuesday to Sunday morning. Closed during the sisters' retreat in January and August; the dates vary each year. Contact the sisters for more information.

Region: East Midlands	County: Derbyshire	City: Derby

Directions

By car: From London take M1, exit at junction 25 and follow the signs to Nottingham/Derby/Ilkeston/A52. At the roundabout take exit 1A (A52) towards Derby. Take A52/Borrowash Bypass and then take the exit towards Spondon/Chaddesen. At the roundabout take exit 4A to Derby Road and turn onto Acorn Way at exit 3A. At the following roundabout turn into Morley Road.

By train: From London St. Pancras take a train to Derby, then a taxi to the Convent.

Contact

Guest Sister
Convent of the Holy Name
Morley Road
Oakwood
Derby, DE21 4 QZ
England, UK
Tel: 0044 (0) 1332 670483 (Cottage phone) or 0044 (0) 1332 671716
Note: Times for phoning 10-12 noon, local time.
Fax: 0044 (0) 1332 669712
Website: www.chnderby.org
Email: bursarsoffice@tiscali.co.uk

Launde Abbey

Order Diocese of Leicester

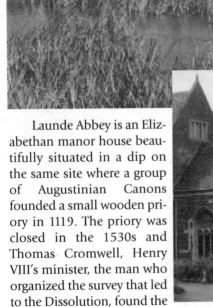

Launde Abbey is an Elizabethan manor house beautifully situated in a dip on the same site where a group of Augustinian Canons founded a small wooden priory in 1119. The priory was closed in the 1530s and Thomas Cromwell, Henry VIII's minister, the man who organized the survey that led to the Dissolution, found the position of the abbey so inviting that he wrote in his journal: "Myself for Launde." This led to the construction of a manor. Although Cromwell never lived there (he was executed for treason in 1540, the very year when the building commenced), Cromwell's son Gregory and his wife Elizabeth inhabited the house for ten years.

Region: East Midlands   County: Leicestershire   City: East Norton

The house was eventually sold by the Cromwell family in 1611 and has been modified over the course of the centuries. The surrounding area was turned into alluring parkland and woodland by the various families that lived in the house. In 1957 the property was donated to the Diocese of Leicester and converted into a retreat house.

Encompassed by peaceful rural farmland, Launde Abbey has preserved a fascinating atmosphere that led it to compete for the BBC Enjoy England Excellence Award in 2007 as one of the best tourist experiences in England. From the original priory church only the early Renaissance chapel remains. This boasts some remarkable medieval stained glass windows and attracts many visitors every year. Launde Abbey offers hospitality to individuals and for organized retreats as well as a meeting venue for religious, cultural and educational purposes.

Six miles from Launde Abbey, Oakham is the nearest village to East Norton. The county town of Rutland, it is rich in history and character. One of its most famous landmarks is Oakham Castle, a fine example of late 12th century domestic architecture. Its Great Hall is decorated with a range of 12th century sculptures. Above the columns

Oakham Castle

are six musicians, each playing a different instrument. They are made of local stone from Clipsham and although damaged, are of superb quality and believed to have been carved by masons who worked at Canterbury Cathedral.

The Great Hall is famed for its collection of horseshoes, 240 of which hang on the walls. These represent the unique custom that every peer of the realm must give a horseshoe to the lord of the manor on the first visit to Oakham. The custom has been followed for at least 500 years and probably dates to the 12th century. The oldest surviving horseshoe is believed to have been given by Edward IV in about 1470. The most recent were given by HRH The Princess Royal in 1999, HRH The Prince of Wales in 2003 and HRH Princess Alexandra in 2005.

South of the Abbey the town of Hallaton is set in rolling country underlain by Jurassic ironstones and clays. Its fine church, St. Michael, dates mainly from the 13th century but there are fragments from Nor-

Region: East Midlands   County: Leicestershire   City: East Norton

Hallaton

man times. In the porch there is a tympanum depicting St. George and the Dragon. The aisles are 14th century and there are some 13th century decorations in the chancel as well as exquisite 19th century stained glass.

Hallaton is mentioned in the *Domesday Book of 1086* under the old name of Alctone. It is believed that Castle Hill, just outside Hallaton, was inhabited more than a thousand years before the Normans and this belief is supported by findings during the 19th century that are on display in the Leicester Museum.

Every Easter Monday about two thousand people visit Hallaton. The point of the day is a bottle kicking game akin to primitive rugby using small barrels of beer instead of a ball. The game starts in the afternoon but is the culmination of a traditional ritual of processions, a church service and the cutting of the hare pie that dates back well over 200 years and may have roots in the Iron Age.

Tilton is just north of East Norton. The crowing glory of the village is its stunning parish church with an intricate needle spire. Sitting at over 700' above sea level, the church stands at the highest point with the village spread out beneath it.

Accommodations

77 beds in 45 single, double and twin bedrooms. 23 rooms have private baths, but all have a washbasin and shaver socket. There are three fully-equipped disabled-friendly en-suite bedrooms and a caregiver's bedroom.

Amenities

All meals are provided with the lodging. Towels and linens are supplied. Meeting and common rooms, dining room, licensed bar, park facilities, shop, gardens and a chapel are available to guests. Tea and coffee facilities are on each landing.

Cost per person/per night

Weekday rate £56.50 full board.

Weekend rate £59 full board.

Other prices and combination of meals to be determined when reservations are made.

Special rules

Closed at Christmas.

A non-returnable deposit is necessary to secure the booking.

Directions

By car: From London take M1 and exit at junction 21, then take M69 and follow the Leciester Ring Road south (A563). Follow the signs for A6 and A47 to Peterborough. Launde Abbey is sign-posted in East Norton (just off the A47). Follow the signs to Launde turning right in Loddington. After about one mile cross the cattle grid to Launde Abbey on the right.

By train: Take a train from London King's Cross to Peterborough and then change to Oakham. From there take a taxi to Launde Abbey (6 miles).

Contact

The Warden

Launde Abbey

East Norton

Leicestershire, LE7 9XB

England, UK

Tel: 0044 (0) 1572 717254 (10AM-4PM)

Fax: 0044 (0) 1572 717454

Website: www.launde.org.uk

Email: laundeabbey@leicester.anglican.org

Morley Retreat & Conference House
Diocese of Derby

Morley Retreat House is a gracious Georgian building set in rural Warwickshire in the small village of Morley, embraced by its own attractive gardens that overlook the verdant countryside. The house, standing beside the historic 14th century church of St. Matthews, is a former rectory built in 1745 to replace another rectory destroyed by fire in the same year. It became a retreat center in 1959 after a new wing with more bedrooms was added to the complex. Additional renovations were completed in 2000: A new chapel was built, the wing became integrated with the main building and the house was made accessible to the disabled. A new project is underway that will turn all rooms into en-suite bedrooms.

ENGLAND

The village of Morley is a rather small entity of 200 inhabitants. It is situated approximately 6 miles northeast of Derby in a rural area of working farms whose elevated position offers wonderful vistas in every direction. The area, formerly the site of quarries that closed in 1917, is now a wildlife reserve managed by Derbyshire Wildlife Trust.

Parish Church of St. Matthew

The main attraction of Morley, however, is the Parish Church of St. Matthew. It lays claim to one of the finest displays of medieval stained glass windows in the country. Much of these came from Dale Abbey at the time of the Dissolution of the Monasteries. There is also a remarkable collection of medieval monuments including those to important local families. The church has a Norman nave, whereas the tower, chancel and north chapel date to the late 14th and early 15th century.

Morley is within easy driving distance to a number of interesting towns that reflect the area's historical ties to the textile industry as well as to the Bronte sisters and their stories; stories set in what is now called Bronte Country, a terrain of deep-sided valleys and glens lying beneath lonely moors.

To the northwest of Morley, the town of Haworth is famous for its connections with the Bronte sisters. They lived at Haworth Parsonage where they wrote some of their most famous novels including *Wuthering Heights, Jane Eyre* and *Agnes Grey*. The Bronte sisters were born in the nearby town of Thornton but in 1820 the family moved to Haworth which remained their home until 1861. The three daughters – Emily, Charlotte and Anne – each wrote books, often inspired by the countryside that surrounded them. *Wuthering Heights* by Emily Bronte is perhaps the most famous: It is the story of the relationship between Catherine and Heathcliffe, set on the moors near Haworth.

The house where they lived is now the Bronte Parsonage Museum. The rooms are meticulously furnished as they were in the Bronte era and include many personal treasures. Evoking the Bronte sisters' novels are a number of local walks such as Bronte Falls and Bronte Bridge.

In the interesting mill town of Hebden Bridge, the houses hang precariously from the steep valley sides. An ancient town, it grew up close to the River Hebden at the point where a stone bridge was built as part of a packhorse route in the 16th century. Heptonstall, above the town, became a center for weavers and Hebden Bridge was the river crossing point for packhorses laden with cloth, salt and food. The bridge that exists today was built in 1510. Heptonstall shows its antiquity in narrow cobbled streets lined with 500-year-old cottages and the ruins of a 13th century church. It is the churchyard though that attracts visitors, it is the place where the poet Sylvia Plath is buried.

At Hebden Water, a few miles from Hebden Bridge, is an area known as the "Crags," an arena of footpaths encompassing a medley of natural and archaeological history, passing through dense woodland, alive with oak, ash, beech and pine. In springtime these lofty trees spread their branches over a carpet of vibrant, gently nodding bluebells. At Hebden Water, Gibson Mill is a three-story building of the early 18th century that has recently been restored. The mill offers hands-on exhibitions and provides insight into the lives of the people who toiled at the mill for up to 72 hours a week, often for very little reward.

Saltaire is a perfectly preserved village of honey-colored cottages that originated as an answer to Bradford's "dark, satanic mills." Now recognized as a World Heritage Site by UNESCO, the town was the brainchild of industrialist Sir Titus Salt who in the early 19th century strove to provide his mill workers with attractive dwellings surrounded by eye-catching buildings with a strong Italianate flavor. He was a firm believer that beauty could be combined with industry and to make this point, he  crowned his mill with a chimney disguised as an Italianate bell tower.

Salt Mill

Today visitors to Saltaire can see Salt's mill in all its glory. It has been transformed into an art gallery and houses works of the famous Bradford born artist, David Hockney. The village is also home to a historic gem – the United Reform Church, a Victorian structure and an exquisite example of Italianate religious architecture.

Nearby Halifax has been influenced by textiles since the Middle Ages. Many of the town's buildings owe their existence to wealthy cloth merchants. Piece Hall is where the wool merchants once sold their goods, trading in one of the hall's more than 300 Merchants' Rooms. The hall preserves an Italianate courtyard built by the town's wealthy industrialists. Shibden Hall, dating from 1420, is a distinctive half-timbered building furnished in the styles of the 17th, 18th and 19th centuries. An important 17th century aisled barn houses a collection of horse-drawn vehicles. In the outhouses, there is a mélange of 19th century craft tools relating to rural industries.

Accommodations
7 twins and 25 singles, all with shared bath.

Amenities
All meals are provided with the lodging. Towels and linens are supplied. There is a range of meeting rooms for a varied number of guests. There are two chapels, a garden with a patio, walled garden, orchard, courtyard and viewpoints, dining room, bookshop and a snack bar.

Cost per person/per night
£52.50 full board, £31.50 B&B.

Directions
By car: From London take M1. Exit at junction 25 and take A52 towards Derby. After about 7 miles there is a Pentagon shaped roundabout. Take the 3rd exit, the A61 (the first after going under the flyover), sign-posted to Chesterfield and proceed for three-quarters of a mile to the next roundabout. Take the first exit, the A608, signposted for Heanor. After about 4 miles and a mile after passing Derby College (Broomfield Hall) on the left, take the turn on the right signed for Stanley, Chaddesden and (on the sign at the junction itself) Morley Church. After 150 meters and immediately by the "Give Way to Oncoming Traffic" sign, bear left into the slightly rising road and easy to miss drive (look for the blue sign). They share the first part of the driveway with St. Matthews' Parish Church. The House is directly ahead and the car park is to the rear of the House.

ENGLAND

By train: Take a train from London St. Pancras to Derby and then take a taxi to Morley. By prior arrangement, taxi service can be provided.

Contact

Anyone
Morley Retreat & Conference House
Church Lane
Morley
Ilkeston
Derbyshire DE7 6DE
England, UK
Tel: 0044 (0) 1332 831293
Fax: 0044 (0) 1332 834944
Website: www.morleyretreat.co.uk
Email: morleyretreat@btconnect.com

Holy Cross Convent
Anglican Benedictine Nuns

The Convent is near the pretty village of Rempstone on the border of Nottinghamshire and Leicestershire. It is enclosed by beautiful farmland. Over the years the sisters have seen the growth of the area and it is becoming too busy for them. Due to their need for a more isolated and quiet environment, in a few years, the sisters plan to move their facility to a farmhouse situated just 1.5 miles from its present location. The sisters suggest that guests contact the convent or check on the Internet to be informed about the up-to-date location.

The community was founded by Elizabeth Neale in 1857 at London Docks. Elizabeth, the sister of a well-known hymnographer, John Mason Neale, had answered the appeal of Father Charles Lowder to create a community to relieve poverty and distress in one of the most sordid areas of his parish. At first the community was not well received but after the major role the sisters played during a severe cholera epidemic, they were finally accepted.

Chapel

The community grew and opened many branch houses until the motherhouse was moved to Haywards Heath, Sussex. As time passed though, the community gradually evolved to a more contemplative and secluded form of life, closer to the Benedictine Office. During WWII the convent was used as an emergency hospital and the sisters slept in bunk beds in the basement. After the war they fully adopted the Rule of Saint Benedict and changed from an active to an enclosed convent.

With a much smaller number of sisters, the community moved to Rempstone in 1979 and continued their enclosed life, blending prayer with manual work and study. Continuing with Saint Benedict's tradition of hospitality, the sisters run a small guesthouse in an external cottage and hermitage.

Rempstone is pleasantly situated on the road from Nottingham to Loughborough and is separated from Leicestershire by a brook. The terrain is hilly and the scenery in many parts is very pleasing, an altogether typical small English town.

North of Rempstone is the university city of Nottingham, a place where creativity and stylishness combine with the legendary medieval rebel and friend-of-the-poor, Robin Hood. Nottingham Castle is linked

Robin Hood Statue

to Robin Hood and his arch enemy the Sheriff of Nottingham. Perched on a rock, Nottingham Castle is a spectacular 17th century ducal mansion with splendid views of the city. The castle harbors over 1,000 years of history and contains an internationally renowned collection of art, silver and glass. An iconic statue of Robin Hood, bow drawn, stands in the shadow of the castle's formidable walls.

Beneath the city is a network of man-made Anglo-Saxon caves dug into the soft sandstone including Mortimer's Hold below the castle. Its name is derived from Roger Mortimer, lover of Queen Isabella, wife of Edward II.

Built on a number of hills, Nottingham is known as "Queen of the Midlands," because of its broad streets and parks. Old Market Square is dominated by the 200-foot high dome of the Council House, traditional seat for the city council. Every third Friday and Saturday of the month, a market takes place in the square.

The environs of Nottingham reveal a rich heritage of market towns, ancient castles and ducal mansions sprinkled throughout tranquil woodlands and countryside. Nearby Newstead Abbey is a beautiful historic house set in a landscape of gardens and parkland within the heart of Nottinghamshire. Founded as a monastic house in the late 12th century, Newstead became the seat of the Byron family in 1540 and was home to the poet Lord Byron between 1808 and 1814. The abbey shelters Victorian room settings and the poet's private apartments, preserved as they were when he resided there. The gardens and parkland cover an expanse of more than 300 acres with paths that meander past lakes, ponds and waterfalls.

Southwell Minster is a minster and cathedral in the nearby town of Southwell. In 2008 the complex celebrated the cathedral's 900th anniversary. Considered one of the county's jewels in the crown, the cathedral has a Norman nave that is one of the finest in Europe and a chapter house that is home to the world-renowned Leaves of Southwell stone carvings. It is considered an outstanding example of Norman and Early English architecture. The distinctive pyramidal lead spires, or "pepperpot" spires as they are known locally are the only example of their kind in Britain.

ENGLAND

Continuing north from Nottingham is the city of Leicester where England's 2,000-year history can be traced to battlefields and fairy-tale castles. Consider the Jewry Wall, one of the highest Roman remains within a city in England. Romans entered through the arches into the Roman baths. Their children played with their toys there – toys later excavated from the site in 1939. Jewry Wall Museum now houses a Roman milestone, one of the few found in Britain in addition to excellent examples of Roman mosaics and wall plaster.

The Jewry Wall is the remaining wall of the public baths of Roman Leicester along with the foundations of the baths that are laid out in front of the wall. The wall is nearly 2,000 years old and is a rare example of Roman walling and the second largest piece of surviving civil Roman construction in Britain. The wall would have separated the gymnasium from the cold room. The name of the wall does not relate to Leicester's Jewish community which was expelled from the city in medieval times.

To experience the very essence of England, consider a day trip to the small towns and quaint villages of East Northamptonshire (northeast of Leicester), a place where time, for the most part, seems to have come to a standstill. This area is a tableau of mellowed, golden limestone villages that offer a glimpse into the past. Interwoven between the villages are a variety of intriguing places to visit: Historic castles, glorious gardens, craft centers, churches and more.

Southeast of Rempstone, Oundle is one of the oldest towns in England. Situated on a curve in the River Nene, it has a collection of old streets full of interesting galleries, a museum and an array of teashops. Honey-colored Jurassic limestone and Collyweston slate roofs of the 16th and 17th centuries distinguish its streets and squares. There's a market every Thursday. Barnwell is an appealing village on the outskirts of Oundle. The oldest cottages were built of local stone and many still have thatch or Collyweston roofs. The manor house at the north end of the village was once the country home of the Duke and Duchess of Gloucester.

Full of charm and character Thrapston was granted its market charter by King John in 1205 and a weekly market is still held on Tuesdays. Wadenhoe is situated midway between Oundle and Thrapston. The village probably dates to Saxon times and is regarded as one of the prettiest in the county. The oldest house is the Manor Farm House, dated from the stone on the rear of the house that reads 1653.

Accommodations

There are two types.

1. One cottage with 4 beds in 2 single and 1 double room with a shared bath.
2. One hermitage with a bed-sitting room, a kitchen and a bath.

Both men and women are welcome.

The guesthouse is closed Christmas and Easter.

Amenities

All meals can be provided with the lodging. Breakfast is eaten in the cottage or hermitage, lunch and dinner with the community. Towels and linens are provided.

Cost per person/per night

Voluntary contribution. For suggestions, speak with the Reverend Mother.

Directions

By car: Exit MI at junction 23 and take A512 towards Loughborough. At Loughborough Ring Road take the first exit A60 towards Nottingham and follow about 4 miles until the junction to A6006 towards Ashby (Ashby Road). The Convent is 0.3 miles on the left.

By train: Take a train to Loughborough from London St. Pancras. Once there take a taxi (3 miles) to the Convent.

Contact

Reverend Mother
Holy Cross Convent
Ashby Road
Rempstone
Loughborough LE12 6RG
England, UK
Tel: 0044 (0) 1509 880336
Fax : 0044 (0) 1509 881812
Website: www.orders.anglican.org.uk or call the convent
Email: chc.rempstone@webleicester.co.uk

London
(and vicinity)

LONDON
(and vicinity)

London is a sprawling combination of two cities, each distinctly different. The City of London is the center of Britain's trade and finance; Westminster is the home of court, government, high society, churches and houses of treasure. Linking both is the River Thames, England's greatest water thoroughfare. The following highlights some of London's most interesting places to visit

London's leading art museum, the grand building of the National Gallery, dominates Trafalgar Square. Its foundation can be traced to 1824 when George IV persuaded the government to purchase 38 major paintings, paintings that continue to be the heart of the museum's European art holdings. Built to a design by William Wilkins and constructed between 1834 and 1837, the museum contains a collection from the British School and is particularly rich in Italian works of art from the 15th and 16th centuries. Some of the masterpieces include work by Leonardo da Vinci, Jan van Eyck, Fra Lippi, Renoir and the only surviving nude by Velazquez. Each month the gallery features a "painting of the month" and there are regular changing exhibitions of the work of a particular artist or those of a famous collection.

ENGLAND

Westminster Abbey is world famous for being the resting place of British monarchs and the place where coronations and other royal pageants are held. Every coronation since 1066 has taken place there. It is an architectural masterpiece of the 13th to 16th centuries and within its walls are some of the most glorious examples of medieval architecture in London. Westminster Abbey contains an outstanding assemblage of tombs and monuments. The interior shelters the Confessor's Shrine, the Tombs of Kings

Westminster Abbey

and Queens and countless memorials to the famous. In 1965-66, Westminster Abbey celebrated its 900th anniversary.

Buckingham Palace is the first home and office of the Royal Family and has been the home of British sovereigns since 1837. Originally a town house built for the Duke of Buckingham in 1703, it was later purchased by George III in 1762 and used as one of the Royal Family's London homes. Fourteen of George III's fifteen children were born at the palace. George IV who reined between 1820-30 employed John Nash to build a new palace around the old Buckingham House. Both he and his brother King William IV died before the new palace was fully completed and so Queen Victoria was the first monarch to live at Buckingham in 1837. The palace is decorated with extraordinary works of art that form part of the Royal Collection. During August and September when The Queen makes her annual visit to Scotland, the palace's nineteen staterooms are open to visitors.

At a height of 450' and weighing 1600 tons, the London Eye Observation Wheel is the biggest of its kind to ever be built. It marked the new millennium and became operational in January 2000. Designed by husband and wife team Julia Barfield and David Marks, the London Eye provides amazing panoramic views of the city of London.

One of London's most celebrated landmarks, Big Ben is famous for being the giant four-faced clock in London. The huge bell was hung in 1858 and named after Sir Benjamin Hall, Chief Commissioner of Works at that time. Big Ben is the largest clock in Britain and has kept exact time for the nation since May 1859. The sound of Big Ben has become famous as the time signal of the BBC.

Houses of Parliament

The Houses of Parliament, also known as The Palace of Westminster, has been the seat of the English government - called the House of Lords and the House of Commons -since 1512. The Commons is comprised of elected Members of Parliament (MPs) from different political parties, Labour, Liberal, Conservative, etc. The party with the most MPs forms the government of England, its leader becoming Prime Minister.

Founded in 1856, the National Portrait Gallery traces Britain's history and famous Britons through portraits, photographs and sculpture from the 15th century to the present. Perhaps though the most visited part of the gallery is the 20th century section with its paintings and photos of the Royal Family, rock stars and contemporary artists and writers.

British Museum's treasures include vast Etruscan, Egyptian, Greek, Oriental and Roman galleries. Founded by an act of Parliament in 1753, the museum is based on the private collections of Sir Robert Cotton, Sir Hans Sloane and Robert Harley, Earl of Oxford. The museum is distinguished by a steel and glass roof, a stunning architectural element. A must-see exhibit is the *Rosetta Stone*, discovered in 1799 and the key to deciphering Egyptian hieroglyphics.

Built as a fortress by William the Conqueror, the Tower of London is infamous as the prison where enemies of the crown were executed. The tower houses the Crown Jewels and is home to Traitors' Gate where prisoners entered the tower by boat. The immense White Tower with its Romanesque architecture and four turrets is perhaps its most striking feature. On the green in front of the church is where seven people were beheaded including Anne Boleyn and Catherine Howard, Henry VIII's second and fifth wives.

Tate Britain is the place to see British Art from the 16th century to the present. Works include Gainsborough, Whistler, Spence and Blake. Open for lunch and tea, the Tate Restau-

Tate Modern

rant is quite popular and boasts an impressive Whistler mural.

Tate Modern houses an illustrious collection of 20th century international art. It is an exciting museum with intriguing artwork presented in a vivid format. The enormous Turbine Hall is a dramatic venue and the highlight of any visit.

Tower Bridge

One of the best-known landmarks of London, the Tower Bridge still opens to allow tall ships to pass beneath. The bridge with its 200' high towers was built in the late 1880s. Its walkways offer splendid views.

Region: London and vicinity   County: Buckinghamshire   City: Iver Heath

The Bridgettine Convent
Sisters of the Order of the Most Holy Saviour (Bridgettines)

The house of the Bridgettine Sisters is a small, pretty Tudor timbered house situated in the proximity of Iver Heath and surrounded by the verdant woods of Buckinghamshire. Iver Heath is a gracious village in the beautiful countryside of Uxbridge, last stop of the "Southwest" line of the London Underground. The Convent was occupied in 1931 by a group of five sisters who came from Rome to open a house of prayer and offer hospitality to all. Over time the house has been enlarged and refurbished to better accommodate a larger number of guests. Nevertheless it has preserved its original style and atmosphere. Individuals and groups of all denominations and nationalities are welcome as befitting the Bridgettines' traditional open attitude to everyone regardless of their creed or background.

Behind the house a local country lane leads to the picturesque village of Fulmer. The village name is Anglo-Saxon in origin and means "lake frequented by birds." In the late 17th century the owners of the manor in Fulmer were forced to sell their house to their servants because they had squandered their money and could not afford to pay them. Eventually the manor passed into the hands of the Duke of Portland. Today the common land that surrounds Fulmer presents the leafy picturesque countryside that typifies Buckinghamshire. Many films have been shot in the area including *Sleepy Hollow*.

The Convent is very close to London but is also near a myriad of towns and villages, each with their own special appeal, interesting histories and architecture. Eton for example is an attractive town dotted with fine historic buildings. The chief attraction, of course, is the famous public school founded in 1440 by Henry VI. The original name of the school was "The King's College of Our Lady of Eton Beside Windsor" and was meant to provide scholars for King's College, Cambridge. The original student body was comprised of 70 poor students who lived at the school and were educated for free as well as several paying students who lived in Eton. Eton Chapel

Eton College

is a wonderful example of the Perpendicular Gothic style. The remainder of the school buildings was added over the course of the next several centuries, notably Lupton's Chapel, finished in 1515.

Percy Shelley

Heading northwest from the Convent, the first town along the route is Amersham whose attractive High Street is a mix of Georgian and half-timbered buildings. Along the Thames are more villages including Marlow, once the home of poet Percy Shelley, it is noted for its suspension bridge across the river and cascading weir.

Continuing northwest, Waddesdon Manor is an ornate French-style country home of the influential Rothschild banking family. Now administered by the National Trust, it was created as a showplace for the

Waddesdon Manor

Rothschild collections of fine art, Sevres porcelain and furniture. French architect Gabriel-Hippolyte Destailleur designed the huge hilltop house overlooking the pastoral landscape. Comprised of Bath Stone it combines a mixture of French traditional chateau elements with round turreted towers soaring high above a mansard roof. A broad avenue leads up the hill to the house and formal terraced gardens.

Near Waddesdon is another historic Georgian house, Claydon, former home of Florence Nightingale. Several rooms in the house feature memorabilia associated with the "Lady of the Lamp." The house itself is an unpretentious 18th century rectangle in the classical style with a large porticoed entry. Claydon is remarkable for its extraordinary rococo interiors, probably the finest example of this architectural style in Britain.

Attractive Winslow reveals half-timbered thatched cottages and ornate Winslow Hall, believed to be the work of Sir Christopher Wren. The unusual central chimney stack, all that remains of William Lowndes' original mansion, marks the three floored central corps de logis of Winslow Hall. Corps de logis is the architectural term that refers to the principal block of a large, usually classical castle, mansion or palace and to the place of the principal rooms.

Nearby the ancient town of Buckingham dates back to the 7th century and contains some fine Georgian buildings as well as an imposing town hall and the distinctive Old Gaol. Just outside of town is Stowe Landscape Garden, an early example of the English Landscape Garden. The lush gardens cover 750 acres and include forty listed historic monuments and temples. The greatest names in English garden design were involved in its creation including William Kent, Charles Bridgman and Capability Brown. The gardens are celebrated for long, sinuous avenues of trees and water interspersed with thirty-two allegorical temples and architectural curiosities.

Region: London and vicinity   County: Buckinghamshire   City: Iver Heath

Accommodations
32 beds in single and double rooms. Some rooms have private baths and all are equipped with telephone.

Amenities
All meals can be provided with the lodging. Towels and linens are provided. There is a conference room, TV, sitting rooms and chapel.

Cost per room/per night
B&B in en-suite single room £32.
B&B in en-suite double room £50.
B&B in single room with shared bath £27.
Lunch and dinner £5 each.
A non-refundable deposit of £15 is necessary to secure the booking.

Directions
By car: From London take A4 towards Uxbridge. At Oxford Road Crossroad take the second road left (A412) and proceed to the Iver Heath roundabout. Take Pinewood Road past the Film Studios and turn left on Fulmer Common Road.

By train: From London Paddington to Slough, then take a taxi to the House of the Bridgettine Sisters.

By underground: From Baker Street to Uxbridge. Continue by taxi to the House of the Bridgettine Sisters.

Contact
Mother Superior
The Bridgettine Convent
Fulmer Common Road
Iver Heath Bucks SLO ONR
England, UK
Tel: 0044 (0) 1753 662073/662645
Fax: 0044 (0) 1753 662172
Website: www.bridgettineguesthouse.co.uk
Email: sbrigittae@iverconvent.fsnet.co.uk

Chester House
Methodist Church Retreat House

The Guy Chester Centre is in Muswell Hill, a popular northern suburb of London, approximately forty minutes from the very heart of the capital city. Formed by Chester House Halls of Residence and the Guy Chester Conference Centre, the complex is encompassed by ten acres of grounds and varied gardens and was founded in the 1960s after Guy Chester donated his property to the Methodist Church. At that time it became the North Bank Centre, a residence for students and young people coming to London to study or work. The Conference Centre opened six years ago and the two activities were unified under the name of Guy Chester Centre.

The Halls of Residence continue to offer long-term hospitality to 120 young people aged 18 to 26. The Conference Centre welcomes groups and individuals (groups have priority) for short stays and organized conferences. In addition to its proximity to London, Chester House is situated in an area close to many small, picturesque villages and towns.

The appeal of nearby St. Albans can be attributed to its 2,000-year history. This old market town is particularly compelling because of its abbey and the Roman settlement of Verulamium, the first Roman municipium in Britain. Its High Street is fringed with many Tudor buildings while the 15th century Curfew Tower is graced with a bell from 1335. In ages past the curfew bell rang twice a day, once in early morning and another at night. A clock was added in Victorian times and the tower is now known as the Clock Tower.

One of the most pleasant parts of St. Albans is quaint Fishpond Street whose name is derived from a fishpond that lay nearby in medieval times, a place where the monks often came to fish. The street is an appealing mix of properties, some with Georgian fronts thought to conceal much older structures.

St. Albans Cathedral occupies a lovely, grassy spot on a hilltop above the city. Its history can be traced to 209 AD when a Roman soldier named Alban became England's first martyr. He was beheaded for giving shelter to a Christian priest. Pilgrims flocked to his tomb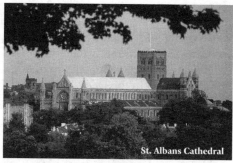

St. Albans Cathedral

especially after it became legal to do so in 313 AD. A church was built on the site sometime in the early 700s. Church historian Bede wrote of "the beautiful church worthy of all Alban's martyrdom where miracles of healing took place." A Saxon abbey was later founded in 793 and established once again under a new monastic rule by St. Oswald in the 960s.

The Saxon abbey was replaced by a Norman one in 1077 and it is this 11th century abbey church that forms the bulk of today's cathedral. In the Middle Ages it was one of the largest in the world. All the monastic buildings and the 14th century shrine of St. Albans were destroyed during the Dissolution of the Monasteries. In 1553 the church was purchased back from Henry VIII by the townspeople.

St. Albans Cathedral

In the late 19th century Sir George Gilbert Scott conducted a major Victorian restoration of the church. In 1862 murals in the imposing 300-foot long nave were uncovered after being hidden under whitewash for nearly 300 years. Further restorations and additions were made throughout the 20th century including a new chapter house dedicated by the Queen in 1982.

At one time Verulamium was the third largest town in Roman Britain. The story of this ancient place is told at the Verulamium Museum in a large park at the western edge of St. Albans. There are interpretive and interactive exhibits built around the archaeological digs that detail every aspect of life in Roman times. The parkland covers much of the ancient metropolis that still possesses Roman walls and intricate, colorful floor mosaics preserved *in situ*.

Berkhamsted, an attractive market town set in a lush green valley, was mentioned in the *Domesday Book* as the place where William the Conqueror took the Throne of England from the Saxons in 1066. There is a lovely old High Street with several noted buildings. To the rear of High Street lies the picturesque Grand Union Canal. Its most scenic part is where the canal passes King's Road, taking in old bridges and lofty warehouse buildings before heading through ancient locks on its journey to the countryside.

Castle Street is over 900 years old and is dominated by 16th century Berkhamsted School. Some handsome additions were made during the Victorian period. The parish church of St. Peter was begun in the 13th century and stands close to a collection of old timber-framed buildings. It has a strong Norman tower adorned with a clock. The interior shelters an intricately carved screen, splendid stained glass, brasses, tombs and a fine organ.

Hemel Hempstead is nestled in a delightful valley of the Chilterns. The town is distinguished by its old structures including the Norman church dedicated to St. Mary. There are a number of Tudor cottages and in the old High Street are buildings dating from the 17th and 18th centuries, many with bow-fronted shop windows.

Accommodations

For short term stays: Two twin rooms and 14 singles all with pull down bunk beds. The rooms can accommodate up to 32 people and each room has private bath.

Long term stays: 120 beds for 18-26 students and workers.

Contact the House for details.

Amenities

For short term stays: Bed, breakfast and dinner are always included. Towels and linens are provided. There are some TV and sitting rooms available to guests. There is also an extensive garden that guests may use.

Cost per person/per night

Single room £55.00 including breakfast and dinner.

Shared room (per person) £42.50 including breakfast and dinner.

Special rules

In line with the Methodist Church rules, alcohol and smoking are not allowed on the premises.

Directions

Very detailed directions about public transport are available on the website. There are also links to the underground, rail and bus maps and timetables.

By car: Chester House can be easily reached from London's North Circular Road, the A406. Exit the A406 at Colney Hatch Lane (the B550) and follow signs for Muswell Hill. Pages Lane is found on the right immediately after a Shell garage (approx. 1 mile from the North Circular). There is some street parking on Pages Lane.

By train: King's Cross, St. Pancras and Euston are the nearest central London stations to Chester House. From any central London station use the underground system to reach Muswell Hill.

By bus: The following buses stop outside Chester House:

43 (Friern Barnet - Highgate - Holloway - City - London Bridge)

102 (Edmonton - Bounds Green - Golders Green – Brent Cross)

134 (Friern Barnet - Highgate - Camden - Oxford Street)
234 (East Finchley - Muswell Hill)
299 (Muswell Hill - Bounds Green - Southgate – Cockfosters)
The Night Bus 134 runs through the night to and from Central
London every 30 mins.
By underground: The closest underground stations are Highgate or
East Finchley on the Northern Line, Bounds Green on the Piccadilly
Line. These stations are approximately 10 minutes away by bus.
Highgate: No.43 or 134
East Finchley: No.234
Bounds Green: No.102 or 299
Finsbury Park on the Victoria Line is 15 minutes away
using Bus No.W7.

Contact
Anyone
Chester House
Pages Lane
Muswell Hill
London N10 1PR
England, UK
Tel: 0044 (0) 2088 838204
Fax: 0044 (0) 2088 830843
Website: www.chestercentre.org.uk
Email: bookings@chestercentre.org.uk

More House

Canonesses of St. Augustine

In the heart of central London, a chaplain and small community of nuns reside on the premises. More House, (after Sir Thomas More), possesses an ideal location near Kensington Palace and Gardens and Hyde Park. Kensington Palace was initially the country home of the Earl of Nottingham. In 1689 the property was acquired by William III and became a Royal Palace. William commissioned Sir Christopher Wren to enlarge the building that was further enlarged and enhanced during the reign of Queen Ann for whom Wren designed the Orangery. The house displays work by Grinling Gibbons; the gardens were laid out by William Kent. Birthplace of Queen Victoria, the palace has provided a home for senior members of the Royal Family including the late Diana, Princess of Wales.

Kensington Gardens is the perfect setting for the imposing Kensington Palace. Queen Ann and Queen Caroline both extended the gardens and they now cover 275 acres planted with magnificent trees and ornamental flowerbeds. Unlike Hyde Park that opened to the public in the 17th century, Kensington Gardens were only opened in the 19th century. There are guided walks featuring wildlife and gardens associated with past kings and queens.

Sir Thomas More

Famous for its Speakers' Corner, Hyde Park is one of the Royal Parks of London. The park is divided in two by a Serpentine Lake and is contiguous with Kensington Gardens.

Royal Albert Hall

More House is also quite close to a number of museums including the Natural History, Science, Victoria and Albert museums as well as Royal Albert Hall. Within walking distance is the renowned shopping district surrounding Harrod's, one of the most famous department stores in the world.

The house was named after Thomas More, the famous British saint who was canonized in 1935. With the publication of *Utopia*, which describes a fictional country in which crime and poverty don't

King Henry VIII

exist and humanistic ideals prevail, More attracted the attention of Henry VIII who appointed him to a succession of high posts and missions. In 1529 the King made him Lord Chancellor. More resigned in 1532 at the height of his career for his principled refusal to accept King Henry's claim to be supreme head of the Church of England, a decision that ended his political career and led to his execution for treason. In the 20th century, Robert Bolt portrayed More as the ultimate man of conscience in his play *A Man for All Seasons*.

Within close proximity to More House are a number of London "suburbs" that have their fair share of charms. Ealing is home to the renowned Ealing Film Studios where many classic British comedies were produced. The studio is now owned by the BBC. Ealing is also home to the Thames Valley University and West London College, the college where three members of the singing group Queen first met: Freddie Mercury, Brian May and Roger Taylor. There was a time in the 19th century when the area was full of gardens and dubbed "Queen of the Suburbs." It remains a pleasant residential neighborhood with many old and new cultures, customs and traditions.

Nearby Kew is best known for the Royal Botanic Gardens, or as they are more commonly known "Kew Gardens." The gardens are set in 300 landscaped acres enhanced with spectacular buildings. 17th century Kew Palace is perhaps the most modest but charming of the Royal residences. The gardens were laid out 220 years ago. The Tropical and Palm Houses preserve rare specimens from the world over.

Region: London and vicinity   City: London

Roral Botanic Gardens or "Kew Gardens."

Notting Hill is defined by quiet tree-lined streets and a beautiful park. It is also the scene of London's biggest annual street party. Each August Bank Holiday Weekend since 1964, the streets of Notting Hill explode with a riot of color, cultural music, dancing and feasting. Notting Hill is home to famous Portobello Road with its shops, galleries, arcades and world famous Saturday antiques market.

Accommodations

From September through the end of June, the house is open only to university students. In July and August, it is open to all guests on a Bed & Breakfast basis. There are about 80 beds in 40 single and 20 double rooms. A few rooms can be used as family rooms accommodating up to four guests. Showers and bathrooms are shared and are located on every floor.

Amenities

In addition to a continental breakfast, a full English breakfast is served and includes bacon, eggs and sausage. Meals are served in the dining room. There is a communal TV room and a conference / meeting room that can be used by groups. Daily papers are also available. Towels and linens are supplied.

Cost per room/per night

Single £38, double £56, triple £69, quadruple £84.
More than a four week stay: Single £170 per week, twin £140 per person per week (£280 per room).

89

A non-refundable deposit is required. Special discounts for groups and longer stays. Credit cards are not accepted.

Directions

Since it is very difficult and extremely expensive to park in London, the nuns suggest public transportation.

By Underground: More House is located between two stops; South Kensington and Gloucester Road on the District, Circle and Piccadilly lines. Piccadilly Line connects London to Heathrow Airport.

Contact

Anyone
Sister Francoise is in charge of hospitality
More House
53, Cromwell Road
London SW7 2EH
England, UK
Tel: 0044 (0) 2075 842040
Fax: 0044 (0) 2075 815748
Website: www.morehouse.co.uk
Email: office@morehouse.co.uk

Note: The house books very early. Sister Francoise suggests booking as early as possible. Reservations can be made via the Internet.

Region: London and vicinity   County: Hertfordshire   City: London Colney

All Saints Pastoral Centre

Diocese of Westminster

All Saints Pastoral Centre is on the west side of London Colney, a large village in the outskirts of London, south of St. Albans. The village is situated on the coaching route that once was the main connection between London and St. Albans. The village, in fact, features the remains of a medieval chapel on a moated island believed to be a stop on the pilgrimage path to St. Albans Shrine.

At one time the Centre was an Anglican convent of All Saints Sisters built in 1901 by Leonard Stokes. The building, bought by the Diocese of Westminster in 1973, is now a conference and retreat center offering a modern venue for both religious and business meetings. Individuals are welcome but priority is given to larger groups.

The complex has preserved the original features of the exterior; the interiors have been

adapted to meet modern conference requirements. It is arranged around a quadrangle garden with an inner cloister. Meeting rooms are on the ground floor; residential accommodations are on the first floor. The Comper Chapel, designed by Sir Ninian Comper, was completed in two periods; the first half in 1927, the second in 1963. It is adorned with beautiful stained glass windows.

The Centre is convenient to a number of appealing towns and villages. During the first century BC, a Roman settlement existed in nearby Baldock. There is evidence to support the theory that occupation continued throughout the Roman period. Baldock lays claim to the lovely church of St. Mary, a spacious structure with a two-story south porch, an early 14th century tower with an octagonal lantern and a small spire. The interior is imbued with an aura of peacefulness and serenity and displays a 13th century octagonal font, 15th century screens, brasses and impressive monuments, one of which is by E.H. Baily, ca. 1846.

The town lies close to the River Beane, in a spot where the river flows through some lovely water meadows and tranquil English countryside. In town and on the fringes are attractive properties, some dating back to the 16th century, a time when the Great North Road that forms part of Baldock's High Street, was not as busy as it is today.

Also in the vicinity, Benington with its curving country lanes presents an atmosphere of cool and calm and the feeling that the modern world has passed by without noticing this classic Hertfordshire village, a commodious place of ancient trees, grassed open spaces, picturesque cottages and gorgeous old farmhouses. It has long enjoyed the reputation as one of the prettiest villages in the area. A row of enchanting black and white cottages edge one side of the village green that boasts a large entitled Georgian Manor House. The interior shelters faded medieval wall paintings and tombs topped by exquisite effigies of a knight and his lady. They date from the 14th and 15th centuries. The knight wears chain mail and the lady has beautiful long hair. The other knight is in plate armor and his lady wears a wimple.

An interesting day excursion can be made to Tring, a market town since 1315. Tring lies on the Ridgeway Path close to the waters of the River Thame and is bordered on one side by the Chilterns, a range of dense wooded hills that span an Area of Outstanding Natural Beauty. Tring Mansion once belonged to the ancestors of George Washington.

Tring Mansion

Years later in 1872 the estate was acquired by members of the famous Rothschild family. The park encompassing the house is extremely scenic. It was planned in the 18th century and presents opportunities for walkers and nature enthusiasts. There is an obelisk in the park known locally as Nell Gwyns Monument. The noble avenue of lime trees is a legacy of the Rothschild's.

The town's narrow streets reveal a rich display of architecture from several periods. The parish church at the center of town is perhaps the oldest building and is dedicated to St. Peter and St. Paul. Historically the first mention of its existence is from 1214. The church of today is mostly from the 15th century. Close to the church there is a war memorial dedicated to those who died during both world wars. The church and its graveyards are enclosed within a low stone wall and highlighted by a number of ancient gravestones and tombs covering hundreds of years. The town's Memorial Gardens offer an oasis of calm and are beautifully designed with lovely flowerbeds, huge trees, shrubs and a pretty pond.

There is a Town Trail leaflet available at the Rothschild Museum. It details the most historic, interesting and beautiful parts of the town. Included in the walk are many Tudor timber-framed properties, the tiny Baptist Chapel of 1832 and the handsome timber-framed Rose and Crown Hotel.

Accommodations
70 singles, 25 twins and 3 suites. Each room has a washbasin; baths are shared except in the 3 suites. Two of the suites are twin bedded and equipped for the disabled; one is a single room with private bath.

Amenities
All meals are provided with the lodging. There is a resident chef who offers traditional English fare as well as occasional dishes from other countries. Cold meals are available from the Salad Bar. Vegetarians and others with special

dietary needs can be provided for upon request. The large dining room can seat 160 people. Towels and linens are provided. There is a wide range of meeting and conference rooms and a chapel, garden with prayer walk, bookshop and licensed bar. There is also a car park available for guests.

Cost per person/per night
£35 B&B.
£53 full board.
The combination of prices to be determined when reservations are made.

Special rules
The center closes at 11 PM.

Directions
By car: Leave the M1 northbound at intersection 6 and join the A405 towards St. Albans. At the roundabout join the M25 towards the Dartford Tunnel. Leave the M25 Motorway at Intersection 22 and follow the signs to Radlett. After about 1/2 mile at the second small roundabout, take the right turn into Shenley Lane. The Centre is immediately on the left.

By train: From London take a train of Thameslink line to St. Albans. The train runs from Brighton in the south to Bedford in the north and passes through the London Bridge, Blackfriars, Thameslink, Farringdon and King's Cross. From St. Albans Thameslink Railway Station take a taxi to the Centre. The taxi ride from St. Albans takes approximately ten minutes and costs around £8. Details of the route and timetables can be accessed on: www.thameslink.co.uk.

Contact
Elias Papadopoulos
All Saints Pastoral Centre
Shenley Lane
London Colney
Herts. AL2 1AF
England, UK
Tel: 0044 (0) 1727 829306 or 1727 822010 (Switchboard)
Fax: 0044 (0) 1727 822880
Website: www.allsaintspc.org.uk
Email: conf.office@allsaintspc.org.uk

NORTH EAST

Region: North East · County: Durham · City: Consett

Minsteracres Monastery and Retreat Centre

Congregation of the Passion of Jesus Christ (Passionists)

Minsteracres is the home of a Passionist Congregation and Retreat Centre set in the comely countryside on the border between Northumberland and County Durham.

Minsteracres is a fine 18th century listed mansion built by George Silvertop in 1758 and then enlarged and remodeled in 1811 and 1865. The Silvertops were a Roman Catholic family who owned extensive portions of land in the area. Henry Charles Silvertop built the chapel by the mansion and dedicated it to St. Elizabeth of Hungary in 1854.

In the second part of the 19th century, the Silvertops, following a fashion of the time, collected various plants and flowers for the grounds. Today Minsteracres is known for its avenue of sequoiadendron giganteum (California giant redwood trees), probably the largest collection of this type of tree in the country. Within the ninety acres of the monastery's grounds and tended by a team of volunteers, The Shrubbery is an attractive wild woodland section of the park that boasts a large variety of plants, trees and shrubs and is a popular diversion for guests.

Avenue of California giant redwoods

The Silvertop family sold the house to the Passionist Congregation in 1949. At that time the fathers embarked on a project of adapting the mansion to the needs of a monastery. In the 1960s the old stables were transformed into a retreat house that opened in 1967. Minsteracres has been active for over forty years. Today it is the residence of a community of Passionists (4) and one lay person. Supported by a group of volunteers, the retreat team and lay staff offer hospitality and spiritual retreats to individuals and groups. A detailed agenda including costs is available on the website. Groups can also organize their own activities, retreats and workshops. Minsteracres offers hospitality to people of all denominations and ages.

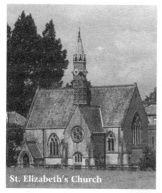

St. Elizabeth's Church

The exterior of the main building has preserved the original details of the structure. Most of the interiors were altered during the 20th century restoration.

St. Elizabeth's Church contains the original stained glass windows and stations of the cross as well as a pretty Carrara marble statue of Our Lady. The ceiling is adorned with the coats-of-arms of the Silvertops and related families.

The area surrounding the center is a medley of charming and historic towns. Nine miles south of Minsteracres is the lovely village of Wolsingham. Lying on the edge of the North Pennines in an area of great scenic beauty, the wild and beautiful landscape is dotted by scattered farms, their meadows full of grazing sheep and cattle. The region has maintained its age-old character exemplified by the typical Pennine cottages and houses. One of the most delightful aspects of Wolsingham is Bradley Burn, a tributary of the River Wear high in the hills above the village. This tranquil locale offers lovely walks with breathtaking views of the countryside. Not far from Wolsingham is Auckland Castle distinguished by its grand arch. Open to the public, it is the official residence of the Bishop of Durham and has been owned by the diocese for 800 years.

Nearby Stanhope is a lovely, bustling little town almost entirely built of stone particularly around the Old Market Square. A largely rural region, its terrain is a patchwork of fields interspersed by a smattering of old farmsteads. The parish church is dedicated to St. Thomas. In its churchyard is a 250-million-year-old fossilized tree.

Corbridge is a quiet town in a peaceful position on the River Tyne that grew from a settlement for Roman troops working on Hadrian's Wall. In spite of the fact that it was razed to the ground several times by border warfare with the Scots, it has many relics from its illustrious past. Corbridge is mostly unchanged with shady, cobbled streets, its houses and quaint shops set haphazardly around a town plan dating to medieval times. There are old stone buildings hung with flower-filled baskets and a bridge built in the 16th century that spans the waters of the Tyne.

Three-story pele tower

Fortified vicarages are rare but one survives in Corbridge. Built during the reign of Edward II, its walls are four feet thick. The Vicar's Pele can be found in the southeast corner of the churchyard. The three-story pele tower, with one room to each story, was built in 1318 and used as a vicarage for the adjacent church. It is constructed mainly of sandstone taken from the nearby Roman fortress at Corstopitum and was used as a vicarage until the early 17th century. Unfortunately the original interior is in ruins.

Another nearby town, Durham was built on Island Hill in 995. The old center with its splendid cathedral and castle perched high above a loop of the River Wear is a spectacular sight. Durham is a place of winding streets, an ancient marketplace, alleyways and rambling old churches that underscore its past as a great place of pilgrimage. The huge cathedral is third only to Canterbury and York in ecclesiastical significance but excels in architectural splendor. The original rib vaulted church was completed in 1133 and took 40 years to build. The cathedral owes its origins to the monks of Lindisfarne who in 875 AD

ENGLAND

Durham Cathedral

fled from Viking attacks taking the coffin of St. Cuthbert with them. They settled where the cathedral now stands and built the White Church for the saint's remains.

The founder of the present cathedral was a Norman who was Bishop of Durham in the late 11th century. He was determined to build a church to replace the small White Church on the scale, splendor and style he had seen in France. In 1093 the foundations were laid for what would become the finest example of Norman architecture in Europe. Durham Cathedral houses fine treasures and is home to two of the greatest figures of the Christian church in England – St. Cuthbert, the shepherd saint of Northumbria and the Venerable Bede, Britain's first historian.

Newcastle-upon-Tyne was known as Pons Aelii in Roman times and it was the Romans who built the first bridge over the River Tyne. Guarded by a Roman fort, in later years it was replaced by a castle erected by Robert Courthose, eldest son of William the Conqueror. It was from this building that the town derives its name. In the 12th century the castle was succeeded by another built of stone. The castle keep can still be seen and is believed to be one of the best examples of its kind in the country. The Black Gate and Town Walls belong to the 13th and 14th centuries, evidence of Newcastle's rich historical past. The popular conception of Newcastle as a place of coalfields and mines has continued since Tudor times but there is more to Newcastle than that.

Tyne Bridge

Newcastle is an attractive, spacious city full of gracious classical buildings. During 1825 to 1840 the vision of three men resulted in a fine town center with many of the elegant structures remaining to this day. On a more modern note is the bridge that resembles a rainbow of flashing steel flying above the River Tyne.

The mechanism of the bridge turns on a central pivot, causing the bridge to open up and allow river traffic to ply the waters of the Tyne. From this massive suspension bridge are sweeping city views. The Baltic Centre is a new art gallery on the river banks that sits in the shadow of the historic Tyne Bridge and Millennium Eye Bridge. The towering Baltic Centre is an international, contemporary arts showplace, the largest such venue outside of London.

The splendid cathedral church of St. Nicholas has stood at the heart of Newcastle for centuries. Its superb lantern tower rises above the rooftops and is a landmark seen from miles around. The cathedral has handsome stained glass, mostly from the 19th and 20th centuries and one medieval window depicting the *Madonna and Child*. Another superb window is dedicated to Danish seamen and is from a design by Queen Margarethe of Denmark. The Thorntown Brass dates from 1441 and is a memorial to Robert Thornton, his wife Agnes and their fourteen children.

Cathedral church of St. Nicholas

A worthwhile day trip can be made to the sparsely populated Northumbrian Coast. There is not much to surpass the beauty of this wild coast with its almost perfect white sandy beaches, natural rock formations and brooding castles, built as symbols of power by Barons and Kings of centuries ago. It is believed that the area may have been inhabited for several thousand years; Bronze Age burial chambers have been discovered as well as the remains of a 13th century chapel at Ebb's Neuk Point. A region steeped in legend and folklore, it is home to the beautiful Farne Islands with their rich wildlife habitation. The lonely outcrops forming the Farne Island Bird Sanctuary off the coast of picturesque Seahouses are unique. In the breeding season, May to July, the islands welcome 100,000 nesting birds including the puffin. There are also colonies of grey seals to be seen languishing on the rocks. In calm weather, sea trips to the islands run from Seahouses. There are picturesque fishing villages with old harbors that offer the enchantment of a bygone era. Among the timeless coastal villages is Beadness, a fishing hamlet crammed with pretty houses and villas. From the newly restored harbor are views of a fortress-like structure built of glowing stone. These are beautifully preserved 18th century Lime Kilns, cared for by the National Trust.

Nearby Bamburgh is known as the ancient capital of the Northumbrian Coast and is home to one of the finest castles in England. Bamburgh Castle sits majestically on a basalt outcrop and looks across the dunes and the sea to the Farne Islands and Lindisfarne. These islands are associated with nearby Holy Island as one of the cradles of Christianity in the north. Founded in 547 by King Ida, the village has a fine Norman church dedicated to St. Aiden.

Also in the vicinity, Craster is a quiet and unspoiled fishing village. Typically the houses and cottages are built of stone, some are quite ancient and have the appearance of growing out from the hard rock on which they stand. They are gaunt and strong and constructed to withstand the harsh weather that pounds this stretch of glorious coastline. The rocky promontory jutting out into the sea is crowned with the romantic ruins of 14th century Dunstanburgh Castle.

Accommodations

There are various types of accommodations.

Main House and Retreat House: Maximum of 86 beds (32 in the Main House and 54 in the adjoining Retreat House) in singles, twins and doubles. Baths are shared except for two ground floor en-suite single rooms in the Retreat House with disabled facilities, one of which has an adjoining room for a caregiver.

Amenities

All meals are provided with the lodging. Linens are supplied. People are asked to bring their own towels. There is a variety of meeting, conference and common rooms. The retreat house has a kitchen area for tea and coffee, including licensed bar, book and souvenir shop, chapel, library and extensive grounds.

Poustina (or Hermitage): The hermitage is in a secluded area on the ground floor of the main house. It has its own chapel, study/dining room, en-suite bedroom creating a silence where one person can to find the 'poustina' of the heart and be immersed in that silence.

Region: North East   County: Durham   City: Consett

Amenities
Guests are required to be self-catering, towels and linens
are supplied.

Youth Centre: The Centre occupies the restored barracks used by
firemen during World War II. It is set in the spacious grounds of the
Retreat Centre and has two dormitories with two-tier bunk beds
each with 16 beds, toilets, washroom and shower. It also contains a
separate adult room.

Amenities
Guests are required to be self-catering. Towels and linens are not
supplied. There is a large well-equipped kitchen, a recreation/dining
room and a covered veranda with a barbecue corner.

Cost per person/per night
Price depends on the type of accommodation and varies each year.
Inquire when reservations are made.

Special rules
Groups' maximum stay 1 week.

Directions
By car: From London take M1 to A1 north towards Newcastle. Go
left after Darlington and take A68 towards Corbridge. About 1 mile
beyond Kiln Pit Hill, follow the signs for Minsteracres and turn left
onto the entrance drive. It is a mile to the house.
By train: Take a train from London King's Cross to Newcastle and
then change to Riding Mill. A car from Minsteracres will provide
transportation from the train station.

Contact
Retreat Administrator
Minsteracres
Nr Consett
Co. Durham, DH8 9RT
England, UK
Tel: 0044 (0) 1434 673248
Fax: 0044 (0) 1434 673540
Website: www.minsteracres.org or www.minsteracres.co.uk
Email: info@minsteracres.org

NORTH WEST

(Includes Lake District)

Rydal Hall
Diocese of Carlisle

Rydal Hall occupies a splendid setting in the heart of the Lake District. Situated in the small village of Rydal, beside Rydal Water and River Rothay, between Ambleside and Grasmere, the Hall is encircled by the wooded fells of Loughrigg and Nab Scar with spectacular views of the mountains, Rothay Valley and Rydal Water.

The village consists of a few houses (some dating back as far as 1535), St. Mary's Church, Rydal Hall, Rydal Mount (home to Wordsworth for over 30 years) and Rydal Hall, a fine Grade II structure dating from the 16th to 19th century. The hall is the prominent building of the village, both visually and historically. It was home to le Fleming family for over 400 years. The family's Flemish ancestry can be traced back as far as 864. More than likely they were linked to the 1066 Norman Conquest and Michael le Fleming was probably related to William, Duke of Normandy, who granted him lands in Cumberland to repay his support during the Conquest. Rydal Hall began as a farmhouse and since 1409 has been associated with le Fleming family by marriage. Initially the family lived at Coniston Hall but moved to Rydal in 1576. At that time it was converted into a primary residence and remained as such until the 20th century when it was bought and transformed into a retreat center by the Diocese of Carlisle (1970).

The house was built in the 16th century by Michael le Fleming, expanded during the 17th century by Daniel le Fleming and refaced in the 18th. The interior has been considerably altered since its original foundation and the facade modified during the Victorian period. The gardens (now partially restored) were designed by Thomas Mawson in 1909. In the garden, a place of formal and informal venues, there are native plants and trees including a remark-

Rydal Gardens

able 500-year old sweet chestnut measuring 36′ in diameter. The grounds and gardens are open to the public every day from 10:00 AM until 4:00 PM.

Today Rydal Hall is a very active Diocesan Retreat and Conference Centre as well as home to the internal Rydal Hall Community. It offers a wide range of courses and retreats (an updated program is available on the Hall's website) and the opportunity of spending a holiday

Rydal Parish Church

in this grand area. Guests may participate in the community's daily prayer and meditation and take advantage of the hall's 30 acres of grounds and attractive gardens.

The Old School Tea Room is a charming stone structure located on the grounds of the Hall. Sir Daniel le Fleming constructed it in the 17th century as a schoolroom for his children. It was beautifully rebuilt in 2007 and today serves as a tearoom. In addition to coffee, tea and a variety of hot and cold drinks and ice cream, it offers homemade soup and cakes prepared with organic ingredients.

Ambleside, meaning "Shieling" or summer pasture by the riverbank, lies beside the northern shore of Lake Windemere. A small but bustling Victorian town, it is an ideal base from which to explore the Lake District. An open-air market is held every Wednesday. The Bridge House is purported to be the most photographed house in the entire Lake District. Originally used as an apple store, it was ingeniously built directly over Stock Beck on a stone arch in order to avoid paying any land tax. Now a National Trust Shop, at one time the small building was home to a family of eight.

There are many pretty villages in the breathtaking Lake District but few possess the quiet contentment of Rydal, a village forever associated with the poet William Wordsworth, one of the founders of the English Romantic Age. The poet lived in Rydal and his works reflect the beautiful terrain that so vividly captured his imagination. Born in Cockermouth, he was locally educated and later married his childhood friend Mary Hutchinson. Together they settled into Dove Cottage in Grassmere but after some time the family moved to Rydal.

Wordsworth home, Rydal Mount

His home, Rydal Mount, provides a glimpse into his life. The Mount has changed little since he lived there and still contains the original furnishings, personal possessions and first editions of his work. The house is embraced by lovely gardens laid out according to his designs. The grounds include waterfalls and a summerhouse. Wordsworth bought and planted a nearby field with daffodils in celebration of his daughter Dora's birthday. Now in the care of the National Trust, Dora's Field comes alive in vibrant color every spring. Rydal Water, though small, is quite scenic. It is not as remote or as spectacular as some of the high upland tarns but its wild beauty and pretty shoreline make it popular with visitors. It is also the locale of Wordsworth Seat, reputed to have been the poet's favorite viewpoint. Nab Cottage, once home to friends of the Wordsworth's, overlooks the lake. It is also near Rydal Cave, a mysterious cavern in the hills above the lake.

Grasmere is a tiny stone village beautifully situated between the tranquil waters of Grasmere Lake and the jagged heights of Helm Crag and Nab Scar. A walk through the village reveals a majestic landscape of towering peaks, stunning lakes and glistening waterfalls. William Wordsworth and his sister Dorothy lived in a stone cottage just beyond the village church. The years of his supreme work as a poet were done during his residence in Dove Cottage. The cottage was once an inn called the Dove and Olive and many of the building's distinctive features date from that time: white-washed

"The Cottage" in Grasmere

walls, flagstone floors and dark, wood paneling. There are many alluring buildings in and around Grasmere including an old creeper-covered house standing by the bridge close to the River Rothay. Grey-green and purple tinged stone shops, houses and cottages flank Broad Street including the village church of St. Oswald described by Wordsworth in his epic poem, *The Excursion*. Near the altar, an inscribed profile in white marble depicts Wordsworth between graceful daffodils and bluebells.

The little hamlet of Buttermere remains serene in its simplicity and beauty. The charms of Buttermere include a bright little beck (a brook or stream) spanned by an old stone bridge. The poet Wordsworth wrote eloquently of Buttermere, especially of the little church that he found deeply inspiring. Crowned with a two-bell tower, the church was built in 1841 to replace one from the 15th century. Considering the charm and natural beauty of the Buttermere environs, it is not surprising that many artists have been inspired by the memorable terrain. The painting by Turner, hanging in the Tate Gallery, depicts the sheer majesty of Buttermere Lake.

Lake Windermere is England's largest lake and one of its most popular. The town's quaint narrow streets sprawl along the shores of the lake. Sweeping upwards from the fringe of the lake, the legacy of the town's Victorian glory can be seen in the fine buildings that remain from that period, a time when wealthy industrialists from Lancashire built extraordinary residences around the lake. Many have since become luxury hotels.

The romantic valley of Borrowdale lies beside the densely wooded shores of Derwent Water and presents an impressive picture of the high peaks reflected in the lovely lake, a quintessential Cumbrian landscape. It is tucked away in a quiet place where streams tumble down crags amidst a patchwork of old packhorse trails. The tiny hamlet of Grange is one of the loveliest spots, the place where the valley narrows dramatically to form the "Jaws of Borrowdale," between Grange Fell and Castle Crag. The double arched bridge was built in 1675 but the hamlet's origins date to a much earlier time. In medieval times the monks of Furness, owners of this part of the valley, built an outlying farm here. Furness Abbey was one of the richest Cistercian monasteries in England, exceeded only by Fountains Abbey in Yorkshire. Located in a peaceful valley, the regal 700-year old remains of the abbey once housed the flourishing community of this wealthy order.

Watendlath is a peaceful hamlet set around a trout-filled tarn. The hamlet is crouched beneath the surrounding fells and mirrored in the waters below. Hundreds of years ago, this isolated spot belonged to the monks of Fountains Abbey. A place of great beauty, Watendlath's dramatic landscape is composed of whitewashed cottages and farms.

It is excellent walking country with sign-posted paths leading through flower-filled hedgerows into leafy dells including a path to Rosthwaite Village and Lodore Falls.

Accommodations
Rydal Hall offers a variety of accommodations.

Main house: There are 30 single and twin bedrooms, half of which are en-suite.

Amenities
All meals can be supplied with the lodging. Towels and linens are provided. There is a chapel, library, meeting/conference rooms, licensed bar, drying room for wet clothing and access to the grounds. The Hall is accessible to the disabled.

Cost per person/per night
B&B £40.50, half board £55, full board £67.50.

Accommodations
Youth Centre: Located on the grounds of Rydal Hall estate, it offers hospitality to groups of all ages. A historical building dating back to the mid-1500s, it has two large dorms with 14 and 18 bunk beds and two rooms, each with two beds.

Amenities
Meals are not supplied but groups can prepare their own meals in a kitchen at their disposal. Towels and linens are not provided. Guests are required to bring their own sleeping bags. There is a dining / recreation room, large equipped kitchen, wood burner and coin laundry machine.

Cost per group/per night
The Centre is let as a unit. November to March £180, April to October and New Year's £270.

Accommodations
Campsite: Within the woodland surrounding Rydal Hall there are four different sized campsites: Large groups, small groups, families and back-packers respectively. There is a water supply and two toilet blocks with hot and cold showers, plus one block for washing up. Electric hook ups are available as well as laundry and drying facilities.

Cost per person/per night
Adults £6.00, under 18 £4.50.

Accommodations
Holiday Cottage - The Stable: The cottage is by Rydal Beck in the former 17th century farm building and stables of Rydal Hall. There is a double and a twin room that share a newly refurbished bathroom.

Amenities
There is a kitchen and dining/sitting room where guests can prepare their own meals, although they are welcome to book occasional meals at the Hall. Guests may also participate in the daily liturgy and have access to the bar and gardens. Bed linens are provided; towels are not. Guests are required to leave the cottage clean on departure. Smoking is not permitted.

Cost per week
The house is let as a unit and costs £260-335 depending on the time of the year.

Directions
By car: From London take M1, exit at junction 19 onto M6 towards Coventry/Birmingham. Exit at junction 36 onto A590 towards A591. Continue on A591 towards Kendal and then reach Ambleside. About a mile after leaving the town take the right turn sign-posted 'Rydal Hall' (blue sign) and 'Rydal Mount' (brown sign).
The Hall is first on the right through wrought iron gates.
By train: From London Euston take a train to Oxenholme or Windermere. From there take a bus to Rydal. 'Rydal Church' bus stop on the A591 road is just 200 yards from Rydal Hall. Guests can be met at this bus stop by telephoning in advance. For information on local bus services, please telephone the Traveline: 0044 (0) 8712 002233.

Contact
Bookings can be made by telephone, or through the website by downloading the Private Guest or Group Booking forms.
The Bookings Co-ordinator
Rydal Hall
Ambleside, Cumbria, LA22 9LX
England, UK
Tel: 0044 (0) 1539 432050
Website: www.rydalhall.org.
Email: bookings@rydalhall.org or mail@rydalhall.org

Region: North West   County: Lancashire   City: Warton (Carnforth)

Monastery of Our Lady of Hyning
Bernardine Cistercian Nuns

Our Lady of Hyning is in Warton in the north of Lancashire on the Cumbrian border, a region designated as an Area of Outstanding Natural Beauty. Surrounded by extraordinary countryside famous for its spectacular limestone crops, it is also the perfect gateway to places like the Lake District, the Yorkshire Dales and North Pennines as well as Morecambe Bay. Historic Lancaster with its dramatic castle is only nine miles from the Monastery.

Founded by a group of four sisters from the monasteries of Slough and Westcliff-on-Sea, the original house, which now serves as a guesthouse, had been a private mansion surrounded by farmland. In 1983 as the number of sisters increased, the nuns built an extension to the house. A year later an old stone barn was converted into the church and in 1999 part of the main house was dismantled and enlarged. The property is encompassed by a lovely garden where guests are invited to wander and enjoy.

Monastery Chapel

Today the Monastery houses thirteen nuns of various nationalities, each actively involved in the work of the guesthouse. Guests of all denominations, individually or as a group, are welcome. A calendar of organized retreats is available on the website.

It is believed that Carnforth derived its name from its position by the ford crossing the River Keer. Settled by invading Danes, many of the place names in the district suggest Scandinavian origins including Hallgarth, Grisdale and Thrang End. Shifts in the salt marsh occasionally reveal artifacts such as remnants of tools and half-wrought shipyard lumber.

Ancient Saxon courts were held on a nearby hill known as Meothaw Hillock. On his way south, Charles II encamped his army at Carnforth in 1651. The market town developed in Victorian times around an ironworks. It is famous for the filming of the romantic classic *Brief Encounter*. Nearby Leighton Hall is a 12th century fortified manor house rebuilt in the 18th century with a neo-Gothic façade set in exquisite grounds. Trained birds of prey give flying displays in the afternoon.

There is a canal network that links Carnforth to many of the nearby villages and countryside and two canal waterbuses

Canal waterbuses

that operate seasonally from Carnforth and Lancaster. The canals, tow-paths and part of the Sustrans Network around Carnforth provide an idyllic way to explore this hidden corner of Lancashire.

The Lake District comprises a spectacular terrain of glacial peaks and ribbon lakes and embraces the five tallest mountains in England. Its rocks provide a dramatic record of nearly 50 million years of natural history, colliding continents, deep oceans, tropical seas and kilometer-thick ice sheets that helped shape the modern landscape. This diverse geographical tableau includes open fells with a mosaic of high craggy peaks and screes, heaths, moorland and grassland as well as remote valleys with fast flowing streams. The lakes, tarns and meres that give the area its name are nationally important for their range of habitats and imbue the Lake District with distinctive scenery and recreational potential found nowhere else in England.

Young Beatrix Potter

The Lakes have been a constant source of inspiration to writers, among them Beatrix Potter who wrote whimsical tales from her home, Hill Top in Near Sawrey, now a living museum. Another writer who found his creative voice in the Lake District was the great romantic poet William Wordsworth, whose poems describe the area's natural wonders. Dove Cottage in Grasmere was his home for nine years and is now a museum dedicated to his life and works.

Morecambe Bay is the largest expanse of intertidal mudflats and sand in England and the place where thousands of wading birds feed and breed. The sands of Morecambe Bay are infamous. At one time travelers cut across the bay at low tide to shorten the long trail around the Kent estuary. But many perished as the rising water turned the beach to quicksand and the fog obscured the paths. It is said that the tide can come in "as fast as a horse can run." Today, there are Royally appointed local guides for crossing the bay in safety.

Quicksand swallows car in Morecambe Bay

Region: North West   County: Lancashire   City: Warton (Carnforth)

Northwest of the Monastery, Grange-over-Sands is a charming Edwardian lakeside resort on Morecambe Bay that offers one of the mildest climates in the North. Traces of its Edwardian heritage remain in the holiday villas and huge hotels. It is a place of hilly streets and a wonderful seafront promenade enhanced with formal terraces and serene manicured gardens.

Quite close to Grange-over-Sands is the village of Cartmel whose town square is surrounded by old shops, pubs and a 14th century gatehouse owned by the National Trust. It is famous for its 12th century Cartmel Priory, a structure of cathedral-like proportions reached via a narrow street crammed with cottages. The priory is one of the few English monastic churches to survive Henry VIII's Reformation. It escaped almost unscathed, leaving its soaring belfry to be seen as a landmark from almost every part of the village. The church displays a magnificent stained glass window of the 15th century as well as outstanding choir stalls.

Accommodations

20 rooms: 7 single, 1 double and 12 twins. There are 12 rooms in the main house and 8 (sleeping 12 people) are in the adjacent cottages. All rooms can be used as singles. Both men and women are welcome. The facilities are accessible to the disabled. Baths are shared now, but will be private in the future (there is no precise date as of this writing).

ENGLAND

Amenities

Towels and soap are not supplied. Linens are provided. All meals can be provided with the lodging. Guests are requested to notify the sisters if they are not going to be at the guesthouse for meals. Guests are also asked to kindly help with washing-up and table-setting. There is a library, bookshop, small gift shop, sitting area with tea and coffee making facilities, meeting room, quiet corners and a church. Most of the garden is available to guests. An Art Studio has recently been established and guests are invited to make use of this amenity. The guesthouse is closed from January 3rd until the end of the month and a variable period between July and August.

Cost per person/per night

Suggested donation - inquire of the Booking Secretary.

Directions

By car: From London take M1 north to the junction with M6. Proceed on M6 to exit 35 and take A601 towards Carnforth. At the roundabout turn right onto A6 and proceed about a mile and then turn left onto Borwick Lane. Once at the T junction turn right into Warton Main Street. The entrance to the Monastery is about 1/2 mile ahead on the right.

By train: From London Euston to Lancaster and then change to Carnforth. Get off at Carnforth (on the Preston Barrow-in-Furness line) and call a taxi or when available, take the local Carnforth Connect Bus Line 1 that serves the Monastery. Ask to be dropped off at the Monastery. The Monastery is about 4 km from the station.

Contact

Booking Secretary
Monastery of Our Lady of Hyning
Warton
Carnforth LA5 9SE
Lancashire
England, UK
Tel: 0044 (0) 1524 732684
Fax: 0044 (0) 1524 720287
Website: www.bernardine.org/hyninge.html
Email: hyningbookings@yahoo.co.uk

Foxhill

Diocese of Chester

Foxhill is a retreat and conference center of the Diocese of Chester. Just a couple of miles from the small town of Frodsham, it is halfway between Chester and Warrington and not far from Liverpool. Foxhill possesses a beautiful setting nestled in the Cheshire Hills and is enveloped by seventy acres of mature woodland.

A charming old country house, Foxhill was built in the 1860s for a local clergyman and then owned by other businessmen until it was acquired by a member of the Pilkington family. The head of the family was a devoted, generous man who decided to donate the house to the Bishop of Chester in 1969. The Diocese converted the house into a retreat and conference center organizing retreats, workshops and conferences for the clergy. Today Foxhill offers hospitality to individuals, groups and families for short holidays when not occupied by those on retreats. "Our main policy is not to turn anyone away," said the Warden.

Region: North West   County: Cheshire   City: Frodsham

Frodsham is a lively market town located where the River Weaver meets the mouth of the Mersey. The town was an important Mersey port during the Middle Ages and a staging post during the stage coach era. 17th, 18th and 19th century buildings flank its spacious tree-lined street. The town hosts a popular weekly market. There are traces of Stone Age and Iron Age settlements on the hills of the area but the first known settlers were Anglo-Saxons of the Kingdom of Mercia.

The entrancing city of Chester is southwest of Frodsham. Founded by the Romans nearly 2,000 years ago as a fort town, Chester was called Deva or Castra Devana by the Romans. It was later named Legaceaster by the Saxons who ruled it before it was conquered by the Danes in 908. After years of resistance, the city surrendered to William the Conqueror and prospered after the building of the port in the 12th century. Chester is the only city in England to have preserved its medieval walls in their entirety. The red sandstone walls cover an almost complete circuit of two miles. They were built during the Middle Ages over the original wooden walls erected by the Romans and form part of the original Roman defenses.

The walls are a popular promenade with many of the towers and gatehouses removed or adapted to allow free movement along the entire circuit of the walls. The Victorians further changed the walls by removing the medieval gates and replacing them with wider ornamental ones. The famous Eastgate Clock was added in 1899 to commemorate the Diamond Jubilee of Queen Victoria. A stroll around the walls provides a sense of the town's history and prime location. From one side, a bird's eye view of the city, from the other, the awe-inspiring mountains of Wales.

Wall walking path

The ruins of the Chester Roman Amphitheatre are the largest as yet uncovered in Britain and date from the first century when the Roman fort was founded. The stone ruins are similar to those found in Continental Europe although a smaller wooden amphitheatre may have existed on the site at one time. The site was only rediscovered in

Roman relics

1929 during construction work. Today only the northern half of the structure is exposed, the southern half is covered by buildings, some of them listed and managed by the English Heritage. The amphitheatre is a true Roman structure built around 86 AD and may have also served as a training ground for Roman troops. In Chester's Grosvenor Museum are Roman relics as well as the original altar from the amphitheatre.

The town itself has a special air to it. The shopping streets are a maze of black and white timbered buildings with courtyard cafes and tucked-away arcades. The Rows, famous galleried structures that fringe the city's main streets, are unique to Chester. No one knows how these two-tiered arcades arose. What is known is that they date

to the 13th century. As an aside, at the Gothic Norman cathedral dedicated to the local Patron Saint Werburgh, Handel rehearsed *The Messiah* for the first time in 1741. The impressive cathedral was founded in 1092 and offers insight into the life of the Benedictine monks and is the venue for recitals and special events.

Chester, like all major towns, has its share of churches. The handsome Norman-Gothic style sandstone cathedral was built in the 10th century to hold the remains of Saint Werburgh and is noted for its intricate and richly carved woodwork, the Lady Chapel and the Cloisters. Historically, the status of the church was changed in 1093 by Hugh Lapus, Earl of Chester, who together

Gothic Norman cathedral

with St. Anselm, founded an abbey of Benedictine monks. The abbey was dissolved in 1540 and the cathedral came into being as a Bishopric in 1541.

Over the centuries this splendid building has hardly changed. It retains the layout of the original monastery building with court, baptistery, cloisters and chapter house. All are equally impressive, showing superb carvings. In the north clerestory of the nave, the Chester Imp is a famous carving of a full-height skeleton standing behind a drape and leering down incongruously from below the garlands. Outstanding features of the church encompass the woodcarving in the choir stalls that dates from around 1380. The bench ends present Arthurian legend, mythical beasts, Aesop's fables and St. Werburgh. The shrine of the saint is evocative of the days when pilgrims came to spend the night with heads bowed in prayer.

The Roman Garden is a misnomer. It did not exist in Roman times but remains as Chester's contribution to the Festival of Britain that took place in London in 1951. Despite its lack of authenticity, the gardens offer a quiet oasis of tranquility and provide access to the River Dee where interpretive panels relate the story of the garden and of the city of Chester in Roman times.

St_Oswald's_Church,

Timber, both inside and out, is the predominant feature of the 13th century St. Oswald at Cheshsire's Lower Peover, a small village mentioned in the *Domesday Book of 1086*. A lovely black and white timber-framed building with a large stone tower, St. Oswald lays claim to being the oldest aisled wooden church in England. Its picturesque exterior is complete with a cobbled lane and ancient graveyard.

Nearby Little Moreton Hall is the most outstanding timber-framed house in Britain. Today the building could be the 'crooked house' of nursery rhyme fame. Little Moreton Hall's aesthetic appeal lies both in the variety of its checkerboard patterns of black timber and white mortar, arranged to dazzle visitors, and the way that the house appears to be collapsing slowly under its own weight. The lack of furnishing and decoration throughout gives visitors a unique opportunity to study Tudor building techniques and architecture.

Little Moreton Hall

An interesting day excursion can include the cosmopolitan city of Liverpool whose long history stretches back in time to the 1st century AD when a settlement appeared on the bank of the Mersey. By the year 1200 it had grown into a thriving fishing village and a charter was granted by King John. The Liverpool of today owes much to the construction in 1846 of the Albert Dock, a stunning architectural triumph that soon became a treasure house of precious cargoes from the world over. Restored in the 1980s, the dock represents the largest collection of Grade I listed buildings in Britain and is the largest floating quay in the world. In 2004 Liverpool's waterfront was declared a UNESCO World Heritage Site.

Standing on the pier head for almost a century are the buildings known as The Three Graces, among Liverpool's most recognizable buildings. Defining the city's skyscape and rising to nearly 295' is the Royal Liver Building with two towers surmounted by the legendary Liver Birds, the Cunard and the Port of Liverpool buildings.

The area around William Brown Street is regarded as the city's Cultural Quarter due to the presence of the William Brown Library, Walker Art Gallery and World Museum Liverpool, just three of the city's neoclassical structures.

Sir Giles Gilbert-Scott designed the New Anglican Cathedral ca. 1904. It features a wonderful organ and fine stained glass windows. In stark contrast is the new Roman Catholic Cathedral of Christ the King with its impressive interior lantern tower of multi-colored glass.

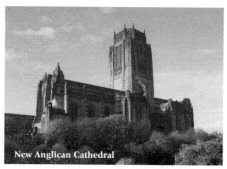
New Anglican Cathedral

121

Roman Catholic Cathedral of Christ the King

This huge circle of stained glass crowns the building and throws rays of light into the church beneath. Above this looms an intricate metal structure, imbuing the cathedral with an almost rocket-like appearance. Sixteen small buildings, eight of which are chapels separated by sheets of deep blue glass, form the outer wall of the cathedral. The interior is also outstanding. Above the high altar hangs a suspended metal structure symbolizing the crown of thorns.

Some of the city's landmarks are better known for their oddness rather than for their role in history. Williamson's Tunnels are architecturally unique as being the largest underground folly in the world. The Philharmonic Dining Rooms are noteworthy for, of all things, their Victorian toilets.

And of course, Liverpool's long history apart, many visit the city to pay homage to the birthplace of the Beatles whose music has an assured place in musical history.

Region: North West   County: Cheshire   City: Frodsham

Accommodations
About 30 beds in single, double and family rooms plus 2 rooms equipped for the disabled. All rooms have private baths.

Amenities
All meals can be supplied with the lodging. The choices range from lodging only to full board and all combinations are possible. Towels and linens are provided. There are three conference rooms, a library, two lounges, a dining room and chapel.

Costs per person/per night
Costs are based on lodging arrangements. Inquire when reservations are made.

Directions
By car: From London take M1 and exit at junction 19. Take M6 towards Birmingham. Continue on M6 until junction 20 then exit M6 and take M56 toward Chester/Runcorn. Leave M56 at junction 12 and take A557 to Frodsham/Widnes. At the roundabout take the first exit on A557 following the signs to Frodsham and A56. Turn right on A56 and continue on A56 for about two miles, then turn left into Tarvin Road (B5393).

By train: Take a train from London Euston to Chester, Warrington or Manchester and then change to Frodsham or Helsby. From either station take a taxi to Foxhill (5 minutes).

Contact
The Warden
Foxhill
Tarvin Road
Frodsham
Cheshire, WA6 6XB
England, UK
Tel: 0044 (0) 1928 733777
Fax: 0044 (0) 1928 731422
Website: www.foxhillconferences.co.uk
Email: foxhillwarden@aol.com or foxhillwarden@chester.anglican.org

Swarthmoor Hall
Religious Society of Friends (Quakers)

Swarthmoor Hall is a handsome historic hall recognized as the birthplace of Quakerism. It lies in a rural setting on the Furness Peninsula, just a few minutes walk from the center of the charming town of Ulverston. Nestled between the mountains of the Lake District and the waters of Morecambe Bay, Ulverston is ten miles off the shore of Windermere and is the ideal site for touring the Lake District National Park, West Cumbria and the Furness Peninsula.

Swarthmoor Hall is a fabled Elizabethan house built in 1586 by local landowner George Fell. In 1634 his son Thomas inherited and moved into the house with Margaret Askew, his wife. In 1652 George Fox, founder of the Religious Society of Friends, visited the couple. Margaret Fox soon converted to the new movement and Swarthmoor Hall became a meeting place for worship by the early members of the society and the "powerhouse of the early Quaker movement" which spread throughout the country, to the Americas and Continental Europe before the end of the century.

George Fox

George Fox, who married Margaret Askew Fell eleven years after Thomas Fell's death, regularly visited Swarthmoor although he spent most of his time traveling through Europe and the United States. He died in London in 1691, Margaret Fell/Fox died in 1702.

John Abraham, Margaret's grandson, sold the house in 1759 and little is known of its history between then and the early 20th century when it was acquired by Emma Clark Abraham, descendent of the Fell family. At that time the house was renovated and sold by her nephew to the Religious Society of Friends. The house is beautifully preserved with the feel of an English country home rather than that of a grand manor house. The design of the house is very appealing with its beautiful mullion windows. Inside is an unusual staircase, rich paneling and excellent English furniture. Today it is managed by the central London Office of the Society and is actively run by a staff of three members. It offers hospitality in Bed & Breakfast and self-catering facilities. It is also a pilgrimage site for Quakers the world over. It is open to the public for guided tours and pilgrimages from mid-March until mid-October, Tuesday to Friday at various times. The Hall displays a fine collection of 17th century furniture although only a few pieces are original. Some of George Fox's personal effects can also be seen.

Ulverston is an ancient town and port with cobbled streets and a pretty market square encompassed by Furness Fells, Coniston Water, Lake Windemere and the spectacular Cumbrian Mountains. Being on somewhat lower land, Ulverston does not necessarily have the dramatic appeal of its illustrious neighbors but it does possess a gentle landscape and a friendly atmosphere. Ulverston is in a part of Cumbria that is a walker's paradise, a network of villages crosscrossed by footpaths, bridleways and green lanes linking together historic sites and waterways.

One note of interest, Sir John Barrow, noted explorer, was born here in 1764. The town is also the birthplace of comedian Stan Laurel who was born in 1890. The Laurel and Hardy Museum contains press cuttings, personal possessions and film archives of the well-beloved comedian.

Laurel and Hardy

Ulverston's quaint market square is dominated by a market cross. Emanating from the square are narrow lanes filled with attractive shops. The town's colorful outdoor market is a fun affair attended from miles around. In the market square stands an attractive former coaching inn with many original features.

The Lakes Glass Center makes an interesting visit. This venue was opened in 1999 by the Cumbria Crystal and Heron Glass factories. Visitors can explore the wonderful world of glass blowing and see the techniques used to make colored glass. Many beautiful pieces are on display.

About five miles from Ulverston, the tall ornamental chimneys, gables and mullioned windows of Holker Hall stand stark against the vast skies covering Grange-over-Sands in Cumbria. The home of Lord and Lady Cavendish, it is one of England's finest mansion houses from the 17th century.

The Hall has been altered on a number of occasions, the most notable are those by Lord Burlington in 1840 when the house was refaced to give it a Gothic look. Lord Burlington also added stables and a conservatory. The most striking renovation was the rebuilding of the entire west wing following a fire in the late 18th century. At that time a grand new wing was designed in elaborate Elizabethan style. Built of red sandstone it remains an outstanding example of the skill of the architects, Paley and Austin of Lancaster. Their creativity is evident in the superb craftsmanship and intricate de-

Holker Hall

tails. It is this part of the house that is open to the public.

Although the house is exceedingly spacious, it exudes an intimate atmosphere enhanced by beautiful marble fireplaces that feature the use of local stone. Mirrors and softly lit lamps complete an overall picture of elegance and comfort. On the ground floor are four rooms in almost untouched condition including the drawing room with stunning silk wall hangings. The duke's bedroom preserves a wonderful collection of Wedgwood's Jasperware in the famous blue, green and lilac. There is also an elegant library sheltering over three thousand books.

The grand staircase is a triumph of design and is elaborately hand carved, with each baluster different from the next. There are memorable collections including decorative arts, paintings, porcelain and fine furniture from several periods including some exquisite Louis XV pieces.

Holker Hall is embraced by a stunning parkland comprised of rare trees and shrubs with one lime tree rising 72' high. In all there are approximately 120 acres of parkland including a garden of 22 acres. The park is also home to a herd of deer.

About 9 miles south of Ulverston, Piel Castle is the place where the last foreign invasion of England took place in 1486 when Irish and Flemish supporters of Lambert Simnel landed at Piel in a bid to seize the crown from Henry VII. The castle's earliest foundation can be traced to the 12th century after King Stephen had granted the island to the monks of Furness Abbey. The monks built a warehouse for the merchandise traded from the abbey. Part of the ruined warehouse can still be seen.

Furness Abbey

Early in the 14th century Furness Abbey was granted permission to crenellate the tower. A new motte and bailey castle was built with a three-story keep. It is the romantic ruins of this later castle that are evident today.

The island of Piel is a lonely, remote place with a haunted atmosphere that speaks of its turbulent past. It has been a place of sanctuary for monks, kings and smugglers. William Wordsworth visited in 1805 and after a stay of four weeks he wrote evocatively of the island as a beautiful swirl of land thrusting above a silver sea and lost in the long ago mists of time.

Also nearby, Dalton-in-Furness is a pretty little town with interesting buildings, the showplace of which is the unique cast iron front of number 51 Market Place. The market place is an attractive affair with a handsome Victorian drinking fountain. Looming over the town is the impressive church dedicated to Saint Mary. A richly decorated structure, it contains a large nave and imposing west tower. Its treasures reflect the past prosperity of the town and include a font from the 14th century.

Like Piel Castle, Dalton Castle was built in 1330 to provide sanctuary for the monks of Furness Abbey fleeing from Scottish raiders. Over the centuries the castle has had a checkered history and has been used as a prison and courthouse. Now owned by the National Trust, the castle retains many of its original features and is open to public view.

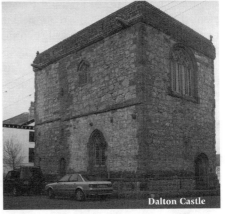
Dalton Castle

Accommodations

Swarthmoor Hall has three facilities used primarily for self-catering holidays or as Bed & Breakfast accommodations when rooms are not in use as self catering. All units have TV/VCRs and fully fitted and equipped kitchens.

Emma Clarke Abraham has an independent entrance from the courtyard. It has up to 6 beds in 1 single room with adjacent bathroom, twin bedroom with adjacent bathroom and another twin bedroom with private bathroom. There is a dining room, kitchen and sitting room with a sofa bed.

Margaret Askew has an entrance from the front door. It has up to 5 beds in 1 single and two twin rooms with 1 shared bath. There is a large room serving as a dining/sitting room and kitchen.

Leopold Muller Cottage is a detached structure reached from the Hall's courtyard. The cottage is accessible to the disabled and built as chemical free as possible. It has 4 beds in two twin rooms with a shared bath. There is a dining room and kitchen area designed with lowered units that is wheelchair friendly.

Amenities

Priority is given to self-catering. When available breakfast can be supplied. Breakfast is a buffet-type arrangement with breakfast foods and drinks in one of the unit kitchens where guests help themselves. Four conference rooms are available for meetings and/or workshops (extra cost) .

Cost per unit/per week

Rates are given per week but short breaks are also available. Ask for details and prices when reservations are made.

Emma Clarke Abraham cost per week £332- £415.

Margaret Askew cost per week £271 - £367.

Leopold Muller cost per week £332 - £415.

Cost per person/per night

£32 B&B.

Special rules

Quiet and peace is required on the premises.

Directions

By car: From London take M40 to Birmingham and then take M6 north exiting at junction 36. Take A590, dual carriage for 3 miles and then turn left following the signs to Barrow and Ulverston. At the roundabout stay on A590 (turn left) and proceed on this road about 20 miles until Ulverston. Once in Ulverston, pass the first set of main traffic lights and then turn left at the second set of main traffic lights, following the signs to the railway station and Swarthmoor Hall (this sign is low down and easily obscured by other traffic). Proceed until next sign to Swarthmoor and enter on the Hall's courtyard.

By train: Take a train from London Euston to Preston or Lancaster and then change to Ulverston. Walk or take a taxi to Swarthmoor Hall. The path is sign-posted across the fields but can be muddy during winter. A taxi service can be obtained from the public phone at Ulverston station

Taxi service - Tel: 0044 (0)1229 582180 / 582779 / 586700 / 587989

Contact

Anyone by email or phone
Swarthmoor Hall
Ulverston
Cumbria, LA12 0JQ
England, UK
Tel: 0044 (0) 1229 583204
Website: www.swarthmoorhall.co.uk
Email: info@swarthmoorhall.co.uk

Region: North West   County: Lancashire   City: Whalley (Blackburn)

Whalley Abbey
Conference & Retreat House

Property of the Anglican Diocese of Blackburn

Ensconced in a handsome woodland, the Abbey lies in the center of Whalley, an inviting little village on the banks of River Calder in the Ribble Valley. In 1170 a group of Cistercian monks founded the Abbey in Stanlow, Cheshire. Due to frequent floods that afflicted the monastery, the monks moved to one of their properties in Lancashire and established a new abbey in Whalley in 1296. The entire complex including the abbey church, monastery and Abbot's Lodging was not completed until 1440. In the interim the institution became a very active spiritual center.

After the Dissolution of the Monasteries, the Abbey became a private manor house. It remained so until 1923 when the Church of England acquired the complex. In 1926 Whalley Abbey passed on to Blackburn Diocese and the retreat house reopened. In 2005 the Abbey underwent a major refurbishment in order to meet higher stands of hospitality. Today it is a very active conference and retreat center offering hospitality to a wide range of guests.

Region: North West   County: Lancashire   City: Whalley (Blackburn)

Near Whalley is the market town of Clitheroe with its amazingly intact 12th century Norman keep. From the keep are impressive views of the river valley. Both Whalley and Clitheroe are in the Ribble Valley, a place thought to have inspired J.R.R. Tolkien's Middle Earth in the *Lord of the Rings*. Many visitors come to this stunning moorland to embark on a Tolkien Trail Tour.

Norman keep

The valley is cut in half by the River Ribble that flows to the Irish Sea through a long, narrow estuary. The northern half is dominated by the moorland of the Forest of Bowland. Gentle and tidy lowlands, crisscrossed with dry stone walls and dotted with enchanting farms and villages, the forest is a place like no other with a strong sense of stepping back in time to a forgotten part of the English countryside. It is a stage of unspoiled and richly diverse landscapes, wildlife and heritage that embraces outstanding heather moorland, blanket bog and rare birds. The deeply incised cloughs and wooded valleys are particularly characteristic of the terrain.

North of the Abbey is the ancient town of Lancaster. The town is dominated by Lancaster Castle. On the site of a former Roman station, nearly 1,000 years old, it is one of the best preserved castles in the country. A place of dungeons and the locale where the Lancashire Witches were convicted and condemned to death, it possesses a Norman keep and tower built with a turret called John O'Gaunt's Chair.

Lancaster Castle

Beside the castle is the Judges' Lodgings, Lancaster's oldest town house and original home to witch hunter Thomas Covell. Now an affiliation of three museums, one displays a wealth of furniture, porcelain, silver and paintings as well as a stunning ensemble of Gillow furniture within its period rooms. The Gillow family founded a furniture business in Lancaster and their products are now highly prized antiques. Nearby Saint Mary is mostly Perpendicular from the 14th and 15th centuries with elements of Saxon and Late-Renaissance styles.

Set high on the hillside overlooking the city are the Victorian neo-Gothic St. Peter's Cathedral and the ancient Priory Church. There is a pedestrianized center lined with shops, restaurants and pubs. The town also holds a number of popular weekly markets.

To the north of the Whalley Abbey, between the historic city of Lancaster and the town of Kirkby Lonsdale, lies the Lune Valley, an undiscovered gem of England's North Country and one of the most attractive stretches of the silvery Lune River. The river meanders through a landscape of outstanding natural beauty that encompasses a pastiche of unspoiled and ancient villages, wild moor and lowland pastures, historic churches, tumbling streams and wooded valleys. The valley has a place in literary history too. Poet William Wordsworth's popular *Guide to the Lakes*, recommends Lune Valley as a place not to be missed.

Accommodations

28 beds in 17 single and double rooms, all with private bath. Individual guests are hosted on a Bed & Breakfast basis. Tea and coffee making facilities, TV and telephone are in each room. Two suites are located on the ground and are equipped for guests with disabilities.

Amenities

Whalley Abbey House has a 4-star rating in B&B standards. Other meals can be catered by the Cloisters Coffee Shop. Towels and linens are supplied. The well equipped conference center offers several conference and smaller meeting rooms and is accessible to the disabled. The Visitor's Centre displays an exhibition of the development of the institution, pre-and post-Dissolution. It includes a gift and coffee shop that supplies homemade lunches and cakes. Guided tours are available.

Region: North West	County: Lancashire	City: Whalley (Blackburn)

Cost per person/per night

£35 per person, per night.

Directions

By car: From London take M6 north, exit at junction 31 and take A59 towards Clitheroe. Whalley is 12 miles further and clearly sign-posted.

By train: Take a train to Whalley from Blackburn or Manchester Victoria. The train station is half a mile from the Abbey.

Contact

Anyone
Whalley Abbey
The Sands
Whalley
Clitheroe, Lancashire BB7 9SS
England, UK
Tel: 0044 (0) 1254 828400
Fax: 0044 (0) 1254 825519
Website: www.whalleyabbey.co.uk
Email: office@whalleyabbey.org

SOUTH EAST

Region: South East   County: Kent   City: Aylesford

Aylesford Priory "The Friars"
Order Carmelite Friars

Aylesford Priory, traditionally known as "The Friars" is a popular pilgrimage site founded in 1242 by the first group of Carmelite Friars arriving from the Holy Land. They came under the patronage of Richard de Grey, a crusader who gave them a small piece of land at his home in Aylesford. The medieval priory is set within acres of verdant landscaped grounds that come alive with colorful plantings in spring and summer.

This chapter of the order effectively changed the lifestyle of the Carmelites from hermits to mendicant friars and over the ensuing fifty years, more than thirty priories were founded in England and Wales. A tradition diffused during the 16th century holds that St. Simon Stock, Prior General of the Carmelite Order, had a vision of Our Lady promising to protect those who wore the Carmelite habit. It was at that time that the brown scapular became an important devotion.

After the Dissolution of the Monasteries in 1538, The Friars became the property of various noble families including the Wyatts, Sedleys, Rycauts and Banks. In the 20th century The Friars became an important center for scouting activities.

A devastating fire in 1930 destroyed the complex. It wasn't until 1949 that the Carmelite Order was able to buy their motherhouse and restore the edifice to its former glory. Shortly thereafter it became a major pilgrimage center. The restoration included creation of an open-air shrine. The Friars possesses some notable artwork such as the ceramics created by Adam Kossowski.

Aylesford is a village on the River Medway in the county of Kent, a place whose very first roots can be traced to Neolithic times. Often described as "The Garden of England" it is a landscape of farmlands, grand country manors and fields of orchards. Its coastline is sprinkled with traditional beach resorts. Within the area are a series of chamber tombs of which Kit's Coty House is the most famous. Bronze Age swords have been discovered nearby and an Iron Age settlement and Roman villa once stood at Eccles. It was in Kent that Julius Caesar landed in 55 BC and uttered the immortal line: "I came, I saw, I conquered."

Nearby Canterbury was an important Roman town centuries before St. Augustine was sent by Pope Gregory to convert England to Christianity in 597. It is of great historical interest with its 14th century gate and the remains of the old city walls. Throughout the years the town rose in importance. St. Martin's Church, established before St. Augustine's arrival, is considered the Mother Church of England.

Canterbury is a prosperous market town charmingly situated on the River Stour. It still retains some of its medieval character clearly visible in narrow passageways lined with timber-beamed structures. The locale is enhanced by a riverside garden and ancient city walls. During the 16th century many Flemish and Huguenot families, fleeing religious persecution, found a safe home in Canterbury. Their weaving skills complemented the growing importance of Canterbury as a wool market. Many attractive houses, known as The Weavers' Houses, remain as testament to that history.

Canterbury Cathedral is a majestic early Gothic structure boasting stunning medieval stained glass, an 11th century crypt, a 12th century quire and a 14th century nave. Particularly noteworthy are the long transepts, the screen separating the raised choir from the Perpendicular nave and the east chapel that reveals the marble chair in which arch-bishops are en-throned. The West Gate Museum is a n impressive medieval gatehouse. Built in the 14th century its round towers harbor an array of arms and armory. In 1170 Archbishop Thomas Becket, friend of the

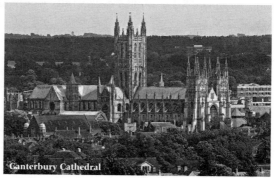

Canterbury Cathedral

Plantagenet King Henry II, was murdered in the cathedral. Since that time it has attracted thousands of pilgrims. The original site of Becket's martyrdom is marked with an evocative memorial. In 1220 Becket's body was transferred from the crypt to a new gold and jewel encrusted shrine in the Trinity Chapel. The pilgrimage inspired Chaucer to write *The Canterbury Tales* in 1387, stories told by a fictional group of pilgrims.

Other interesting castles nearby include Dover Castle, one of England's most formidable. Built on the original site of an ancient Saxon fortification, it sits strategically atop high cliffs and reveals a secret labyrinth of tunnels used during the WWII Dunkirk evacuation. It shelters a museum highlighting the local history. On the grounds are ruins of a Roman lighthouse and Saxon church.

Balanced on two islands, enormous Leeds Castle is surrounded by a lake that mirrors its crenellated turrets. Considered England's most romantic castles, it was a favorite of Henry VIII and contains a bust of him from the 16th century. The castle was a Royal residence for more than 300 years and home to six medieval Queens. Over the centuries it metamorphosed from a fortress to an elaborate palace.

A comparatively small building, Hever Castle dates from the 13th century and is famous as the childhood home of Anne Boleyn. It provided a backdrop for her courtship with Henry VIII, first as his mistress and then his doomed second wife. Quite close to the castle are many stately homes including medieval Penshurst Place and Chartwell, retreat of Sir Winston Churchill. Furnished as it was when he lived there, it is filled with Churchill memorabilia, from cigars to paintings to war correspondence. The manor house at Penhurst dates from the 13th century and includes a spectacular chestnut roof. Its famous walled gardens were designed in the middle of the 14th century and remain virtually unchanged. A number of pretty riverside walks lace the grounds.

The quaint charm of Chilham lies in its near perfect representation of a medieval town with its Tudor and Jacobean timber-framed houses. It has an appealing village green known as "The Square," around which stands the parish church of St. Mary's.

Accommodations
100 beds in single, double or family rooms (up to 4 beds). Baths are shared. The Friars is closed between Christmas and New Year. The Friars welcomes thousands of guests from throughout the world. Group retreats and conferences can also be organized.

Amenities

Rooms are located in two separate blocks called the Old Block and the New Block. Both have lounges and meeting rooms accessible to all guests. Towels and linens are supplied. All meals including after-noon tea can be provided with the lodging. All meals are freshly prepared each day.

Cost per person/per night

Full board: Adults £41.50 single room, £40.50 double or shared room. Children £11.50 to £34.50 (no charge for children under two).
Bed and English Breakfast: Adults £23.50 single room, £22.50 double or shared room. Children £6 to £18.00 (no charge for children under two).
Meal prices (Wine and beverages not included): Continental breakfast £5.50, English breakfast £6.50, three-course lunch £9.50. Light supper £6.75, packed lunch £5.50.
Note: Deposit required. Special prices for senior citizens.

Directions

By Car (From London):
1. Take M20 exit at junction 6 and follow the signs to The Friars.
2. Take M2 exit at junction 3 and proceed towards Maidstone on A229 and then follow the signs to Eccles and The Friars.
By train: From London Victoria to Maidstone East, then bus #155 or taxi to The Friars; or London Victoria to West Malling and then a taxi to The Friars.

Contact

Anyone
The Friars
Aylesford
Kent ME20 7BX
England, UK
Tel: 0044 (0) 1622 717272
Fax: 0044 (0) 1622 715575
Website: www.thefriars.org.uk
Email: guesthouse@thefriars.org.uk

Saint Michael's Abbey

Benedictine Monks

The Abbey is a magnificent French Gothic edifice built by Empress Eugenie (1826-1920) as a mausoleum for her late husband Napoleon III (1808-1873), Emperor of France and their son, the Prince Imperial (1856-1879), both of whom are buried in the Imperial Crypt, as is Empress Eugenie. The Prince was killed in South Africa by the Zulus. The red brick Abbey sits beside an original medieval monastery and together they present an unusual visual juxtaposition. The monastery was built after the church and was intended to be a more modest enterprise in order to suit the finances of the Empress. She lavished her finances on the church and it quickly became clear that the monastery, modeled on the chateau of Blois, would have to be a less expensive version.

After its foundation, the Abbey was entrusted to the Premonstratensian Canons, later replaced by the Benedictine Monks of Solesmes, France. By 1947 the number of French monks had declined and another group of monks from Prinknash Abbey (see page# 391), Gloucester, came to reside with the French order.

Today the Abbey is managed by a small contemplative community. Their liturgy is offered entirely in Latin and Gregorian Chant for which they are renowned. The community also runs a small farm and apiary. They enjoy a fine reputation for the restoration of historic books as well as for their printing and publishing skills.

The complex, encircled by secular trees, is isolated from the rest of the small village and presents a spectacular sight. The abbey church is a unique example of French Flamboyant Gothic designed by Gabriel-Hippolyte Alexandre Destailleur. The church is a stunning structure whose features recall many famous churches and buildings in France. The architecture is an elegant blend of splendor and austerity with simple, lofty arches and an Italian marble pavement. The dome evokes the dome of Les Invalides in Paris, where Napoleon I lies. The interior of the church shelters the crypt and reveals the simplicity of the Romanesque style, although richly decorated with a marble floor.

Also preserved in the church is an organ built by Aristide Cavaille-Coll, the artist considered the greatest organ designer of the 19th century. Its golden pipes enhance the quality of the sound of the music that accompanies the Gregorian Chant.

Farnborough was founded in Saxon times and is mentioned in the *Domesday Book of 1086*.

The old parish church of St. Peter is quite possibly the town's oldest building. The Hill, highest point in Farnborough, provides panoramic views over the town and countryside and overlooks Ship Lane on the old main road from London to Portsmouth.

To the southwest of the Abbey is the quaint market town of Farnham with roots established in the Bronze Age when traveling merchants passed through a prehistoric settlement at Farnham. The town is bedecked with narrow streets fringed with some of the finest Georgian architecture in the south of England. Its parish church and castle date to the 12th century.

Farnham has been an important site for thousands of years. The Romans used its plentiful clay to make pottery and the Saxons gave it its name. Farnham Castle dates from Norman times. Its chapel, great hall, first floor hall and kitchen were built in the 12th and 13th centuries by Henri de Blois, grandson of William the Conqueror. An early Tudor brick tower was added at a later date followed by an Elizabethan wing. The halls were redesigned and a new chapel and staircase with Grinling Gibbons carvings were built during a period of restoration. Gibbons was the most famous English woodcarver of all time. Oddly enough though, he was not born in England but in Rotterdam (what is now Holland) in 1648. He did not invent the type of carving with which he is most closely identified, namely decorative overmantels and architectural embellishments. One form of carving he did invent was the trophy panel, a freestanding carved tableau somewhere between a painting and a sculpture.

Grinling Gibbons

Just as the castle was central to the life of the town so too was the parish church of St. Andrew. The church dates from the 11th century, and is a mix of late Norman and early English with later additions; including a Perpendicular top. The Lady Chapel contains early tables and plaques. The Museum of Farnham is installed in an elegant Georgian townhouse built in the early 1800s and traces the history of Farnham with unusual themed exhibits.

ENGLAND

Farnham Potter is one of the best preserved examples of a working Victorian pottery left in England. A major pottery industry has existed in the area since Roman times. In the 16th century it supplied London with a substantial part of its pottery requirements. The Pottery still contains many examples of the original molds and a number of local houses were built using architectural fittings made on the site.

In the vicinity of Farnham is Waverley Abbey, the first Cistercian monastery on English soil. Built by French monks in 1128, for the next four hundred years, the abbey was home to 2,000 monks until its dissolution by Henry VIII. In 1723 the Chancellor of the Exchequer, Sir John Aislabie, used materials from the old abbey to build a country house nearby. In the 19th century the house passed into the hands of George Nicholson, brother-in-law of Florence Nightingale, a frequent visitor to Waverley, as was Sir Walter Scott, whose Waverley novels took their name from the Abbey.

Just a few miles south of the Abbey, the Devil's Punchbowl is in the east of Hindhead, the largest area of open heath in Surrey. The punchbowl has a long history and tradition. Legend holds that the devil spent his time tormenting the god Thor by pelting him with enormous handfuls of earth, leaving the great bowl that visitors see today. In reality the depression was created by erosion as water percolated down and hit the impervious layer of clay. A number of small springs were formed across the area as the water pressure built up.

Not far from the Abbey, the town of Guildford has been settled since Saxon times and incorporates the remains of a small Norman castle. The town's High Street is one of the steepest and most alluring in England with numerous old buildings, many from the Tudor period. At the top of the street is the Grammar School founded by Edward VI with fine Tudor buildings and the "Chaines Library," so-named because it contains nearly 90 books chained up to prevent theft. From its commanding hilltop position, Guildford Cathedral is an impressive landmark. The interior is a space of tranquility, peace and dignity made all the more handsome by the pale Somerset sandstone and white Italian marble floors. Guildford is also home to Clandon Park, an outstanding Palladian house with an extraordinary Marble Hall and one of the finest English interiors of the period. Several other impressive rooms conserve the Gubbay collection of porcelain, furniture and needlework.

Between Farnham and Guildford, Wanborough Barn is a medieval barn built by the Cistercian Monks of Waverley Abbey. It harbors a permanent display of local and historic interest and hosts special events and exhibitions throughout the summer.

Also nearby is Hampton Court and Gardens, a grand Tudor and English Baroque structure. Situated on the meadows of the River Lugg, the castle is backed by a steep wood escarpment and encompassed by grounds of 1,000 acres. Built in the early 16th century as the private residence of Cardinal Wolsey, it was presented to Henry VIII at a time when the Cardinal's fate hung in the balance. All of the king's wives, with the exception of Catherine of Aragon, lived in the palace. As recently as a hundred years ago it is believed to have extended to over 60,000 acres. Original Victorian garden walls enclose stunning new flower gardens divided by canals, island pavilions and pleached avenues. There is a centuries-old maze of a thousand yews with a Gothic tower at the center of the garden and an underground tunnel that leads to a waterfall in the sunken garden. Beautiful herbaceous borders stretch out from an ancient wisteria tunnel to vast lawns and age-old trees beside the castle. Beyond the lawns are riverside and woodland walks. Adjoining the castle is a grand conservatory housing a restaurant where lunch and tea are served.

Due east of the Abbey, and worthy of exploration, is the enormous Tudor Knole Mansion. Henry VIII liked it so much that he forced Thomas Cranmer, his Archbishop of Canterbury, to hand it to him in 1538. But others have either been delighted or displeased with the edifice. These mixed emotions can be partly explained by the many faces Knole presents on different days and at different times of the year. On a dull winter's day Knole's sprawling mass of sodden Kentish ragstone strikes a somber note. But on a sunny day in summer, the south front, with its colonnade of seven highly colored marble arches, comprises an altogether alluring picture.

There has been a garden at Knole for five centuries, ever since the days of Archbishop Bourchier. In the 16th century, under the aegis of Henry VIII, the garden was extended and the Kentish ragstone walls, which run for almost a mile around the 24-acre garden, were added. Punctuating the walls is a series of wrought-iron gates most dating from the 17th century.

Region: South East   County: Hampshire   City: Farnborough

Accommodations
Hospitality inside the Abbey is reserved to male guests for spiritual retreats. There are also some rooms reserved for males guests who aren't necessarily seeking spirituality. In addition, there is a small self-catering bungalow with three en-suite rooms (1 double) and sofa beds when families are using the facility.

Amenities
Meals are provided for guests in the Abbey but not in the guest-house that is self-catered. There is extensive parking on the grounds. The abbey church and its grounds are open exclusively to guests.

Cost per person/per night
£20 per night is the suggested donation.

Directions
By car: From London take M3, exit at junction 4 and follow the signs to Farnborough on A325.
By train: Take a train from London Waterloo and get off at Farnborough Main Station (35 minutes from London Waterloo) and walk five minutes to the Abbey entrance. Gatwick and Heathrow airports are easily accessed from the Farnborough train station.

Contact
The Guest Master by fax or email
St. Michael's Abbey
Farnborough
Hampshire GU14 7NQ
England, UK
Tel: 0044 (0) 1252 546105
Fax: 0044 (0) 1252 372822
Website: www.farnboroughabbey.org
Email: guestmaster@farnboroughabbey.org

Alton Abbey
Anglican Benedictine Monks

Alton Abbey

Alton Abbey is ensconced on a hill surrounded by the woodland and farmland of Beech, a small village of Hampshire, two miles from the market town of Alton, an ideal place for visiting this pristine region. The Abbey's foundation dates to the ordination of Reverend Charles Plomer Hopkins who was appointed River Port Chaplain and worked among merchant sailors in Rangoon, Burma in the late 1880s. In order to recruit others to work with him, he began a parish brotherhood in Shoreditch. At a later date, after Rev. Hopkins took his vows, the community was regulated by the rules of the Order of Saint Benedict and Alton Abbey became the motherhouse. Fr. Hopkins died in 1922 and since that time the community gradually concentrated more on the monastic life rather than apostolic service and the work with the seamen was interrupted in 1989. Nevertheless, the community continues to administer the Seaman's Society as a charitable trust. There are six permanent members of the community living at the Abbey. They lead a life of prayer and study but are also very active offering hospitality.

Alton Abbey

The Abbey was built by the monks under the guidance of architect Sir Charles Nicholson. At one time part of the Abbey served as home for retired seamen. Today this section of the complex has been converted into a guesthouse with 23 beds. The Abbey church is an imposing stone building, its interior dominated by heavy wooden beams, beautiful oak stalls and an altar.

Beech is a peaceful, charming, albeit isolated village near the home of Jane Austen in Chawton, an area known as Jane Austen Country. Jane Austen lived and worked in an unassuming 18th century cottage. It is where she wrote some of her most famous works: *Emma, Mansfield Park* and *Persuasion.* The cottage looks much as it did when Ms. Austen was alive. It is said that she planted the two oak trees that stand on the Winchester Road a little beyond her garden wall. One of the monks at Alton Abbey is considered an expert on the subject of Jane Austen and conducts workshops related to the author.

Alton is a market town with a history dating back as far as Roman times. Its gracious streets are fringed with fine examples of Georgian architecture. The dominant feature of Alton is its church. Dedicated to St. Lawrence, the earlier parts of the structure date from 1070 and over the centuries it has been enlarged many times. The style is mainly Perpendicular with a fine Norman tower. The interior preserves the Henry Speechley organ. Built in 1866 it is one of the finest organs in the south of England. The church offers a series of organ recitals during the winter months when organists of national and international acclaim perform. FYI: The bullet holes in the west door remain as evidence of the Civil War skirmishes during which men were shot in the church pulpit.

There are many villages in the vicinity of Alton worthy of exploration and some of the most interesting follow. Beautiful Itchen Abbas is adorned with pretty cottages, an old mill and sparkling river. Lodged in a serene and beguiling valley, its meadows are watered by the gently flowing River Itchen. The parish church is a splendid 19th century reconstruction of an earlier structure that most likely dates to Saxon times. Dedicated to St. John the Baptist, it is lodged in a lovely quiet spot close to the river and has a well-tended churchyard with interesting tombstones.

St. John the Baptist

Just a few miles from Itchen Abbas are the outstanding remains of Wolvesey Castle, once the principle residence of the powerful Bishops of Winchester. It was a keep and bailey castle built around 1100 on a site used by the Anglo-Saxons. The ruins consist mainly of the massive walls to the towers and impressive great halls. The site is the parvenu of the English Heritage.

South Harting is another nearby village. There is something quite special about the view of the slender spire of the church of St. Mary and St. Gabriel as it rises above the wooded farmland. An idyllic Downland destination, the main street is thronged with exquisite old properties, some brick, some tile hung and some built of Sussex clunch – a building material of soft limestone. The rolling downland and wooded glens there provide opportunities for wonderful country walks.

Midhurst is an enchanting example of the perfect English market town and is in one of Sussex's most stunning regions, a place with little gems of villages strung out like pearls dotting the downs. Midhurst is distinguished by properties from all periods including half-timbered houses dating back to Tudor times. Walking the atmospheric streets is like stepping back in time. The houses close to the river near the church form a lovely backdrop for the graceful swans and ducks making their way in the waters of the Rother.

Cowdray House is the ruins of one of great houses of England, located just outside of Midhurst on the north bank of the River Rother. It was gutted by fire in 1793, but what remains hints at its former glory with many significant parts of the walls standing at full height. Started in

Cowdray House ruins

the early 16th century on the site of an earlier building, this noble house became the home of the Browne family, later the Viscounts Montague and a repository of some key artifacts from English history. Its heyday was during the Tudor period; architecturally it compared to many of the great palaces and country houses of that time.

One of the attractions of the region is the fabled Highclere Castle. Built for the 3rd Earl of Carnarvon, it was designed by Charles Barry during the 1830s. Medieval in style it has a celebrated grand staircase. The castle houses Egyptian findings from the tomb of Tutankhamen. Highclere is now the home of the 8th Earl and his family. It is encompassed by landscaped gardens and grounds laid out by Capability Brown.

Accommodations

Individuals and groups are welcome at the Abbey by previous arrangement with the Guest Master. The Abbey also offers a series of organized retreats on a variety of themes such art, icons and literature (see the website for an up-to-date schedule). There are 12 single and 6 double rooms. All baths are shared.

Amenities

Linens are supplied, towels and soap are not; meals can be supplied.

Products of the institution

The monks have a Wafer Bakery that manufactures and distributes communion wafers to the local religious institutions. They also mix and sell incense.

Cost per person/per night

Costs vary depending on the type of stay and start at a minimum of £25 per day.

Directions

By car: From London take A31 (London-Winchester). Bypass Alton and turn north on A339 (towards Basingstoke), then left towards Beech and follow the signs to the Abbey.

By train: Take a train from London Waterloo to Alton and a taxi to the Abbey (5 miles).

Contact

The Guest Master by phone 0044 (0)1420 562145
(Between 9:45 AM – 10:15 AM or 4:00 PM- 4:45 PM on weekdays).
Alton Abbey
Abbey Road
Beech, Alton
Hampshire, GU34 4AP
England, UK
Tel: 0044 (0) 1420 562145
Fax: 0044 (0) 1420 561691
Website: www.altonabbey.org.uk
Email: altonabbey@supanet.com
Note: Email is checked twice weekly.

Charney Manor
Religious Society of Friends (Quakers)

Charney Manor is a 13th century stone building originally constructed as a grange for Abingdon Abbey when the abbey owned extensive portions of the land in the area. Today the Manor, known for being one of the oldest inhabited houses in Britain, is a conference and retreat center, managed by the Religious Society of Friends (Quakers). It offers hospitality to groups (guided and self-organized) in the main house and to individuals in a recently restored cottage on the grounds of the manor.

Charney Manor is in Charney Basset, a small attractive village fourteen miles southwest of Oxford in the center of the imaginary triangle formed by three historical towns: Abingdon, Wantage and Faringdon. Charney Basset's origins date to Anglo-Saxon times when the environs were marshland. The name Charney means Cearn-isle or Island in the River Cearn.

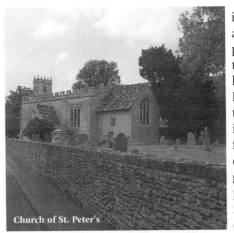

Church of St. Peter's

In the center of the village is a small triangular green and the remains of what was probably an ancient cross although only the stump is left. The village church of St. Peter's features a turret containing two medieval chiming bells. Built on the foundations of a Saxon church, the present structure gradually evolved with improvements and alterations in the 14th, 16th and 18th centuries.

Nearby Standford-in-the-Vale was named after a stone ford. An appealing green earmarks the center of the village with the Church of St. Denys on the western edge and picturesque old cottages and a manor house on the others. Numerous lime trees planted to celebrate Queen Victoria's Diamond Jubilee in 1897 enhance the setting. Anne Neville, daughter of the Earl of Warwick, once occupied the Manor House. The south porch of the church was built to mark her marriage to the Duke of Gloucester, later Richard III.

The church of St. Denys is named after the patron saint of France and was founded about 939. Its present external appearance is mostly as it would have looked in the 16th century, by which time a steeple had fallen or been blown down.

The nearby Vale of White Horse District derives from the figure of a horse carved into the hillside above the village of Uffington. This is the oldest chalk figure in Britain and dates to around 1000 BC. The inviting Thames-side is home to Abingdon, main town of the Vale of

Vale of White Horse

White Horse. Occupied in prehistoric times by settlers of the Bronze and Iron Ages, it was a flourishing town in the Roman period that, in turn, gave way to a Saxon settlement. The earliest documents tell of a hamlet called Sevekesham sited at a ford of the Thames. A nephew of King Cissa was granted land for founding a Benedictine monastery called Abbandun (Abingdon) at the same time that his sister founded the Nunnery of Helnestowe. When Henry VIII dissolved the monasteries in 1538, Abingdon Abbey was the sixth richest in Britain. The County Hall dominates the marketplace and has existed since the mid 16th century. Noted almshouses flank 13th century St. Helen's Church. Two of the main roads into Abingdon cross the Thames and the Ock over bridges listed as ancient monuments. The bridge over the Thames dates back more than 550 years.

Ancient Faringdon is a beautiful small town whose strategic position has given rise to a long history. Faringdon, meaning fern-covered hill, was the first capital of the ancient Kingdom of Wessex and Alfred the Great had his castle there. The tithe barn at nearby Great Coxwell by the Abbey of Beaulieu bears evidence to the fertility of the Vale. The town was granted a royal charter by King John in 1216 for a weekly market that continues to this day. The 17th century Town Hall remains the focal point of Faringdon and is encircled by Georgian-fronted inns and shops.

Wantage in Oxfordshire is a lovely market town whose links to the past are very strong. Its mostly 17th and 18th century architecture defines the narrow cobbled streets and passages. There is a market held every Saturday and Wednesday. Outdoor enthusiasts will appreciate the ancient Ridgeway National Trail just a couple of miles out of town.

Apart from its proximity to Oxford and other historical sites, Charney Manor is also within the eastern section of The Cotswolds, designated as an Area of Outstanding Natural Beauty, the largest in England and Wales. The region is famous for its bustling market towns and ancient mellow honey colored limestone villages that blend perfectly into the countryside. Many of the towns look today as they have for centuries when they prospered with the medieval wool trade (15th and 16th centuries) before being forgotten for more than 300 years. This sequence of events contributed to the pristine landscape that now makes the Cotswolds one of the most treasured regions in England.

To the west of Charney Bassett, Cirencester, Capital of the Cotswolds, has the unmistakable air of a lively market town. Its street market is still a colorful twice-weekly feature of town life. Cirencester began during the Roman period and was one of the regional capitals of Roman Britain. Although little of the Roman town survives above ground, the large grassed over amphitheatre is worth a visit as is the award-winning Corinium Museum that relates the Roman history. The parish church of St. John Baptist dominates the town center in "woolgothic" style, a reference to the importance of

Parish church of St. John Baptist

income from the wool trade in medieval times. Often called the "Cathedral of the Costwolds " (although other churches also claim this distinction), it is a lasting symbol of the town's wealth and influence in medieval England. The church's unique three-storied porch is the physical link between the church and town and was the town hall until 1897. The porch is an unusually grand landmark built by the abbey in 1490 and designed to serve as a public meeting place as well as the main entrance to the church.

From Cirencester an itinerary can include the towns of Burford, Bibury, Northleach and Bourton-on-the-Water. Burford is considered the gateway to the Cotswolds. Approached from the east, its steep main street leading down to the medieval bridge over the River Windrush provides the first typically Cotswold scene. The town presents some of its best 17th and 18th century frontages on High Street with earlier buildings often visible through atmospheric alleyways and courtyards. Burford was the site of a fortified fort in Anglo-Saxon times. The town grew to be an important crossroads and a very wealthy wool town. Many of the town's dignified houses and ancient cottages appear little changed since Tudor times as witnessed by the precarious angles of the buildings.

Arlington Row, Bibury

William Morris called Bibury "the most beautiful village in England." Two communities (the other is Arlington) form the village. Overlooking a water meadow and river is Arlington Row, a group of ancient weavers' cottages with steeply pitched roofs dating back to the 16th century. The National Trust owns the cottages and Arlington Mill is now a museum housing a fine collection of furniture from the Cotswold Arts and Crafts movement.

There is a rich blend of properties in Bibury, some are timber-framed with thatched roofs but most are built of honey-colored Cotswold Stone. Presenting the quintessential Cotswold scene, they are defined by steep gables and tall chimneys, often with small stone clad windows and nearly all submerged in green foliage.

The modest size of Northleach belies its former importance. The Abbey of Gloucester owned the area from 800 AD, granting the town a charter in 1220 to hold a weekly market. The town was transformed by the wool trade and from 1340 to 1540 it flourished as the center of a large sheep rearing area. The grand church of St. Peter and St. Paul dominates the town. A fine example of 15th century Perpendicular, it is adorned with some of the best wool merchants' brasses in the country. The church is large and impressive and is also referred to as the "Cathedral of the Cotswolds." It has a lofty west tower and a fine south porch with pinnacles and niches filled with statues. The church is adorned with stained glass windows and among its treasures are a font from the 14th century and a Goblet pulpit. A walk along High Street reveals the medieval property boundaries – the burgage plots – that can still be traced from the town's foundations in the 13th century. In medieval England, burgage plots were enclosed fields extending the confines of a medieval town and established by the lord of the manor.

Bourton-on-the-Water straddles the River Windrush with its series of elegant low bridges beside neat, tree-shaded greens and tidy stone banks. It has been described as the "Little Venice" of the Cotswolds. Its streets are lined with gorgeous old Cotswold stone buildings, pretty lawns and public gardens.

Bourton-on-the-Water

Region: South East   County: Oxfordshire   City: Charney Bassett

Accommodations

Inside the Manor: 36 beds in 14 singles with private bath and 11 twins (two of which can be family rooms) with shared baths. Both men and women are welcome, but only as a group (20 people minimum).

Amenities

All meals are supplied with the lodging. Linens are provided, towels are not (exceptions can be made for guests coming from abroad). There are two meeting rooms (one dates back to 13th century), a dining room, two common rooms and a library.

Cost per person/per night

£79 for full board.

Accommodations

The Cottage: The Gilletts were originally two separate cottages that have been recently restored to form one single larger cottage that can sleep up to 10 people in 3 twins, two singles plus a sofa bed and folding beds. Baths are shared.

Amenities

Meals are not supplied and guests staying at The Cottage are not admitted in the Manor. Towels and linens are supplied only on request. There is a patio, large sitting room, dining room and adjoining kitchen.

Cost per person/per night

£21.

Directions

By car: From London take M4 and exit at junction 15. Follow the A420. About 4 miles after Faringdon take a right turn at sign-posted "Stanford in the Vale & Pusey for Charney Bassett."
By train: Take a train from London Paddington to Didcot Parkway (they run every hour) and then a taxi to Charney Bassett.

Contact

Anyone
Charney Manor
Charney Bassett
Wantage, Oxon, OX12 0EJ
England, UK
Tel: 0044 (0) 1235 868206
Website: www.charneymanor.demon.co.uk
Email: charneymanor@quaker.org.uk

Saint Cuthman's Retreat House

Property of the Diocese of Arundel and Brighton

Saint Cuthman's Retreat House is ensconced in the midst of its own twenty-acre park, in a tiny village south of London and north of Brighton, an area designated by West Sussex as being of Special Nature Conservation Interest.

The House is a beautiful country home of Jacobean origin built in the 1650s with views across the lake to the South Downs. In became a retreat house, property of Saint Julian's Community, in the late 1940s. The Diocese of Arundel and Brighton took over management of the House in 2000. Today it offers a venue for reflection and relaxation on its extensive grounds that include a large lake and a chalk downland formed by two areas of Outstanding Natural Beauty: East Hampshire and Sussex Downs. The property also encompasses formal gardens, woodlands, orchards and fields and is rich in bird and plant life. Full of character and inviting charm, the House is open to people of all denominations and offers peace, comfort and tranquility in a wonderful setting. Its chapel is a lovely, simple space.

The village of Coolham is distinguished by a 17th century half-timbered cottage and Quaker chapel oddly named "The Blue Idol." It remains a Friends Meeting House. The famous Quaker William Penn met and worshipped here with the Warminghurst Quakers before he left for America.

Steeped in history, the market towns and quintessential English villages of Sussex are highlighted by welcoming village greens, beaches backdropped by high cliffs, Roman remains, monasteries, forts and castles. Stroll down an ancient Saxon twitten (an old Sussex word for a path or alleyway still in common use) and come face to face with a flint-walled thatched cottage, a 16th century half-timbered inn or a grand 19th century windmill. There are dozens of churches spanning the last thousand years, their towers and spires forming a distinctive feature on the landscape. Notable examples include the 11th century Church of St. Botolph at Hardham which contains one of the most complete sets of early wall paintings of any church in the British Isles.

North of the Retreat House is the town of Horsham with its inviting town center, narrow, paved twittens, pretty tree-lined streets and medieval and Tudor buildings. The attractive, pedestrianized center combines the trappings of a provincial Sussex town with the distinctly cosmopolitan air created by the outdoor cafes, markets, shops and historic buildings. The "Riverside Walk" is a self-guided nine-mile trail circling the town alongside the River Arun and its tributary streams. Along the path is an ancient monument that was the site of an 11th century motte and bailey castle. The earth works (or motte) on which the timber tower was situated are still visible. Horsham Museum is in the Causeway House, a medieval timber-framed building. It offers a treasure trove of local history objects and is home to the famous dinosaur bones of the Rudgwick Polacanthus.

Amberley is also on the River Arun and boasts many flint walled thatched cottages and a medieval castle (now a hotel). Its early Norman church contains a 12th century font. An impressive river bridge with superb views is an ideal starting point for walks through the "wildbrooks" an area known for its wildlife.

Billingshurst is in the heart of the Sussex Weald. Built on the

Roman Stane Street, it features many old houses including a 16th century half-timbered inn on High Street and a Unitarian Chapel, ca. 1754, one of the oldest of its kind in southern England. As an aside, when William Penn, who lived at Warminghurst, sailed to America to establish the state of Pennsylvania, sixteen people from Billingshurst comprised part of the hundred settlers.

Heading southwest, an interesting day trip can be made to Chichester, minutes from the classic South Downs countryside and minutes to the coast, Chichester Harbour and the wild, windswept beauty of East Head's sand dunes. Built by the Romans after their invasion in 43 AD the well preserved market town is compact and intimate with Roman walls and a medieval heart. Chichester's history is revealed on nearly every corner, from the Tudor Market Cross to the stunning cathedral spire, a landmark over the Sussex plains. For

Chichester Cathedral

900 years the cathedral has stood at the heart of Chichester. Famous for its art, it safeguards medieval stone carvings, vibrant 20th century works by Piper, Sutherland, Skelton and a stained glass window by Marc Chagall.

Ancient Lewes on the South Downs of East Sussex takes its name from the Saxon word for hills or slope. A historic market town, it rises along several steep hills interlinked by a series of narrow passageways. A very pleasant town it grew up on the River Grand Ouse and presents a number of Georgian shops on its High Street. Lewes is the boyhood

Lewes

Lewes Castle

home of the famous diarist, John Evelyn (1620-1706). He lived at Southover Grange, an Elizabethan house close to the castle. The house that Henry VIII gave to Anne of Cleeves following their divorce can also be seen on Southover High Street. It is now an interesting museum. Lewes Castle is a motte and bailey affair and from the castle's high towers, views encompass the ancient town and the distant vistas of downs, river and forest.

Accommodations

There are 8 single and 8 twin rooms, all with a shower, WC and washbasin. One bedroom, for twin or single use, is adapted for wheelchair users and is accessible by lift. The house is centrally heated. There is a bathroom on each floor for general use as well. There is an art room and summerhouse with lovely views of the lake and Hermit Huts for solitary guests. The huts are for single guests and are equipped with towels, linens and simple self-catering facilities. Guests staying in the Hermit Huts do not have access to the main house.

Amenities

Towels and linens are supplied. All meals are supplied and full
board is mandatory. The chef offers creative, wholesome home
cooking using fresh ingredients, seasonal local produce and
whenever possible, fairly traded goods. Vegetarians and most special
dietary needs can be catered but arrangements should be made
when reservations are being determined. Sitting and dining areas
are divided into one silent and one non-silent.

Cost per person/per night

£63 full board. Hermit Huts from £18 to £26 depending on the hut.

Special rules

A deposit is required to secure reservations.
Minimum stay is two nights. The house closes at 10 PM. Closed at
Easter and Christmas.

Directions

By car: From London take M23, A23 or A24 and then take A272
westbound towards Billingshurst. St. Cuthman's House is
approximately 2.5 miles from the intersection of A24 with A272.
By train: Get off at Billingshurst and take a taxi to St. Cuthman's (3
miles). Taxi, phone 0044 (0)1403 786818 – book in advance to meet
train if possible. Or get off at Horsham (7 miles from St. Cuthman's)
and take a taxi – phone 0044 (0)1403 254321.

Contact

The Booking Secretary
St. Cuthman's Retreat House
Cowfold Road, Coolham
West Sussex RH13 8QL
England, UK
Tel: 0044 (0) 1403 741220
Fax: 0044 (0) 1403 741026
Website: www.dabnet.org/stcuthmans
Email: stcuthmans@dabnet.org

Region: South East   County: Kent   City: Minster-in-Thanet

Saint Mildred's Abbey
Benedictine Nuns

The Abbey lies just outside the small, attractive village of Minster-in-Thanet, ancient capital of the Isle of Thanet. The earliest foundation dates to 670 (by a widowed Princess of Kent). The Princess' daughter Mildred, great-great-granddaughter of King Ethelbert became the second abbess and one of the most beloved Anglo-Saxon saints. Tradition holds that the Abbey was granted as much land as a hind could run in a day, resulting in the hind becoming the village emblem. In 804 the Abbey was destroyed when the Danes invaded the land and wasn't rebuilt until 1027. The institution was later enlarged and flourished until 1538, when, at the time of the Dissolution, it was partly destroyed.

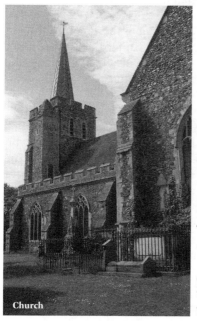

Church

In 1937 the Abbey was returned to a group of Benedictine nuns who came from the Monastery of Saint Walburga in Germany. The nuns were refugees fleeing the Nazi government and until 1997 depended on their former Bavarian affiliation until they became part of the Subiaco Congregation of Italy. The thirteen nuns in residence lead a simple life of prayer, farming and attending to guests. They also do a bit of weaving and card making.

The Abbey is an austere stone complex dominated by a slender tower bell. Most interesting are the remains of the oldest settlement as well as the Norman Crypt. The church is Saxon in style and the oldest church within the city walls, much of it dating from the 8th century. The chancel is Early English with later flying buttresses. It shelters a fine set of misericords dating to around 1400. The tower has a curious turret at its southeast corner that is locally referred to as a Saxon watchtower but is built at least partly from Caen Stone. The chapel preserves a 17th century statue as well as the saint's relics. The sisters live in what remains of the 11th century buildings while the guesthouse is a new construction.

Although the village is now miles from the coastline, until the 11th century, it lay right on the estuary to the River Wantsum, making it one of the nearest ports to the continent. Ships regularly sailed past on their way to London and often anchored at what are now arable fields below the church grounds. Minster was once again the site of major change in the year 597 when St. Augustine landed on the shores and brought Christianity to Britain.

Nearby Ramsgate is the largest of the seaside towns on the Isle of Thanet and is linked to France by ferry. A handsome place, the seafront is lined by stately, red-brick Victorian and Georgian buildings overlooking the harbor. St. Augustine's Church is a neo-Gothic masterpiece (see page # 385) built by A.W.N Pugin, the most prominent British architect of the 19th century. Pugin paid for the construction from his own funds and is buried in the churchyard. The Grange, the neighboring house, was completed in 1843 and is adorned with a tower fortified with battlements.

South of Ramsgate is the town of Sandwich which preserves the remains of its 14th century medieval walls, narrow alleyways and several historic buildings. The town boasts timber-framed houses typical of the region in addition to a number of ancient churches. The foundations of a Roman amphitheatre and a pre-Norman chapel have been excavated. Finds from the site are exhibited in a small museum. Richborough Castle, one of the most important Roman sites in Britain, is just outside of Sandwich.

Still further south is the peaceful little town of Deal, thought by some to be the place where Caesar landed and began his first exploration of Britain. An outstanding highlight of the town is its castle, one of more than twenty that Henry VIII had built along the coast. They were constructed to defend England against the threat of invasion from Catholic France and Spain, At the same time, similar castles at Walmer and Sandown were constructed and together they provided a formidable defense line along the coastal stretch of The Downs.

Based on a "walls within walls" plan, Deal Castle is shaped liked a Tudor rose, perfectly symmetrical, with a low, circular keep at its center. All outer walls of the castle and sturdy bastions are rounded to provide more protection from attack than

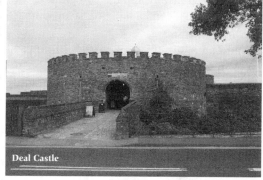

Deal Castle

flat walls. To further secure the castle, the entire structure was completely surrounded by a very deep, wide moat. Upon entering Deal Castle across the drawbridge and through the first bastion, there is an overwhelming sense of power and foreboding lurking among the grey, stark walls of this vast fortification. But the fortress is a delight to explore with its endless circuit of passages, both below and above ground.

The town of Dover is a little further south. Famous for its steep chalk white cliffs it is England's closest geographical point to Continental Europe. Every day of the year ferries travel between the port, Calais and Dunkirk in France and Ostend in Belgium. Dover is a place of fairy tale castles and imposing fortresses by the sea. For a different per-

Dover Castle

spective, sail around the harbor on a tour boat or travel back in time on a historic railway.

Dover Castle, one of England's most invincible, was built on the original site of an ancient Saxon fortification. Sitting strategically atop high cliffs, the castle shelters a secret

167

labyrinth of tunnels used during the WWII Dunkirk evacuation. The tunnels were created by prisoners in the Napoleonic Wars and detail the history of those turbulent times. The castle is also home to a museum of local history. On the vast grounds are ruins of a Roman lighthouse, ca. 50 AD and a restored Saxon church.

Accommodations
About 16 beds in single and double rooms. Baths are shared in the single rooms. Double rooms are accessible to the disabled and are en-suite. Hospitality is offered to single women, families, married couples and groups. Single men are not allowed.

Amenities
Towels and linens are supplied. All meals are included. There is a meeting room for 40 people that can be used for residential or day guests. For those who are not residential, food catering is not provided.

Cost per person/per night
Full board £35.

Special rules
The sisters ask that guests respect the atmosphere of the Abbey. Curfew based on arrangement. Closed from October 1st until the beginning of January.

Directions
By car: From London take M2 to Ramsgate exit 7. Then take A253 to Ramsgate (about 1.5 miles) and then B2048 to Minster. The Abbey entrance is on the left after Minster Village Center.
By train: Take a train from London Victoria to Minster. The train station is 200 yards from the Abbey. Or take a train from London Victoria to Ramsgate and from there to Minster.

Contact
Call or write to the Guest Sister
Saint Mildred's Abbey
Minster-in-Thanet
Ramsgate
Kent, CT 12 4HF
England, UK
Tel: 0044 (0) 1843 821254
Note: Contact via post and NOT via email or telephone.
Website: www.minsterabbeynuns.org

Region: South East   County: Isle of Wight   City: Ryde

Saint Cecilia's Abbey
Cistercian Nuns of the Solesmes Congregation

Overlooking the sea from a hill, St. Cecilia's Abbey is an oasis of peace and tranquility. St. Cecilia was a Roman virgin martyr and is the subject of one of the *Canterbury Tales* as well as a song of Dryden and an ode by one of the popes. The first community of nuns was started in 1234 in Orchies, Belgium. In 1637 the sisters moved to Liege and founded a monastery at Ventnor on the Isle of Wight. In 1922 they moved to St. Cecilia's Priority at Ryde. Some of the nuns live in seclusion and are renown for Gregorian chant that accompanies daily mass.

The origins of Gregorian chant can be traced to early Christian times and seem to have derived from musical practice in the Jewish synagogue and Greek musical theory. Named for Pope Gregory I, it is also known as plainsong or plainchant and refers to early unharmonized melody in free rhythm but is usually synonymous with the liturgical music of the Roman Catholic Church. In the Western church there were four main dialects of plainsong but only two have survived. Ambrosian chant was introduced by St. Ambrose into the cathedral of

Milan and is still used in that diocese. In the 19th century the Benedictine Monks of Solesmes undertook many years of research to restore the Gregorian chant to its original form and establish its proper rhythm. In 1903 Pope Pius X decreed the use of the chant in the Solesmes version as the official music of the Catholic Church. The texts of plainsong are the words of the Mass and the Psalms in addition to certain verse hymns.

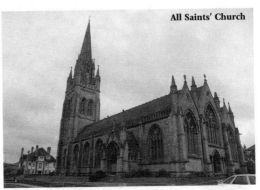

All Saints' Church

Ryde is the largest town on the Isle of Wight and boasts wide sandy bays and a half mile long pier. The town's architecture reflects its Victorian roots and is dominated by the tall tower of All Saints' Church. Completed in 1872 it is the symbol of Ryde. There are numerous walks from Ryde including one to Seaview (4 miles east) a small resort with a good beach and an iron pier.

Conquered by the Romans, the Isle of Wight became the headquarters of the Danes at the end of the 10th century. In 1293 it was returned to the Crown. Three miles from the south coast of Great Britain, the island is separated from the mainland by the Solent. It is 23 miles long from the Eastern Foreland to The Needles, three towers of rock jutting out of the sea at the island's western end. Famous for their multi-colored cliffs and sand, The Needles are a very short walk from Alum Bay and are among the most photographed aspects of the island. Numerous streams have carved a series of picturesque gullies and sea ledges into the soft rock. Quaint villages, a lovely coastline and the fact that Queen Victoria made Osborne House her summer home all contributed to the island's popularity as a holiday resort at-

The Needles

tracting fashionable Victorians and members of European royalty. It is home to the Bestival (held in mid-September) and Isle of Wight Festival (held in June).

ENGLAND

The lovely Isle of Wight is diamond in shape and slightly more than half is designated as the Isle of Wight Area of Outstanding Natural Beauty. The landscape is remarkably diverse leading to its oft-quoted description of "England in Miniature." Abundant with flowers and gardens, it is the perfect venue for outdoor enthusiasts with hundreds of miles of paths meandering through the verdant terrain and along coastal routes. As an aside, the island is noted as an important area for finding dinosaur fossils. Standing on the site of a former Roman fort, Carisbrooke Castle, now in ruins, was the place where King Charles I and his daughter were imprisoned in the mid-17th century. Mostly dating from the 13th century, the castle's keep is Norman and offers outstanding views.

Nearby Cowes is a hilly harbor town and the island's yachting center. This world-famous sailing milieu reaches the high point of its year with Cowes Week, held in early August. Close to 200 years old, it is among the longest running and largest annual sailing regattas in the world.

Cowes Week Yachting

Another highlight of the town, Osborne House, reflects the height of Victorian opulence and contains extravagant rooms including the remarkable Indian décor in the Durbar Room. A stroll through the Queen's bedroom, the nursery rooms and even the Royal bathrooms provides an intimate glimpse into the life of the Royal Family. The

Osborne House

grounds include a Swiss Cottage, a structure that was dismantled and brought piece by piece from Switzerland and reassembled. It was the Queen's gift to her children on her birthday in 1854. The Royal children were encouraged to garden. Each child was given a plot in which to grow fruit, vegetables and flowers that they would then sell to their father, Prince Albert. This was the Royals' way of teaching the basics of economics to their children. The house is located across the River Medina from West Cowes and is reached via a chain ferry.

Heading south from the Abbey, the towns of Shanklin and Godshill make for an interesting excursion. Shanklin is popular with artists due to its idyllic locale. The old town is characterized by thatched cottages with enchanting gardens. The village features a good beach and delightful promenade walks. FYI: John Keats lived in Englatine Cottage in 1819.

Inland, the village of Godshill is highlighted by thatched stone houses, a Methodist chapel from 1838, a small natural history museum, toy museum and medieval St. Lawrence Church which shelters the tombs of the Worsley family as well as a 15th/16th century fresco in the South Chapel. The painting *Daniel in the Lions' Den* is most likely the work of Rubens or one of his pupils.

Accommodations
The Garth Retreat (the name of the guesthouse) is a charming stone edifice a few meters from the main house. It offers accommodations to all guests. There are 3 twin beds and two larger rooms that can host up to 7 guests. Married couples and single women are welcome, single men are not allowed. Bathrooms are shared.

Amenities
Meals are not offered with the lodging but there is a kitchen that guests may use. Shops are not far from the Abbey. Linens are supplied, towels are not. There are common rooms and a library.

Cost per person/per night
Voluntary contribution.

Special rules
Closed at Christmas. Arrival time for check-in must be before 7 PM.

Products of the institution
The nuns sell Gregorian chant recordings as well as altar bread.

Directions
By car-ferry:
Portsmouth to Fishbourne (35 minutes), 20-minute drive to Ryde.
Southampton to East Cowes (1 hour), 30-minute drive to Ryde.

Southampton West Cowes (high-speed transport – 22 minutes), 45-minute drive to Ryde.

Lymington to Yarmouth (30 minutes), 50-minute drive to Ryde.
Note: Reservations for the car-ferries must be made in advance. Log onto www.directferries.co.uk or call 0044 (0) 0871-222-3312 in England. The car-ferries also take passengers (without cars). The bus journey to Ryde takes much longer than by car.

By train: Book your ticket to either Ryde Pier Head or Ryde Esplanade and take the train to Portsmouth Harbour. The 15-minute crossing is by catamaran to Ryde Pier Head. Take the train (three minutes) along the pier to the Esplanade. Taxies and buses are available at the Esplanade. The closest bus stop to the Abbey is in East Hill Road. It is clearly marked on a map on their website. If walking from the Esplanade (20-30 minutes), turn left upon leaving the station. Continue along the seafront until a boating lake on the left, a roundabout on the right and a thatched-roofed restaurant in front. Cross one road and turn up Appley Rise alongside the restaurant. The gateway to the Abbey is a short distance up on the left.

By bus: Either take the bus to Portsmouth and then make the crossing by catamaran or take the bus to Southsea and make the crossing by hovercraft. Instructions for walking are the same as above.

Contact

Call, write, send a fax or email to the Guest Mistress
Saint Cecilia's Abbey
Ryde
Isle of Wight, PO 331 1 LH
England, UK
Tel and fax: 0044 (0) 1983 562602
Website: www.stceciliasabbey.org.uk
Email: info@stceciliassabbey.org.uk

Malling Abbey
(Saint Mary's Abbey)
Anglican Benedictine Nuns

Malling Abbey lies on the outskirts of West Malling, a historic market town of Kent. "It is a town which likes to define itself as a village because the atmosphere is that of a village, "said the Guest Sister. With its long and rich past, West Malling offers fascinating corners and back streets replete with Norman ruins and medieval houses and wells whose spring waters brought prosperity to the village in years gone by. West Malling is also famous as the site of the first cricket match played in Kent, the same match at which Charles Dickens assisted and inspired the "All Muggleton vs. Dingley Dell" (from Dickens' *Pickwick Papers*) cricket match featured on a £10 note. West Malling has been visited by many famous people and was featured in the Beatles' movie, *Magical Mystery Tour*.

Enveloped by an engaging countryside of rolling hills and orchards, the nuns of Malling Abbey lead an enclosed lifestyle. The present Benedictine Anglican community was founded in Edmonton as an active community in 1891 but gradually moved to a more contemplative life, closer to the Benedictine's rule until it fully joined the order by pronouncing the vows in 1906. The nuns moved from Edmonton to Baltonsborough in 1906 and from Baltonsborough to West Malling in 1916 occupying the buildings of Malling Abbey vacated by a community that now inhabits Curzon Park Abbey in Chester (see page # 380).

The Abbey is an ancient building whose Benedictine foundation by Gundulf, Bishop of Rochester, dates to 1078. The Abbey prospered and the village itself revolved around the life of the Abbey. A fire destroyed the structure in 1190 but it was soon rebuilt and continued to exist until the time of the Dissolution by Henry VIII in 1538. After the Dissolution, the complex fell into the hands of private owners until the 1890s when it was returned to the Benedictine Order. "It is one of the few abbeys in England that was built for the Benedictines and then restored for the Benedictines," said the Guest Sister.

Norman tower and guesthouse

A new church was erected in 1966. The exterior is cement. "It is very simple but it was all we could afford," said the sister. Today the complex is a mix of medieval, 14th and 20th century structures. Very little of the original building remains: The tower whose Norman bottom is topped with Early English stories, one of the transepts, the wall of the nave, the refectory and the 14th century cloisters.

The sisters work a large vegetable and fruit garden and have a printing works where they produce handicraft printing. They also weave and make their own clothes, but "our main ministry is hospitality," said the Guest Sister.

Guesthouse on a snowy winter day

The 15th century timbered guesthouse is warm and inviting. Its grounds provide an atmosphere of quiet and spaciousness, an ideal environment for contemplation and reflection. In fine weather guests may enjoy the extensive garden or sit beside the tranquil Ewell stream that runs through the property.

The Heart of Kent is English countryside at its best, a landscape of rolling hills and wooded valleys dotted with orchards and vineyards. It is a place where each season yields its treasures in a myriad of colors. There are quiet byways and splendid castles, gardens and historic country houses. During spring and summer the chalk grassland of the Kent Downs is carpeted with wildflowers including orchids and shaded bluebell woods, while the lowland orchards are veiled with delicate blossoms.

A pistache of inviting towns and sites populate the region. Maidstone is a lively mix of history, arts and culture. The town's colorful past is mirrored in ancient buildings that sit alongside more modern styles and provides an interesting juxtaposition of old and new. The parish church of All Saints is distinguished by elaborate misericords and splendid glass windows. Within the medieval stables of the Archbishop's Palace which adjoins the church, is a fascinating collection of horse-drawn vehicles at a namesake museum. Fremlin Walk is a modern open-air shopping complex on the site of a former brewery. Just opposite is Chillington Manor, a grand Elizabethan manor house and home to the Maidstone Museum and Bentlif Art Gallery, one of England's finest regional museums.

Tonbridge

South of the Abbey are three interesting towns. Tonbridge has been a market town since the Middle Ages. Built on the River Medway, it presents fine streets with a rich variety of architecture including typical Wealden tile-hung properties and handsome Georgian and Victorian buildings. The ancient church of St. Peter and St. Paul sits close to a number of timber-framed black and white houses. The Normans chose Tonbridge for their motte and bailey castle, a structure that dominates the town to this day. It is encompassed by fourteen acres of lawns and gardens alongside the river. Motte and bailey castles were built in a very interesting manner. The construction began by digging a deep circular ditch and piling up the earth taken from the ditch into the center that became the motte. Mottes were generally crowned with a wooden tower that was basically a lookout. Motte and bailey castles often evolved into large and impressive stone fortresses when walls, gatehouses, towers and other structures replaced the timber defenses. However, in most cases, what remains is just a tree-covered mound. Baileys were large areas of additional space adjacent to the motte that were enclosed with a circular earthwork, a mound lower than the motte.

At Royal Tunbridge Wells, the Chalybeate Mineral Spring was discovered in 1606 and led to the town's popularity with royalty and the aristocracy particularly in the 17th and 18th centuries. A stroll along High Street leads to the Pantiles, the town's historic colonnaded and paved promenade, named after the original square tiles.

The pretty Kentish market town of Cranbrook retains its medieval layout of streets and alleys. Known as "The Capital of the Weald" it was once the center of the region's medieval cloth industry and the skyline is still dominated by its most famous landmark, the Union Windmill. Sissinghurst Castle is just two miles away. Of the original Tudor mansion, only the four-storey gate tower survives. Its beautiful gardens are separated by walls or hedges and linked by paths and vistas, each with a theme including the Herb Garden and the White Garden.

A few miles west of the Abbey, the country town of Sevenoaks traces its roots to Saxon times. Set amidst the woods, hills and valleys of the North Downs, there are many splendid reminders of the town's historic past including England's largest private house, Knole, set in a 1,000-acre deer park. A vast Tudor mansion and one of the finest houses in the country, it dates from the late 15th century. At the time of the Dissolution of the Monasteries, it was seized by Henry VIII from Thomas Cranmer, Archbishop of Canterbury. In 1566 Elizabeth I gave Knole House to her cousin Thomas Sackville whose descendants still own it today. Knole is filled with a wonderful 17th century Royal Stuart furniture collection unrivalled in England for its rarity and quality. The house also shelters an extraordinary amount of Renaissance, Tudor and Stuart artworks including plasterwork ceilings, grand tapestries, carved marble, silver furniture, painted walls and portraits by Van Dyck, Gainsborough and Reynolds.

Region: South East   County: Kent   City: West Malling

Accommodations

11 single rooms with 3 shared baths. Both men and women are welcome.
Note: The Abbey is closed during January and part of February. The times in February vary. Check with the Guest Sister for exact dates.

Amenities

All meals are provided. They are simple, hearty and homemade. Lunch and dinner are eaten in silence. At lunch one of the sisters reads for the guests. It is possible to forgo meals but guests must provide prior notice. Towels and linens are supplied. There is a sitting room and library that guests may use. There is also a kitchenette for making hot drinks. It is possible to participate in the Divine Office but guests are asked to sit in a separate chapel as the nuns live in seclusion.

Special rules

Curfew is at 7:45 PM.

Cost per person/per night

Voluntary contribution.

Directions

By car: Take M20 and exit at junction 4 and then take A228 about 0.2 miles and take A20 towards West Malling. Swan Street is on the left of High Street.
By train: Get off at West Malling (from London Victoria or London Bridge Station). The Abbey is within walking distance of the station.

Contact

Guest Sister (By phone or letter)
Saint Mary's Abbey (West Malling Abbey)
Swan Street
West Malling
Kent, ME19 6JX
England, UK
Tel: 0044 (0) 1732 843309 (call in the morning, local time)

Douai Abbey

Monks of the English Benedictine Congregation

ENGLAND

Douai Abbey is ensconced in the Berkshire countryside. It is embraced by its own well tended park and peaceful woodland and is the perfect venue for relaxing walks in the natural landscape. The Abbey was founded in 1615 in Paris, the place where Benedictine monks took refuge from the British persecutions. In Paris the exiles maintained the British Catholic traditions. As happened with many other institutions, the monks served the English mission and often returned to their homeland to preach or serve as priests at the risk of their own lives.

The community managed to resist the French suppression of the monastic orders that followed the French Revolution but after many vicissitudes, they moved to Douai, Flanders where they founded a school for English boys, most of whom were destined for priesthood.

In 1903, three years after having been raised to the rank of Abbey and during a second wave of persecutions of religious orders, the community was expelled from France and settled at Woolhampton. The Abbey kept the name of Douai in recognition of the hospitality the town had offered to the monks. The classic plan of the church is mixed with modern elements and comprised of brick, cement and stone with wide windows that illuminate the interiors with natural light.

North of Douai Abbey is the famous university town of Oxford. It is the quintessential college town with its old walls, delightful gardens, serene courtyards and inviting squares. But it also a place of hustle and bustle and of pedestrian-only areas that invite exploration. The prestige of Oxford can be noted in the fact that it received a charter from King Henry II that granted its citizens the same privileges and exemptions as those enjoyed by the populace of London. The University of Oxford is first mentioned in 12th century records.

University of Oxford

Its earliest colleges were University College, Balliol, and Merton. They were established at a time when Europeans were starting to translate the writings of Greek philosophers. These writings challenged European ideology – inspiring scientific discoveries and advancements in the arts – as society began seeing itself in a new way.

St. Mary the Virgin Church is the official church of the university. It was here that the first library of the university was established. Legend holds that the first gatherings of master and students was held here as early as the 12th century. St. Mary was the site of the trial of the "Oxford Martyrs" when Bishops Latimer and Ridley and Archbishop Cranmer were tried for heresy in 1555. They were found guilty and burnt at the stake on what is now Broad Street.

St. Mary the Virgin Church

The most notable feature of St. Mary is its spire that contains elements of the original 13th century construction. 127 stairs lead to the top and extraordinary views encompassing the quads of several nearby colleges including All Soul's College and a confection of spires and towers.

There are numerous buildings of stature throughout the city and university such as the Radcliff Camera. Built in the late 18th century, its classical rotunda sets it apart from any other structure in the city. The Bridge of Sighs was copied from a steeply arched bridge in Venice. The landmark bridge was built in 1914 and connects the new and old buildings of Hertford College.

The Sheldonian Theatre is where traditional graduation ceremonies are held. Built in the mid 1700s after a design by Christopher Wren, it is named after Gilbert Sheldon, Chancellor of the university at the time. In addition to graduation ceremonies, the theatre is used for music recitals and conferences. As an aside, Handel performed in the theatre including the first performance of his third oratoria *Athalia* in 1733.

The River Thames is quite close to the Abbey and offers easy strolls along the Thames Path. The following highlights some of the towns along the way. Nestled alongside the river, Pangbourne has been the subject of much literary inspiration. Kenneth Grahame, author of *Wind in the Willows*, lived in the town. The Swan Public House is referred to in Jerome K. Jerome's *Three Men in a Boat*. An inviting place full of character, with individual shops, pubs and cafes, it is encircled by pretty countryside that cradles the river. The tranquil water meadows are a popular spot for a picnic or stroll.

ENGLAND

Set on the banks of the river and backdropped by wooded hills, Henley is an ancient town with elegant stone houses from the 15th and 16th centuries. St. Mary is an imposing checkered flint and stone church with a 16th century tower topped by four octagonal turrets. The town is legendary for its extremely popular Royal Regatta held every July.

One of the most visited Thameside resorts, the village of Cookham is famous as the home of Stanley Spencer, one of Britain's leading 20th century artists. His old studio is now the Stanley Spencer Gallery where images of Cookham can be viewed. The artist was strongly influenced by the river and his religious beliefs. Many of his works depict villagers and village life. This pretty enclave is a mix of rustic workmen's cottages and grand Georgian and Victorian houses, its High Street lined with excellent restaurants and pubs, the oldest dating from 1417.

Marlow has the allure of a modern town but upon closer inspection, a number of fine Georgian buildings on High Street and West Street come to light. In addition there is a pretty suspension bridge dating from 1832. The bridge was built by W. Tierney, the same engineer who constructed the bridge between Buda and Pest in Hungary. This charming town is surrounded by beautiful countryside and with the Chiltern Hills to the north, makes for an ideal riverside locale.

The woodlands at Bisham provide a dramatic setting for its many historial structures. Bisham is best known for its abbey, founded by the Knights Templar in 1338. Despite its name, it was never inhabited by monks.

East of the Abbey is the town of Windsor and its famous castle. Windsor preserves its beguiling medieval flavor with half-timbered houses, ancient inns and winding cobbled alleyways. A significant town in the Middle Ages and one of the fifty wealthiest towns in the country by 1332, its prosperity arose from its close association with the Royal household. The development of the castle under Edward III (1350-68), it was the largest secular building project (in England) of the Middle Ages and work continued into the 15th century. Windsor also became a major pilgrimage destination. Pilgrims came to touch the Royal shrine of murdered Henry VI and the fragment of the True Cross in St. George Chapel.

During the Tudor and Stuart periods the town began to stagnate, its

Windsor Castle

castle considered old fashioned. *The Merry Wives of Windsor* is set in Windsor and it is believed that Shakespeare walked the town's streets. The Georgian and Victorian periods saw a resumption of the Royal presence and new development in Windsor.

The majority of the present streets date from the mid-19th century however the main street, Peascod, is very ancient. It predates the castle by many years and formed part of the tenth century parish structure in east Berkshire. By this measure, the thousand-year-old Royal castle, although the largest and longest occupied in Europe, is a relatively recent development.

Windsor Castle was built by William the Conqueror after the Norman Conquest of 1066. It has been remodeled by successive Kings and Queens including Henry II, Charles II, George IV and Queen Elizabeth II. Their legacy can be seen throughout the castle. Today the Queen spends most of her private weekends at the castle that is also used for ceremonial and state occasions. It preserves some of the greatest paintings and works of art in the Royal Collection.

Accommodations
The guesthouse has 22 rooms, 14 of which are en-suite; the other 8 have showers. There are also hostel-style self-catering cottages that can accommodate up to 15 guests. Both men and women are allowed. Hospitality is offered to individuals or those seeking personal or spiritual retreats.

Amenities
Meals are provided to guests at the guesthouse. For guests in the cottages there is a kitchen and dining room at their disposal. Towels and linens are supplied only to those in the guesthouse. There are three conference rooms, two lounges, a parlor and parking on the abbey grounds.

ENGLAND

Cost per person/per night
For full board approximately £40 per day, plus VAT. Other costs to be arranged with the guest master.

Directions
By car: From London take M4 towards Reading and exit at junction 12. Take A4 to Woolhampton and follow the signs to the Abbey.
By train: Take a train from London Paddington, Reading or Newbury to Midgham train station (actually in Woolhampton) and walk to the Abbey about a mile away.

Contact
Email the Guest Master, Br. Christopher Greener
Doaui Abbey
Upper Woolhampton
Reading, Berkshire RG7 5TQ
England, UK
Tel: 0044 (0) 1189 715399 (Guest Master) 1189 715300 (Abbey)
Fax: 0044 (0) 1189 715303
Website: www.douaiabbey.org.uk
Email: guestmaster@douaiabbey.org.uk

Park Place
Pastoral Centre

Franciscan Sisters of St. Mary of the Angels

Park Place is a Grade II listed Georgian building only a five-minute walk from Wickham. At one time a private mansion, in 1968 it became the Pastoral Centre and Retreat House for the Diocese of Portsmouth. Initially under the guidance of the Bishop of Portsmouth the house is now managed by the Franciscan Sisters of St. Mary of the Angels. The Centre is an important meeting place for  people of all faiths who come to attend conferences and various types of courses as well as those seeking retreats and holidays. The Centre, through the presence of Indian/Franciscan members of the community, offers an East/West feeling and spirituality.

Wickham is a small market town ideally sited in the rural countryside of the Meon Valley, the scenic attractions of the New Forest, the Solent and the South Downs. It is within easy reach of many historic cities including Winchester, Southampton and Portsmouth.

Wickham's origins probably date back to the Stone Age but it was during the Roman occupation that it became a military settlement of the important Roman road system that connected Chichester and Winchester. It was also involved in the Roman industries for the local production of pottery.

During the ensuing centuries the town flourished and became a center of skilled craftsmen and merchants. At one time it was an intermediate stop along the Victorian Meon Valley Railway that closed in 1955. The railway has since become a scenic bicycle path.

The County of Hampshire lies in the south of England and offers an enchanting blend of coast and country. It is home to the New Forest an area west of the Centre covering 145 square miles. It is England's largest, intact venerable woodlands and has earned national and international status. The New Forest is a former Royal hunting area created in 1079 by William the Conqueror. The landscape is imbued with an atmosphere of peace and tranquility. A unique mélange of historical, ecological and agricultural significance, it retains many of the rural practices conceded by the Crown in historical times to local people. Principal of these is the pasturing of ponies, cattle, pigs and donkeys in the open forest by local inhabitants known as Commoners. The New Forest has also been an important source of timber for the Crown and an outstanding recreational area for walking and riding. Within the New Forest are many intriguing villages. The quaint and historic village of Beaulieu, nestled on the bank of the Beaulieu River, was where (in 1204) King John gave the area known as Belus Locus to the Cistercian monks. Many of Beaulieu's present buildings are Georgian, built in red brick with attractive dormers. The gently sloping High Street lays claim to a number of structures with bow windows that add an old-world charm to the setting.

William the Conqueror

Burley depicts a traditional New Forest village. Settled in the lee of a hill enveloped by an area of outstanding natural beauty, the terrain is a dramatic contrast of colorful heathlands, mighty oaks, beeches and lofty pines. Ponies and cattle roam freely around this lovely village, following forest tracks used for centuries by Commoners and their livestock. Quaint thatched cottages tucked away in unexpected places evoke the way of life in centuries gone by. Burley remains untouched by time, its atmospheric setting steeped in old customs and history.

The cobbled streets of the old town of Lymington lead to a High Street filled with quintessential shops and pubs. There are great walks along the tidal salt marshes that are designated a Site of Special Scientific Interest and comprise ten miles of nature reserve. Lymington remains a busy fishing port with the quay providing a scenic viewing point for the arrival and departure of boats, from the smallest dinghy to luxury yachts.

Lyndhurst is considered the capital of the New Forest. Dominating the skyline stands St. Micheal and All Angels Church where the influence of the Pre-Raphaelite Brotherhood is everywhere. In the churchyard is the grave of Alice Liddel, Lewis Carroll's inspiration for *Alice in Wonderland*.

Heading in a northwesterly direction is the town of Winchester. A capital of Saxon kings, the city's rich past is mirrored in heroic statues, handsome Elizabethan and Regency buildings, narrow winding streets and a cathedral that punctuates its center. Winchester has always been an eminent town as witnessed by the sum and substance of its ancient buildings and historic facts. During the 13th century it was second only to London in importance.

Today Winchester presents a sharp contrast to its early beginnings. It has become a resort destination, its popularity owing as much to its

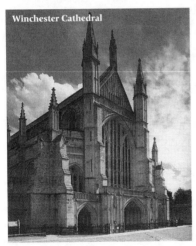

Winchester Cathedral

delightful situation on the South Downs as to the town's age old roots. The biggest draw historically is the cathedral, a building of extraordinary beauty. Begun in 1079 in the Romanesque style, the cathedral is at the heart of Alfred's Wessex and a diocese that once stretched from London's Thames to the Channel Islands. Its bishops were men of enormous wealth and power, none more so than William of Wykeham, twice Chancellor of England, Founder of Winchester College and New College Oxford.

The cathedral was also the church of the community of Benedictine monks from its earliest days. Elements of the monastic buildings can still be traced through the Cathedral Close. Central to the life of the monks was the *opus dei* (The Work of God), the regular offering of prayer sung in the choir. Evensong still takes place in the choir of the cathedral that is highlighted by glorious gabled canopies.

Winchester's fine college buildings are noteworthy as well. They cover over 500 years of history. Lying at the heart of the college is a chapel from the 14th century. The City Museum celebrates the heritage of Winchester through a series of displays and exhibitions and the beautiful 13th century Great Hall offers a dramatic view of life during the reign of Henry III. The King was born at Winchester Castle in 1207, the Great Hall is said to be a reflection of his taste with exquisite columns and extravagant decoration.

There are two significant attractions easily reached in a day's excursion from the Centre. Both are located in Romsey just southwest of Winchester. The first is the Mottisfont Abbey Gardens, a former Augustinian priory on the banks of the River Test. The abbey was powerful in its day but it is for the gardens that Mottisfont is principally known today. The park has ancient trees and an 18th century summerhouse.

In the 19th century the garden at Mottisfont Abbey was typical of the period with sweeping lawns and stands of trees, much in the Capability Brown style. The garden as seen today is the result of the work of several well-known garden designers. Norah Lindsay originated the parterre in the south front of the house and the flower-filled knot garden that remains today. One of the 20th century's foremost landscape architects, Geoffrey Jellicoe, designed the Lime Walk to a yew octagon, with an avenue of limes leading away from it above the croquet lawn. In 1971 the garden feature for which Mottisfont is so famous today was developed to hold a collection of heritage roses and many old French roses. For rose aficionados this collection is a must-see as it includes roses so old that they are prehistoric. There are also many that Empress Josephine grew in her famous garden at Malmaison in France. Since the roses are predominantly older varieties, visit in June for the best display. The grounds are also defined by a wonderful collection of oaks, chestnuts, beech, hornbeam and a huge plane tree thought to be the largest in the United Kingdom.

The second attraction is Broadlands, a part of English history for centuries. Home to statesmen, host to royalty and the celebrated of their time, Broadlands remains one of England's most alluring country homes, a gem of mid-Georgian architecture. The elegant Palladian house and lovely landscaped setting beside the River Test are a tribute to the genius of Capability Brown. The 18th century grace of Broadlands' exterior is complemented by its harmonious interior. The house shelters many of the original paintings, furniture, porcelain and sculpture collected by the second Viscount Palmerston.

Accommodations
Main house: 60 beds in single and twin rooms, half of which have private baths. One twin bedded en-suite room is accessible and equipped for the disabled.

Amenities
All meals can be provided with the lodging. They can also be vegetarian, Indian or meet special dietary requirements. Towels and linens are supplied. There are meeting and conference rooms, a dining room, ample gardens, chapel and a parking lot.

Accommodations
Assisi House: 10 beds in 2 single and 6 twin rooms, each with private bath. Assisi House can be rented by the day or week - either in total or on a room only basis.

Amenities
Meals can be self-catered by the guests or taken in the dining room of the main house. There is a lounge, sunroom and a well equipped kitchen (with a washing machine). Towels and linens are supplied. A chapel, ample gardens and parking lot are available for guests.

Accommodations
Youth Wing: 25 beds in 12 and 13 bed dormitories with shared baths and adjacent supervisor's rooms. This separate structure is intended for groups of young people led by a supervisor.

Amenities
Self-catering basis. There is a kitchen, dining rooms, various meeting rooms, gardens, a chapel and parking lot.

Cost per person/per night
Costs to be determined when reservations are made.

Directions
By car: From London take M3 to Southampton and then M27 towards Fareham. Exit at junction 11 and take A32 to Wickham. In Wickham take A334 west and follow the signs to the Centre. Or take M3 until Winchester, exit at junction 11 and then take B3335 to Bishop Waltham's. From there take B2177 to A334. The Centre is before the entrance to Wickham on A334.

By train: Take a train from London Victoria or London Waterloo to Fareham and then a taxi to Wickham and the Centre.

ENGLAND

Contact
Anyone (Preferably via email)
Park Place Pastoral Centre
Wickham, Fareham
Hants PO17 5HA
England, UK
Tel: 0044 (0) 1329 833043
Website: www.parkplacepastoralcentre.co.uk
Email: pastoralcentre@aol.com

Saint Columba's House

Sisters of the Anglican Community of St. Peter

Saint Columba's House is on the outskirts of Woking. It was founded in 1968 by the Anglican Community of St. Peter, a group of sisters who do not reside at Saint Columba's House but in a nearby convent. Built in the 1960s the structure is enclosed by its own garden. The house has recently undergone complete refurbishment to improve its accommodations and conference facilities.

Woking is in the heart of Surrey and combines the excitement of nearby London with the serenity of the countryside. In the 17th century the old part of Woking was a thriving market town. In more recent times it has become a commuter community for those working in London. An attractive leafy town with quiet lanes, waterways and a peaceful atmosphere, it features modern museums and a wealth of famous gardens and historic houses.

Interestingly the town has the first mosque to be built in Britain. Dating from 1899, it was financed largely by the Begum Shar Jehan, the immensely rich ruler of Bhopal State in India following her visit to Woking that same year. The town was once the home of H.G. Wells and formed the setting for his novel *The War of the Worlds* that is celebrated by The Martian, an piece of modern sculpture to be found in the town center.

The Surrey Hills Area of Outstanding Beauty is one of England's 37 protected landscapes. This treasured district stretches across a quarter of the county of Surrey and includes the chalk slopes of the North

Woking Mosque

Downs from Farnham in the west to Oxted in the east and extends south to the deeply wooded Greensand Hills in Haslemere. Surrey Hills is rich in wildlife, woodland, appealing market towns and villages and boasts some of the best walking in southern England.

Just outside of Woking and stretching over 240 acres, Wisley is the flagship of the Royal Horticultural Society and demonstrates the best in gardening practices. Highlights include the Rock Garden, rock pools and Alpine House. There is also a 16-acre fruit field containing over 700 apple cultivars. Model gardens demonstrate design ideas reflecting changing styles and new techniques. The Wisley Glasshouse is filled with exotics from around the world. During every season the Garden serves as a working encyclopedia for gardeners of all levels.

North of Woking the town of Egham's High Street commemorates the sealing of the *Magna Carta* with statues of King John and coats-of-arms embedded in the pavement. Egham Museum, Strodes College, Royal Holloway College and Runnymede Meadow are within walking distance of the town center. The museum preserves a number of local history collections.

Not far from Woking, the ancient town of Godalming lies in the heart of the Surrey countryside halfway between London and the south coast. The polygonal white market hall of 1814 distinquishes the center of town. Locally known as "The Pepper Pot" it displays arcades and a cupola and is a striking structure especially when lit against the evening sky. A feature of the town is its long narrow streets that stretch out from the River Wey and are lined with gracious his-  toric properties. One, the noted Kings Arms Hotel, traces its history to the 14th century. The town's church is dedicated to St. Peter and St. Paul and stands on a Saxon site. A cruciform church, it is earmarked by a central tower and spire and preserves work from all periods, showing parts of its Norman origins through to restoration work of the 19th century. The interior harbors frescoes from the 12th century, statues, paintings and carved Saxon stones.

The Pepper Pot

Accommodations

27 beds. Most rooms are single but there are some twin rooms, each with private bath. Both men and women are welcome, individually and as a group. One twin en-suite room located on the ground floor is accessible to the disabled.

Amenities

All meals can be provided on either a Bed & Breakfast or full-board basis. Towels and linens are supplied. There is a wide range of meeting rooms, a library, reading room, garden room and chapel.

Cost per person/per night

B&B from £45.
Full board from £66.
Weekend full board from £138.

Special rules

Closed at Christmas and Easter.

Directions

By car: From London take M25 and exit at junction 10 or 11 and follow the signs to Woking. Once there ask for Maybury Hill.
By train: Take a train from London Waterloo to Woking (40 minutes). The house is a 15-minute walk from the station.

Contact

Anyone
St. Columba's House
Maybury Hill
Woking
Surrey, GU22 8AB
England, UK
Tel: 0044 (0)1483 766498
Fax: 0044 (0)1483 740411
Website: www.stcolumbashouse.org.uk
Email: james@stcolumbashouse.org.uk

SOUTH WEST

Buckfast Abbey
Monks of the English Benedictine Congregation

ENGLAND

Situated between Plymouth and Exeter in South Devon, the Abbey is on the River Dart and represents one of the most interesting English monasteries due to the combination of the outstanding beauty of the landscape, a lively monastic environment and a rich heritage. Buckfast is one of the very few institutions in England that have been rebuilt for their original purpose after destruction by Henry VIII.

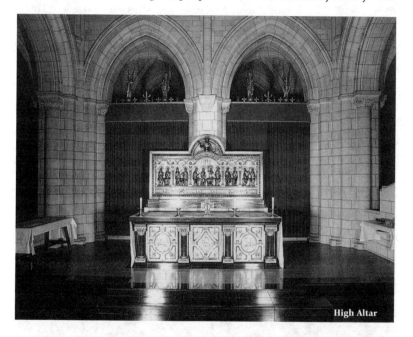

High Altar

The long, extraordinary history of the Abbey can be traced to 1018 when it was constructed under the reign of the Saxon King Knut. The first structure was small and unimpressive compared to others of the time. In 1136 a group of Benedictine monks from Savigny, Normandy, took charge of the monastery. It wasn't until 1147, however, that the Abbey became part of the Cistercian Rule and underwent a drastic change. The monks rebuilt the complex following the dictates of Cistercian simplicity and austerity. The monastery flourished with the successful production of wool exported to Italy and other European countries. The Cistercians became the country's main wool producers and established an industry whose influence affected the entire country.

The Cistercian monks also became wealthy landowners and Buckfast prospered until the Dissolution in 1539. At that time Buckfast was stripped of its possessions and left to decay. In 1800 Samuel Berry purchased the property and built his own mansion. The property changed hands four times before the last owner, Dr. James Gale, decided to sell it. In 1882 a group of monks exiled from the French monastery of La Pierre-qui-Vire bought the Abbey and made it their home. The community restored the complex and appointed an architect to design a new structure. During the rebuilding, one of the monks discovered the 12th century Cistercian foundations while digging in the vegetable garden. It was then decided to restore the monastery in keeping with its original plan and the restoration was completed in 1938. During the ensuing years the church and monastery were embellished with various works of art and one of the monks, a talented artist, Dom Charles Norris, created and influenced the style of the decorations including the stained glass windows, painted ceiling and marble pavement.

Stained glass window

In 1960 the community joined the English Benedictine Congregation. In the 1970s Buckfast began to attract hundreds of thousands of visitors every year. This brought more changes to Buckfast as the monastery had to deal with the influx of visitors while keeping spirituality as its main focus. During the final restoration of the medieval structures and the former almshouse, Southgate was converted into the main residential center for Buckfast retreats and guests.

The Lady Chapel contains a statue that is a replica of the original medieval seal of the Abbey, now preserved in the British Museum. A series of chapels called "Ambulatory Chapels" are dedicated respectively to the Resurrection, Saint Benedict, Christ the High Priest and St. Joseph. In contrast to these more traditional chapels and the simple style of the church is the Blessed Sacrament Chapel, distinguished by splendid modern stained glass windows depicting Christ at the Last Supper. The windows were designed and made by the monks in their workshop.

Abbot Anscar Vonier was the second abbot of the restored Buckfast Abbey. He was a monk as well as a builder and the key figure in the restoration. He died three weeks after the completion of the works. A plaque dedicated to him is on the right side of the south aisle. It was decorated by the refugee monk and artist Benno Elkan.

Abbey Ceiling Detail

Buckfast monks live a very active life of prayer and work. They are excellent beekeepers and produce honey. They also produce the famous Buckfast Tonic Wine based on the recipe of the French monks who occupied the Abbey in the 1880s. The base wines originally came from Spain, today they come from France. The wine is marketed and distributed by a private company. The monks of the Abbey have also created remarkable works of art that can be admired in the church. The products of the Abbey are sold in three shops on the grounds.

Region: South West   County: Devon   City: Buckfastleigh

Choir and Sanctuary

The Abbey is in Buckfastleigh, a quaint town within the Dartmoor National Park, a place where wild ponies still roam free. The park possesses a wealth of historic sites and monuments. It is a tableau of rolling moorland, wooded valleys and windswept Tors (the old Celtic word for tower). A wide open expanse covering nearly 370 square miles, it features some of the wildest and bleakest country in England. This isolated landscape is known for its uncommon weather conditions that can change in minutes. Prehistoric remains can be found throughout the moor as well as ancient clapper bridges, stone crosses, standing stones, circles, tumuli and cairns, each contributing to the unusual ambience of the park.

East of the Abbey is an area known as the English Riviera, twenty-two miles of spectacular coastline. From a background of pirates, smugglers and fishermen, the town of Torquay developed into a fashionable haven in the 19th century and features a lively harbor and palm-fringed promenade that frame an international marina. An icon of the seafront, Torre Abbey was founded in 1196. The Torquay Museum is a journey of discovery with an interactive Explorers' Galley that travels around the world to discover cultures, objects and artifacts from the past and present including the way of life in a reconstructed Devon farmhouse.

Nearby Maidencombe is a pristine coastal hamlet marked by a sheltered beach, picturesque coastal walks and protected woodlands. The gardens planted by the engineer Isambard Kingdom Brunel now form Brunel Woods, a setting of exotic trees and shrubs that Brunel had planted with an eye for both texture and color. Some of the specimens include Monkey Puzzles and Monterey Cypresses.

An interesting day trip can include a section of the Jurassic Coast, a beautiful terrain of natural features. The variety of beaches, bays and cliffs results in a constantly changing landscape. The red cliffs of East Devon date back 240 million years to the Triassic Period when vast deserts covered the area. The dark clay cliffs of West Dorset, at 200 million years in age, are the earliest Jurassic rocks and were formed in a tropical sea that flooded the desert. About 140 million years ago sea levels dropped again and forests grew. They were surrounded by swamps and lagoons across which dinosaurs prowled. The Jurassic Coast, England's first natural World Heritage Site, joined the ranks of the Great Barrier Reef and the Grand Canyon as one of the wonders of the natural world.

Region: South West   County: Devon   City: Buckfastleigh

The layers of pebbles found in the cliffs at Budleigh Salterton orig-inated over 400 million years ago when sandstones formed in what is now called Brittany. These rocks were then eroded and transported by vast rivers during the Triassic Period to form the Budleigh Salterton Pebble Beds. The famous bun-like pebbles or cobbles then fell onto the beach and were transported to the east by the sea.

Budleigh Salterton derives its name from the manufacture of salt in large salt pans. They belonged to the priory of Otterton and the monks were in charge of the salt makers and the packhorses used to convey the salt to the towns and villages along the course of the river. Situated at the mouth of the River Otter, the town's sheltered location has made it popular since Roman times. A walk up the sandstone cliffs provides outstanding views of Budleigh.

Otterton is a picturesque village with many thatched cottages. It provides easy access to the cliffs and Ladram Bay, home to the stacks, among the most dramatic sights along this part of the coast. The stacks were formed from caves that over time were hollowed out by the sea. Eventually they became arches that collapsed and formed the stacks of today. The red color of the stacks and the cliffs is due to iron min-erals that have weathered over time. These Triassic rocks are more than 200 million years old. The Undercliff between Lyme Regis and Ax-mouth is a massive landslide area now colonized by woodland – the nearest thing to a rainforest in Britain.

Sidmouth is an elegant seaside town that became a popular re-sort in the 19th century. Beautiful gardens, pleasant walks and Re-gency history add to the allure of the town. One of the best vantage points to view the extraordinary scenery is from halfway down the Peak Hill coastal road from Otterton. The backdrop of red sandstone cliffs, the buildings nestled among the wooded hillsides and the pas-tures of Sid Valley mirrored in the sparkling water are impressive. Fur-ther up Peak Hill is Mutter's Moor, an area of heath named after the notorious local smuggler Sam Mutter.

Seaton is situated at the mouth of the River Axe and features a pebble beach, walled promenade and pleasant harbor. The town cen-ter offers a mix of Victorian and Edwardian architecture. There's a tramway that runs inland to the medieval market town of Colyton.

Lyme Regis is on the border where Dorset meets Devon. With a history stretching back to the 8th century, this one-time farming village is defined by its narrow tangle of streets that wind their way to the 13th century Cobb Harbor. The steps leading to the upper part of the Cobb, made from protruding stones, are known as the Jane Austen Steps and are featured in her novel *Persuasion*. Locally they're known as Granny's Teeth. The movie, *French Lieutenant's Woman*, was set in Lyme Regis. Retrace the footsteps of the famously cloaked Meryl Streep as she walked along the old stone jetty (The Cobb) looking out across the English Channel to France, lovesick for her soldier across the sea.

The Lyme Regis area is fossil hunting country. Ammonites, Belemnites and even bones from Ichthyosaurs, extinct marine reptiles, are frequently uncovered. Rocks formed during the Jurassic Period are constantly being eroded to reveal new finds. Note that it is safer to search on the beach, not the cliffs. The ideal time to find fossils is during the winter months after rough seas have washed away the soft mud and clay.

Accommodations, Amenities and Cost

Monastery main guesthouse: Situated in the monastery, hospitality is offered only to men for spiritual retreats. There are 17 single rooms, 10 of which have private baths. Guests are asked to participate in the Divine Office and Mass and take all meals with the monks. Towels and linens are supplied. There is no fixed charge. The suggested basic contribution for this type of full-board hospitality is £35 per person per night. Curfew is at 10 PM. The guesthouse is closed at Christmas. Maximum stay 1 week.

Southgate: Renovated guesthouse where both men and women are welcome for individual spiritual retreats. They are asked to participate in the Divine Office and Mass. They can spend the rest of the day relaxing, taking walks or visiting the surroundings. There are 12 rooms, 3 of which are double, the rest are singles. Baths are shared. Breakfast and dinner are supplied. Lunch can be provided by the Abbey restaurant. Towels and linens are provided. The cost per person per night to be determined when reservations are made. Maximum stay 1 week. The guesthouse is accessible to the disabled.

There are three other houses within a 3 to 5 minute walk from the Abbey and each can accommodate small to large groups. The houses offer an excellent opportunity for those who wish to visit the interesting surroundings without participating in a spiritual retreat. All three houses are equipped with washers/dryers and travel cots.

ENGLAND

North Gate House: Previously a private home, it can sleep 13/15 in 4 twin rooms, 2 rooms with double bed and 2 singles. Baths are shared but rooms are well served by separate toilets and bathrooms. Towels, linens and breakfast are supplied on request. There is a large kitchen, lounge and dining room. Fully self-catering £16, self-catering with towels and linens supplied £20, B&B (towels and linens included) £24. Maximum stay two weeks. A detailed room plan of the house is available on the website.

Avila House: The smallest of the three houses, it is ideal for a family or a small group. There are 8 beds in 1 twin, 1 single, 1 double and 1 triple room. Baths are shared. Like North Gate, Avila was also originally a private residence. Towels, linens and breakfast are supplied on request. There is a kitchen, lounge with a fireplace and dining room. Fully self-catering £16, self-catering with towels and linens supplied, £20, B&B with towels and linens included £24. An extra charge of £10 per person is required when staying only one night. Maximum stay two weeks. A detailed room plan of the house is available on the website.

Grangehurst House: A guesthouse for over 12 years, it is the largest of the three houses. It was refurbished in 2006 and can accommodate up to 56 people in 6 double rooms, 2 single rooms and 7 larger rooms with bunk beds or regular beds. Nine of the rooms have private baths and two are accessible to the disabled. Access to the house is permitted for one group at a time. Towels, linens and breakfast are supplied on request. There is a large kitchen, a large lounge and activity room with TV/DVD player and tennis table available to guests. Fully self-catering £16, self-catering with towels and linens supplied £20, B&B (towels and linens included) £24. Maximum stay 2 weeks. A detailed room plan of the house is available on the website.

Restaurant

The Grange Restaurant occupies part of the Abbey's 12th century North Gate and in 1992 was the winner of the Civic Trust Award for Architecture. It can seat 200 people. An outdoor patio offers views of the Abbey and gardens.

Directions

By car: From London take M4 west and then M5 south towards
Plymouth. After Exeter take A38 towards Plymouth. Leave A38 and
take A384 following the signs to Buckfastleigh. Before entering
Buckfastleigh turn right following the signs to Buckfast.

By train: Take a train from London Paddington to Plymouth and get
off at Newton Abbot or Totnes, both about a twenty minute drive
from the Abbey. There is regular bus service from Newton Abbot
and Totnes, as well as from Exeter and Plymouth.

Contact

Contact the Guest Master via email, telephone, letter or send an
email using the "Booking Enquiry" window on the desired type of
accommodation on the website (more direct).

Buckfast Abbey
Buckfastleigh
Devon, TQ11 0EE
England, UK
Tel: 0044 (0) 1364 645558 (Guest Master)
For group accommodation only: 0044 (0) 1364 645532
Fax: 0044 (0) 1364 645615
Website: www.buckfast.org.uk
Email: brdaniel@buckfast.org.uk or use the link on the website

Region: South West   County: Somerset   City: Compton Durville

The Community of Saint Francis
Anglican Franciscan Sisters

The Franciscan Community of Sisters of the First Order is lodged in the Somerset countryside in a hamlet one mile from South Petherton and seven miles from Yeovil. The convent is surrounded by attractive rural lanes and a verdant landscape and offers a tranquil setting for a relaxing stay in the South West of England.

The Community was founded in 1905 and occupies a 17th century manor partly enlarged in recent years. The main guesthouse is in the converted barn and a wing of the modern building. The sisters welcome guests of all denominations. Guided retreats are also available. A detailed calendar is on the website.

South Petherton is a small country town distinguished by the traditional golden-hued Ham Stone construction of many of its buildings. It is home to St. Peter and St. Paul, a church with an octagonal tower believed to be the tallest octagonal church tower in the UK.

The busy market town of Yeovil is the center of an agricultural area of apple orchards, farmland and ancient hamlets. The handsome Early Perpendicular St. John's Church reveals an unusual copper lectern and several rather curious bosses including some carved with African masks from the time of the Crusades.

Continuing eastward from Yeovil is the historic town of Sherborne, cozily ensconced in green valleys and wooded hills. Founded by the Saxons, Sherborne is a living pageant of history whose ancient and beautiful buildings, constructed from local Ham Stone, possess a very pleasing, very distinct golden tone and celebrate the glories of church, military might and renowned schools.

The 15th century Sherborne Abbey Church was consecrated in 705 by King Ine of Wessex and Saint Aldhelm, the first literate Saxon. In its 1,200-year history the church has been a cathedral, abbey and monastery. Its heritage includes a battle between the monks and the townspeople in 1437 that resulted in destruction of the roof. The bell tower contains the heaviest set of eight bells in the world. The av-

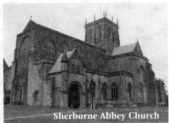

Sherborne Abbey Church

erage weight of the bells is over one ton. They date from 1350 to 1653. The church is defined by its delicate stone, fan vaulting and stained glass windows. The town is also home to a 15th century almshouse of

Region: South West   County: Somerset   City: Compton Durville

Sherborne Castle

St. John the Baptist and St. John the Evangelist. Sherborne Castle was built by Sir Walter Raleigh on the site of a former hunting lodge. It harbors a fine collection of paintings, porcelain and furniture. Lovely lakeside gardens and grounds surround the castle. Capability Brown created the lake in 1753 and gave Sherborne the very latest in landscape gardening. There are thirty acres of lakeside gardens with sweeping lawns, borders and majestic specimen tress that extend around the 50-acre lake.

Just a few miles from the community is the village of Martock. This village of golden glowing stone has an ancient history and was mentioned in the *Domesday Book of 1086*. The interior of Martock's Ham Stone church is perhaps the grandest in Somerset, the startling effect of the golden stone against the most lavishly decorated of the country's great tie-beam roofs is quite remarkable. The building dates to the late 15th century but displays stonework of an earlier period. The village also preserves many fine Ham Stone buildings ranging from cottages to grand houses. The most impressive is The Treasurer's House, so-named because the local vicar was formerly Treasurer of Wells Cathedral. This property dates mostly from the 13th century with work from the 14th and 15th. At the head of the main street, Market House is a handsome structure of the Georgian era.

Charming Beaminster's town center is protected as a conservation area with 200 listed buildings. A vibrant and prosperous market town Beaminster stands at the head of Dorset's "Hidden Valley" – the historic Vale of the River Brit whose quiet beauty features rare flowers, old water mills and delightful walks.

The ancient borough of Chard has a spacious High Street flanked by two streams and a wide variety of shops. It is the most southerly town in Somerset and only a mile from the Devon border at the foot of the unspoiled Blackdown Hills. The town itself has many interesting buildings: A fine parish church, prestigious museum and the recently refurbished Guildhall. Now privately owned, Forde Abbey was founded by the Cistercians in 1140 and became one of the richest and most learned monasteries in the country. The church was demolished in the Dissolution but in 1649 Sir Edmund Prideaux transformed the abbey into a sumptuous commonwealth house. Of particular note are the splendid tapestries and ceilings from the 1650s and the crucifixion painting dated 1320. The thirty-acre gardens include a walled, working kitchen garden, ponds, cascades, ionic temple, bog garden and the Centenary Fountain, the highest-powered fountain in England.

Nearby Neroche Forest provides fascinating insight into the history of the area. The site of Castle Neroche was a small settlement over 2,600 years ago when it probably supported a farming and hunting community. In Saxon times, over a thousand years later, the north slope of the hill became an important hunting forest and by the time of the Norman Conquest of 1066, the site was an important stronghold. The forest offers far-reaching views over the Vale of Taunton towards the Quantock Hills and Exmoor.

Accommodations

Main guesthouse: 14 single and 2 twin rooms, all with shared bath but each with a washbasin. Both men and women are welcome.
Dower Cottage: A five-minute walk from the main buildings, it has three single bedrooms suitable for self-catered retreats.
The Hermitage: Set in an isolated position nearby, it offers self-catered accommodations for one person only and is suitable for a solitude retreat.

Amenities

Towels, linens and all meals are provided for guests staying in the main guesthouse. Breakfast can be prepared by guests in a small kitchen; lunch and dinner are taken with the sisters. It is possible to miss meals but it is necessary to provide prior notice. There are sitting rooms, a chapel, refectory, large conference room and large library that guests may use.

Cost per person/per night

Voluntary contribution. Suggested contribution will be given by the sisters when bookings are made or are available on the website. Working guests are also welcome.

Region: South West   County: Somerset   City: Compton Durville

Special Rules

Hospitality in the main guesthouse is offered from Tuesday to Sunday morning. Hospitality in Dower Cottage and the Hermitage is available for longer periods but a minimum of two nights in any case. A non-refundable deposit is necessary to secure the booking.

Directions

By car: From London take M3 and then leave it following the signs to Andover on A303. Continue on A303 until Hayes End Junction. Turn right towards South Petherton and follow the signs to Compton Durville on Compton Hill Road.

By train: Take a train from London Waterloo to Crewkerne and then a taxi to Compton Durville (7 miles) or Yeovil Junction (11 miles). It is necessary to book a taxi in advance. Travel directions as well as taxi phone numbers will be provided when reservations are made. They are also available on the website.

By coach: From London Hammersmith Bus Station to Taunton. The bus stops in South Petherton about two miles from Compton Durville and the convent. There are also buses available from Taunton to Compton Durville but they are infrequent and not available on holidays.

Contact

Guest Sister (preferably by email)
The Community of St. Francis
Compton Durville
South Petherton
Somerset, TA 13 5ES
England, UK
Tel: 0044 (0) 1460 240473
Fax: 0044 (0) 1460 242360
Website: www.franciscans.org.uk/h-compton.html or www.franciscans.org.uk then click on "Where we are," then on Compton CSF.
Email: comptondurvillecsf@franciscans.org.uk

Abbey House Glastonbury

Property of the Diocese of Bath and Wells (Anglican Church)

The Abbey House is a retreat house situated on the grounds of the ruins of Glastonbury Abbey Gatehouse, the first Sanctuary of Great Britain and "traditionally the oldest above-ground Christian church in the world."

ENGLAND

Built as a private residence in the 1830s, the retreat house is not connected to the Abbey. In 1907 the Diocese of Bath and Wells purchased the property and later converted it into a retreat house. The beautiful building has preserved its original 19th century features. The guests of Abbey House have the privilege of accessing the ruins of the ancient abbey from the gardens.

The ruins of Glastonbury Abbey Gatehouse are enveloped by a plethora of fascinating legends and myths beginning with the pre-Christian tradition of spiritual rites held on the enigmatic Glastonbury Tor, the 500-foot rise dominating Glastonbury. This site is believed to have been the center of spiritual fertility rites and spiritual energy.

Region: South West   County: Somerset   City: Glastonbury

Glastonbury Tor

   A landmark that can be seen for miles around, the Glastonbury Tor is a natural hill crowned by the remains of a 14th century church. Two thousand years ago the area was flooded and the Tor could have looked like an island. Myth holds that this was the legendary island of Avalon, the place of passage to another level of existence. It was in this enchanted place that Joseph of Arimathea (Jesus' great uncle, who donated his tomb to him after the crucifixion) is believed to have landed carrying the Holy Grail, the cup used by Christ at the Last Supper and later by Joseph to catch his blood at the crucifixion. On disembarking he stuck his staff into the ground and by the next morning, the staff had miraculously flowered into a thorn bush later called the Holy Thorn (or Glastonbury Thorn). Legend holds that for safety the Holy Grail was buried just below the Tor at the underworld entrance. After Joseph had done this, a spring, now called Chalice Well started to flow, bringing eternal youth to those who drank from it.

   The Holy Grail is a feature of medieval legend. It appears in various forms, from a chalice to a caldron. It was identified as the chalice of the Last Supper and was miraculous in its powers. Those powers, however, would only be revealed to a pure knight. In Arthurian Legend the purest knight is Parsifal or Galahad. The Grail has many facets in tradition and can include a Christian story, Celtic myth and ancient fertility cults.

Myths entwined with King Arthur, the legendary English King raised by the wizard Merlin, hold that he was the King who gained the throne by extracting the sword Excalibur from a stone and establishing the Knights of the Round Table. According to tradition the King was supposedly buried under two pillars of the abbey.

Falling under the same legendary myth, the monks of Glastonbury discovered the remains of the King and his beloved wife, Guinivere during the Middle Ages. The bodies were placed in caskets in front of the main altar of the church. After the Dissolution, the relics were vandalized and dispersed. Since that time the spirit of the king is believed to haunt the ruins of the church.

Apart from the myths, Glastonbury and the ground on which the present ruins stand is one of the most sacred and historic sites in England. Facts state that the wattle and daub church was most likely built in 63 AD. Years later in the 7th century, Ine, the King of the Saxons who had converted to Christianity, built the first stone church, the base of which forms the end of the nave. The church was enlarged and Saint Dunstan became its abbot from 940 to 956. In 1184 a violent fire destroyed the entire complex. Once rebuilt it became a very active spiritual center visited by many Celtic saints. Its fame and power made it one of the main objects of Henry VIII who ordered it destroyed in 1539. Nevertheless it continued to be a site of intense mystical and spiritual interest. The imposing Gothic ruins have been turned into an open-air museum set in 36 acres of verdant parkland.

Only a few miles from the Abbey, Wells is a quaint village that seems a place untouched by time. The name Wells derives from the three wells dedicated to Saint Andrew, one in the market place and two within the grounds of the Bishop's Place and cathedral. During the Middle Ages these wells were thought to have curative powers. Wells was a Roman settlement and only became an important center under the Saxons when King Ine of Wessex founded a minster church in 704.

Region: South West   County: Somerset   City: Glastonbury

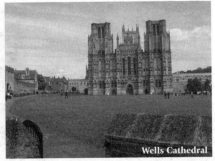
Wells Cathedral

Imposing Wells Cathedral is one of the architectural highlights of Britain, replete with outstanding Gothic carvings, a unique scissors vault to brace the building against shifting medieval foundations and a grand chapter house. The northwest transept preserves a renowned astronomical clock, ca. 1392. When it strikes on the hour, four mounted knights ride into action. The tournament between the knights continues for a quarter of an hour and presents a captivating picture.

Begun at the end of the 12th century, the cathedral was completed in 1260. The remarkable west front contains about 400 carved figures, some larger than life size. Originally the statues were painted beautiful, vivid colors and gold but time has taken its toll. The vault that springs from a series of marble shafts forms a netlike pattern, accentuated by intricate boxes of blind tracery. The interior reveals a triple-aisled basilica with double pointed inverted arches. The large stained glass Golden Window at the end of the chancel depicts the *Tree of Jesse*.

The cathedral is reached via Pennyless Porch where beggars once received alms. Linked to the cathedral by a covered bridge, the Vicar's Close is a winsome row of 14th century houses on cobbled streets. Built to accommodate the clergy of Wells Cathedral, they have been preserved and continue to be inhabited by church employees and students. The streets radiate from the cathedral green to the main marketplace and the fortress-like Bishop's Palace. Encompassed by a wall and a moat, the palace highlights an inner courtyard, a chapel built by Bishop Brunel and the palace gardens. The swans of the moat were and still are trained to ring a bell hanging from the gatehouse at feeding time.

Accommodations

The Retreat House offers hospitality mainly to groups and to individuals as space permits. There are 36 beds in 18 single and 9 double rooms. Two of the twin rooms have private baths, the rest have shared baths. Rooms are on the ground floor and are accessible to wheelchair users.

ENGLAND

Amenities

Linens are provided; towels are not. The house operates on a full-board basis but it is possible to make different arrangements. There is a library, meeting room, two chapels and parking near the house that guests may use.

Cost per person/per night

Approximately £50 for full board.

Directions

By car: From London take the M3 to junction 8 (A303) and continue until either B3151 (signs to Glastonbury), A37 (signs to Shepton Mallet, picking up signs to Glastonbury) or A371 (signs to Shepton Mallet, picking up signs to Glastonbury) and then follow the signs.

From Bristol take A37 south until the intersection with A361 and then follow the signs to Glastonbury.

By train: Take a train from London Paddington to Bristol, Bath, Bridgewater or Castle Cary. There are buses from Bath, Bristol and Bridgewater. Castle Cary is connected to Glastonbury by taxi (15 minutes). An updated bus timetable is available on the website.

By coach: Coach service to Glastonbury is available from Bath or Wells. An updated timetable is available on the website.

Contact

Anyone
(Reservations can be made through the website, by telephone or email)
Abbey House Glastonbury
Chilkwell Street
Glastonbury
Somerset, BA6 8DH
England, UK
Tel: 0044 (0) 1458 831 112
Website: www.abbeyhouse.org
Email: info@abbeyhouse.org

Hilfield Friary

Anglican Franciscan Friars

The Friary is set in rural Dorset, more precisely on the north Vale and towards the Mendip Hills, the north facing slope of the Dorset Downs, an Area of Outstanding Natural Beauty with views over the Blackmore. Not originally founded as a Friary, Hilfield developed into one as a result of the amalgamation of two separate communities that came to live here the 1920s.

The property was once part of the large estates owned by the Earl of Sandwich in Dorset. In 1888 he turned a simple farmhouse into a place where his guests could rest after a day of shooting. In 1912-1913

the Earl allowed his nephew to turn the lodge into a school for children with social and behavioral problems that was run by American psychologist Homer Lane. Due to the difficulties of WWI, the school was closed and in 1921, the 9th Earl agreed to let the place to Brother Giles and a group of Franciscans so they could establish a home for wayfarers (homeless men traveling about the roads of England searching for work). Homer Lane enlarged the original property to suit his purposes and then the friars rearranged it over the ensuing years to better suit the needs of a religious community.

Today the community of friars has reduced in numbers but at the same time, the friars diversified their goals. They offer hospitality year-round to guests staying in the Friary guesthouse, organize youth campuses and have recently started a project that focuses on environmental issues. Hilfield Project is "A Franciscan Initiative for

Peace and the Environment" based on St. Francis' spirituality which combined love of nature and animals with harmony and peace among human beings. Hilfield Project activities are separate from those of the Friary and hospitality is managed by lay personnel.

The county of West Dorset is a setting of unspoiled charm and uncommon natural beauty, of sweeping coastlines and gentle chalk downlands, sleepy villages and bustling market towns, wooded hills, river valleys and beaches that seem to stretch for miles. The Friary is very close to the historic county town of Dorchester. Built on a low chalk hill beside the River Frome, it is the ideal location for exploring both the beautiful countryside of West Dorset and the celebrated Jurassic Coast. It is a place of 18th century houses, alleys and precincts. A place where Roman relics and vestiges of Saxon royalty vie with reminders of Tutankhamun's Egypt. A market has been held in Dorchester for as long as records have existed. The Hangman's Cottage along the River Frome once served as lodgings for the hangman. The Dorset County Museum delves into the town's past. The unique structure with its splendid Victorian Hall and mosaics houses permanent exhibitions on Dorset wildlife, prehistoric times and Roman Dorset. Dorchester is still recognizable as the town that Thomas Hardy used in his novel *The Mayor of Casterbridge*. The Dorset County Museum preserves the original manuscript.

To the south of town is the Iron Age Hill Fort of Maiden Castle. Situated on 47 acres, it dates back 4,000 years and is the largest in Europe. The defenses visible today date from around 800 BC when the powerful Celtic tribe, the Durotriges, were at the height of their power. This was almost certainly their capital until the Roman conquest of 60 AD. The Maumbury Rings were originally constructed as a Neolithic henge monument at least 4,500 years ago, probably by the inhabitants of Maiden Castle. The Romans made some major changes by lowering the central area and raising the banks to create an amphitheater capable of holding 10,000 people. The site is still used as the Romans intended, with outdoor performances and historical reenactments during the summer.

An easy day trip can be made to the Jurassic Coast. Just east of Lulworth Cove, an extraordinary fossil forest is exposed on the cliffs. It formed when sea levels dropped and land emerged. The trees grew but were then submerged in a swamp. Thick layers of sticky algae grew around the tree stumps and fallen logs. Sediments stuck to the algae and turned into limestone "burrs" - the donut shaped structures that remain today.

The beaches between Bowleaze Cove and Osmington contain visible traces of the past in the form of fossilized burrows and ripple marks. These provide evidence that Dorset was once a tropical paradise similar to the present day Bahamas.

To the north and northeast of Dorchester are villages seemingly as old as the hills. The village churches in the high chalk downland and vales of Dorset offer insight into the history of the area and depict the evolution of style over the centuries, from post-Roman to Gothic and on through the Stuarts and the Georgians to the Victorians and sometimes beyond.

Accommodations, Amenities, Cost and Contact

Friary: At the Friary there are 9/10 beds in the Friary Guesthouse. Two rooms have twin beds, the rest are singles. Baths are shared. Both men and women are welcome. The guesthouse has been recently renovated.

All meals are provided with the lodging. Guests may opt out as long as they provide notice to the friars. Linens are provided but guests should bring their own towels. There is a common room and library that guests may use. Voluntary contribution. Suggested minimum for full board is £27.

Contact

Guest Brother
The Friary
Hilfield, Dorchester
Dorset DT2 7BE
England, UK
Tel: 0044 (0) 1300 342313
Email: hilfieldguests@franciscans.org.uk

Accommodations, Amenities, Cost and Contact

Bernard House: A thatched roof stone building with 8 beds in 4 single and 2 double rooms. All rooms have washbasins, one single room has a private bath. There is a large kitchen and sitting room. Linens and towels are provided. The cost, to be determined when reservations are made, includes electricity and gas.
Meals are not supplied.

ENGLAND

Juniper House: Part of the original 19th century building, it has 8 beds in 6 single and 1 twin room. All rooms have a washbasin, one single has a private bath. There is a large sitting room and kitchen. Linens and towels are provided. The cost, to be determined when reservations are made, includes electricity and gas. Meals are not supplied.

Special rules
Maximum length of stay is one week.

Contact
Sarah Hargreaves
Tel: 0044 (0) 1300 341741
Email: hilfieldproject@franciscans.org.uk
or Br Samuel
Tel: 0044 (0) 1300 342314
Email: samuelssf@franciscans.org.uk
The Friary
Hilfield, Dorchester
Dorset DT2 7BE
England, UK

Directions
By car: From London take M3 and then A303 towards Yeovil/Exeter. Follow the signs to Yeovil on A37, pass Yeovil and follow A37 south about eleven miles. At the Clay Pigeon corner (at the top of the hill after a sign to Batcombe) turn left at sign to Minterne Magna then right again on Haydon Lane (the Celtic escarpment road). Travel a mile or so, then take the second left down a steep hill (called Great Head Lane, though not indicated). The Friary is in the center of the triangle at the bottom of the hill. If you get lost the friars will provide directions on the phone.

By train: From London Waterloo take a train to Exeter and get off at Sherborne. Guests can be met at the train station by prior arrangement.

Website: www.hilfieldfriary.co.uk or www.franciscans.org.uk (click on "where we are" and then on Hilfield) or www.hilfieldproject.co.uk.

Region: South West   County: Avon   City: Stratton-on-the-Fosse

Downside Abbey
Monks of the English Benedictine Congregation

Ensconced in a lush countryside milieu, the Abbey is an important spiritual center. The Downside Community started at the monastery of Saint Gregory in Douai, Flanders then under Spanish authority. In 1606 a group of monks who had entered Spanish monasteries after the suppression of monastic life in England established a house and school near the English Channel. They chose their location so they could easily cross the Channel to serve the Catholic community in secret. When arrested they faced the death penalty. Six of the monks were beatified in 1929 and two canonized in 1970.

The community returned to England after the French Revolution when Douai was captured by the French. Upon their arrival, they settled at Acton Burnell, Shropshire before establishing their present community in 1814.

The complex was started in 1876 and the development of the first structures led to the growth of a large range of new buildings. The imposing neo-Gothic complex was completed in 1935 with the consecration of the monumental Abbey.

The church is one of only two in the United Kingdom to be designated a Minor Basilica. It is dedicated to Saint Gregory the Great. Despite the fact that construction took place in three different stages under the direction of various architects, the result is a harmonious blend that resembles the great Gothic churches of the Middle Ages and is the largest neo-Gothic Catholic church built after the Reformation. It boasts a majestic central nave and beautiful stained glass windows. The interior preserves a number of 14th to 15th century paintings of the Italian School. With a reredos and altar furnishings incorporating medieval fragments, the chapel, dedicated to Our Lady, is a remarkable structure designed by Edward Hansom and decorated by Sir Comper and is acknowledged as one of the latter's most successful accomplishments. Dedicated in 1905 the choir is the masterpiece of Thomas Garner and its stalls are modeled on the famous stalls at Chester Cathedral. At 168' the church tower dominates the entire complex and surroundings and is the second tallest church tower in Somerset. It harbors only one bell, known as the Great Bede, in memory of Dom Bede Vaughan who became Archbishop of Sydney.

The monks also founded other monasteries including Ealing and Worth in England and were involved in the foundation of Portmouth Abbey, Rhode Island. A number of monks also helped to establish the Catholic Church in Australia. Today the community is employed outside the monastery in parish and chaplaincy work.

Stratton-on-the-Fosse occupies one of the most fertile and pleasant parts of the Mendip Hills. Stratton means flat stone, possibly from the large flat stones laid by the Romans as the base for their road. The village lies between the Roman city of Bath and the town of Shepton Mallet where a large Roman settlement was recently excavated. The modern road follows the line of the old Roman road, The Fosse, the main Roman road linking Lincoln and Exeter.

There is evidence of early man having occupied the parish. In 1905 Father Ethelbert Horne, a monk at Downside Abbey led the excavations of a cave at Nettlebridge. The skeletons of a male and female were discovered along with Bronze Age pottery. A second and lower cave at the same location revealed more human bones together with that of several animals. Late Neolithic grooved ware pottery and flint implements were also uncovered.

Mendip Hills represents an Area of Outstanding Natural Beauty and comprises some of the finest countryside in Britain. Composed primarily of limestone, the hills shelter numerous caves that show signs of prehistoric occupation as well as the ruins of Roman lead mines, an amphitheater and Roman road. Sprinkled with caves, Cheddar and Wookey Holes have become very popular attractions. The Cheddar is a series of limestone caverns that extend deep into the surrounding rock. A few are open to the public. Two of the most impressive are Cox's Cave and Gough's Cave, both showcased by an extraordinary array of stalactites and stalagmites lit to enhance the colors in the rock. Wookey Hole features a subterranean lake as well as enormous dripstone grottoes. Inhabited by prehistoric people, archaeologists have unearthed bones, tools, cooking utensils and ornaments in caves throughout the Mendips. Many of these relics can be seen at the museum in Wookey.

The town of Bath is quite close to Stratton-on-the-Fosse. Bath has the only natural hot springs in the country and remains one of England's most elegant and attractive towns. Hundreds of its buildings are protected for their historical or architectural importance. The hot springs were originally discovered by the Celts who believed that the act of hot water rising from the ground came directly from the goddess, Sulis. The Romans arrived around 44 AD and deduced that the goddess Sulis was none other than their own goddess Minerva. They named the site Aquae Sulis "waters of the sun" and built elaborate lead-lined baths.

The remarkable Romans Baths complex is located in the heart of the city center. Walk where Romans walked on ancient stone pavements and imagine the grandeur of their town. Archaeological excavations have revealed that the human use of the hot mineral springs at Bath began at least 10,000 years ago and have continued to the present. First frequented by Neolithic hunter-gatherer tribes, the springs were later venerated as sacred by Celtic, Roman and Christian peoples.

Region: South West   County: Avon   City: Stratton-on-the-Fosse

Life in Bath revolves around the three natural springs that bubble up near Bath Abbey, the last of the great medieval churches in England. The Gothic cathedral known as "the Abbey" reflects the long history of abbey churches preceding it on the site. It is an Anglican parish church and former monastery and represents many elements associated with Perpendicular Gothic

Romans Baths Complex

architecture. The present building was started by Bishop Oliver King who immortalized his dream in stone on the west front where, above olive trees encircled by crowns, angels can be seen ascending and descending tall ladders surrounded by apostles.

Built on a cruciform plan, the structure has fifty-two windows, occupying about 80% of the wall space, that imbue the interior with light. The church has three aisles and shallow transepts. Superb fan vaulting adorns the chancel and side aisles. The building was completed at the end of the 16th century but its fan tracery and flying buttresses date from the late 19th.

In the 18th century the classically inspired architect John Wood and his son transformed Bath into England's most fashionable spa. The Woods, using creamy gold Bath Stone from nearby quarries, built Queen Square with its beautifully symmetrical facades, the Circus with its perfectly proportioned classic design and the Royal Crescent, a monumental semi-circular sweep of residential town houses with a singularly uniform, palace-like façade. The grand houses overlook a private lawn and the verdant swath of Royal Victoria Park. Each represents an excellent example of Georgian architecture and the recurring and powerful influence of Palladian design.

Spanning the River Avon, Pulteney Bridge was built by Robert Adam for Sir William Pulteney in the late 18th century. The bridge with three distinctive arches and lined on either side with little shops is reminiscent of the Ponte Vecchio in Florence and opens onto the regal rows of neoclassical houses in Great Pulteney Street.

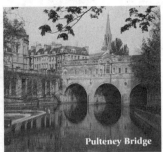

Pulteney Bridge

Accommodations

Bainesbury House: Self-catering hospitality intended for groups of young people is available in Bainesbury House on the monastery grounds. There is 1 single room, 1 double and 3 dormitories. Extra beds can be provided on request.

Amenities

Linens are supplied, towels are not. Meals are not supplied. Guests are to be self-catering and clean up upon leaving the guesthouse. There is a kitchen, living room with a small library of religious books and other literature. The dining room is next to the kitchen. There is central heating and carpeting throughout the house. Shops are a few minutes away.

Cost per person/per night

£6.

Accommodations, Amenities and Cost

Monastery guesthouse: The monastery has a guesthouse with 11 rooms (en-suite) open only to men for spiritual retreats. The suggested daily charge is £25. Contact the Guest Master, Dom Martin Gowman, Downside Abbey, Stratton-on-the-Fosse, Radstock BA3 4RH. Tel: 01761 235153
Email: dommartin@downside.co.uk.

Directions

(The abbey is approximately a 2 1/2 hour drive from London.)
By car: Take M4 to exit #18 and then take A46 to Bath. Once in Bath take A367 (Bath-Shepton Mallet) to Stratton-on-the-Fosse. On entering Stratton-on-the-Fosse turn right and the Abbey will be on the right. To enter the Abbey, turn right down a sign-posted narrow road about fifty meters before the Stratton-on-the-Fosse War Memorial.

By train: Take a train from London's Paddington Station to Bath, then a taxi or local bus to Stratton-on-the-Fosse (get off at the War Memorial). From the North, Midlands or West, take a train to Bristol's Temple Meads Station and a taxi to the Abbey.

Contact
Dom Alexander George
Downside Abbey
Stratton-on-the-Fosse
Bath BA3 4RH
England, UK
Tel: 0044 (0) 1761 235114
Fax: 0044 (0) 1761 235124
Website: www.downside.co.uk
Email: domalexander@downside.co.uk
Email: monks@downside.co.uk

Region: South West   County: Wiltshire   City: Salisbury

Sarum College
Southern Theological Education & Training Scheme

Sarum College is a 17th century building located within Salisbury Cathedral. It is a theological college open to all with hospitality extended to individuals, groups and conferences.

Salisbury is a historical town whose earliest foundation (11th century) was two miles from the modern town on a hill called Old Sarum by St. Osmund. Its imposing cathedral and close attracted students and scholars throughout Europe and made Salisbury one of the important centers for theological training of the Middle Ages. Although the city never reached the importance of Oxford or Cambridge, the theological college established in the Cathedral Close continued to offer specialized training for the clergy throughout the 13th and 14th centuries.

A new college for theological studies was founded in the Close of the new cathedral by Bishop Gilbert Burnet in 1677 under the name of School of Divinity. By the 18th century it ceased to exist. This constitutes the oldest part of the present Sarum College and is attributed to the respected architect Sir Christopher Wren.

Thanks to a donation made in 1860, Walter Kerr Hamilton, Bishop of Salisbury, was able to purchase the property and enlarge it. Architect William Butterfield was commissioned to design the additions to the original buildings that included a library and

Cathedral view from college

chapel. In 1994 the college was converted to a theological college open to all.

The college has continued to offer theological training throughout the centuries despite temporary interruptions, religious disputes and vicissitudes. It is now the property of an independent institution, the Southern Theological Education and Training Scheme and home to the administrative core of the Royal School of Church Music. Today, apart from offering courses on theology and spirituality, college activities include organizing conferences and offering hospital to individuals on a B&B basis and to groups for meetings. The beautiful historical complex includes a library opened in 1860 by Bishop Hamilton. It preserves an outstanding theological collection of over 35,000 books.

Known as the city in the countryside, medieval Salisbury has much to offer including historic chequers (squares) and alleyways, charming half-timbered buildings and Britain's finest medieval cathedral. Salisbury Cathedral is unique in Britain. Unlike its cousins, Salisbury did not evolve gradually over centuries with constant additions and renovations. Rather it was built nearly to completion within a single generation. As a result, it presents a remarkable unity of vision. The cathedral was begun in 1220 and finished, with the exception of the tower and spire, in 1258. At 404' the spire is the tallest in Eng-

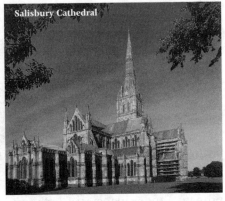

Salisbury Cathedral

land, a fact known by most English school children. What is not as well known is that the medieval builders of the spire accomplished their masterpiece with foundations only five to six feet deep in the wet ground to bear the strain of 6400 tons.

There are 323 steps to the spire and excellent views of Salisbury and the encompassing countryside. A stroll along the Town Path across the water meadows comes complete with a memorable sight of the cathedral rising up from lush green fields.

The Cathedral Library houses an original copy of the *Magna Carta*, brought here by William Longpre, Earl of Salisbury and half-brother to King John. Longpre is buried in the cathedral, the first person so honored. In the nave is probably the oldest working mechanical clock in the world dating to 1386. There are no hands and no clockface, rather, it rings a chime of bells every hour. It was originally built to call the bishops to services.

Just as there is more to the cathedral than the spire, so there is more to the city than the cathedral. A wide green space, The Close envelops the cathedral. Essentially it is a walled city within the city and ringed by wonderful period houses. Among the most memorable is Mompesson House, an elegant and spacious 18th century house built in 1701. It displays magnificent plasterwork, a fine oak staircase and splendid period furniture as well as a walled garden with a garden tearoom. The house also contains the Turnbull collection of 18th century drinking glasses.

Just a few miles north of Salisbury is Old Sarum, site of the original cathedral and castle, now impressive ruins. The massive Iron Age hill fort of Old Sarum was re-used by the Romans, Saxons and Normans before growing into one of the most flourishing settlements in medieval England. This intriguing and dramatic site contains the ruins of a castle, cathedral and royal palace. From the Iron Age ramparts, there are fine views of the countryside.

Region: South West   County: Wiltshire   City: Salisbury

There are a number of country towns and villages in the vicinity of Salisbury, an area characterized by rolling chalk downlands and tree-lined river valleys. These ancient quintessential landscapes epitomize rural England at its very best.

Downton, six miles south of Salisbury, is an ancient settlement with links to the Romans, Saxons and Normans. Once a market town, it is one of Wiltshire's loveliest villages with the River Avon forming a division between the old and the new. Downton features thatched cottages and appealing greens rising up to the church of St. Lawrence. Cruciform in design and constructed of flint and stone, most of the church's features date between the 12th and 15th centuries with the central tower and intricate stained glass dating to a later period. Held on the first bank holiday in May, the annual Cuckoo Fair, with hundreds of stalls and street activities, is a popular event and has been a highlight of village life since the 16th century. The Townton Moot is a Grade I listed 18th century ornamental garden reputed to have been a Saxon meeting place. Along with Redlynch, Woodfalls and Whiteparish, Downton is one of a handful of south Wiltshire villages that lie on the fringes of the New Forest, an ancient woodland and national park.

Accommodations
45 beds in 27 standard singles, 2 standard twins, 5 standard doubles, plus 7 en-suite singles, 6 en-suite twins, 5 en-suite doubles. All rooms have washbasins. Some rooms enjoy a magnificent view of the cathedral (Wren Rooms).

Amenities
Towels and linens are provided. Breakfast is always included; lunch and dinner can be included on request (lunch is served daily, but dinner is catered only for a minimum of ten guests). A variety of meeting and conference rooms is available for rental. Chapel and library are available for guest use.

Cost per room/per night
Single room, standard £50, en-suite £55. Twin/double, standard £80, en-suite £85-105 (depending on the type of room – with or without a view of the cathedral).

Special rules
Closed at Christmas and New Year. The Close closes at 11 PM every night.

Directions

By car: From London, take M4, M25 and then M3 south until the intersection with A303 to Salisbury. Follow the signs to the city center and the cathedral. The only vehicle access to the Close is from High Street.

By train: Take a train from London Paddington to Salisbury. The train station is about 15 minutes walk from Sarum College.

Note: Public transportation is the best way to reach Salisbury. In addition, the Close is a pedestrian area, whose only car access is on High Street and parking inside the Close is not permitted. When arriving by car, use the Salisbury District Council's Park & Ride service (a link is available on Sarum College website).

Contact

Anyone who answers the phone
Sarum College
19, The Close
Salisbury
Wiltshire SP1 2EE
England, UK
Tel: 0044 (0)1722 424800
Fax: 0044 (0)1722 338 508
Website: www.sarum.ac.uk
Email: Use the contact link on the website.

Region: South West   County: Wiltshire   City: Warminster

Ivy House
St. Denys Sisters

Ivy House consists of two linked 18th century houses (Ivy House and St. Denys Lodge). Ivy House is the Retreat Centre of the Community of St. Denys Sisters founded by Reverend Canon Sir James Erasmus Phillips, Vicar of Warminster (1859-1897). During his 40-year vicarage Sir Phillips founded many institutes, one of which, the Training Home for Women Missionaries, became the Community of St. Denys. From 1881 until 2004 the Sisters of the Community served as missionaries in England, India and South Africa. Today the  eight members of the community who do not live in the former convent hold daily worship and services in Ivy House.

The House offers hospitality for individuals seeking a peaceful stay or for guided and private retreats. The community, now open to lay members as well, has vegetable and fruit gardens in the extensive property that includes the gardens of the former convent. The gardens are divided into four parts: The main lawn, the garden by the stream, the hidden garden and the kitchen garden. There is also a summerhouse and plenty of garden seating. "Although very accessible from the town, Ivy House is also a tranquil place," said Helen, the Warden.

Ivy House is half a mile from the center of Warminster, a peaceful market town whose origins date to Saxon times. A former wool and corn town, it sits comfortably beneath the chalk downland of the Salisbury Plain at the head of the beautiful Wyle Valley. Warminster is

233

noted for historic 17th and 18th century houses. Topping the modern storefronts in the shopping area are attractive mullioned windows from another age. Warminster was once a popular stopping place for coaches as witnessed by the beautiful buildings of the Bath Arms, dating back to the 1600s, the Anchor and the Old Bell Inn dating from 1483. All have preserved period features from these bygone eras.

Dazzling views of the town can be had from Cop Head and Cley Hill Iron Age Hillfort about three miles west of Warminster. Now the property of the National Trust, Iron-Age Hillfort is just one of several such sites in Wiltshire but differs in that it occupies an unusual location built upon a segment of chalk rising to around 775' above the countryside.

Ivy House is situated in the Salisbury Plain, a place of great natural beauty and renowned throughout the world as the home of Stonehenge. Standing proudly amid an ancient landscape high on Salisbury Plain, Stonehenge is a prehistoric monument of unique importance. Erected between 3,000 BC and 1,600 BC its orientation on the rising and setting sun is one of its many remarkable features. Why it was built in this way remains unknown. Whether it was simply because the builders came from a sun-worshiping culture or because, as some scholars believe, the circle and its banks were part of a huge astronomical calendar, remains a mystery. Designated a UNESCO World Heritage Site and recently voted Britain's Best Historic Site, Stonehenge is surrounded by the remains of over 400 ceremonial and domestic structures – some older than the monument itself. Many of these features - earthworks, burial mounds and other circular "henge" monuments - are accessible by road or public footpath.

Due south of Stonehenge, Wilton was once a county town as well as a bishopric, a Royal residence and one of the oldest boroughs in England. In 871 King Alfred founded an abbey here. This stood on ground now occupied by Wilton House, designed and rebuilt by Inigo Jones following a fire of 1647. The house contains sumptuous furnishings and fine paintings including work by Rubens, Van Dyck and Tintoretto. Today the town is best known for the Wilton Carpet Factory where visitors can explore the world of carpet manufacturing in its authentic setting around an 18th century courtyard. On display are exhibits from 300 years of carpet making as well as demonstrations of hand weaving.

| Region: South West | County: Wiltshire | City: Warminster |

The church of St. Mary and St. Nicholas is one of the town's most treasured possessions. It is a true architectural showplace that was built at the behest of the Russian Dowager Countess of Pembroke in the mid- 1800s. The church is in the Romanesque style depicting the look of the

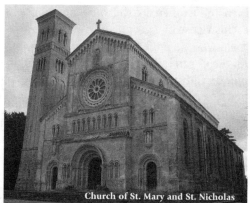

Church of St. Mary and St. Nicholas

basilica in Lombardy. Both the interior and exterior are breathtaking in their beauty. There are fine marble columns that came from Portovenere and stained glass from France.

South of Ivy House, ancient Tisbury is the largest village in the Nadder Valley and has been a settlement for over 2,000 years. Most of the older houses in the village were built with locally quarried Chilmark Stone, in contrast with the Victorian red brick found on Tisbury's High Street. Place Farm a 15th century thatched tithe barn is supposedly the largest in England and includes the farmhouse and gatehouses. It is considered one of the finest surviving groups of monastic grange buildings in England. Closely associated with Shaftesbury Abbey, it was founded by King Alfred the Great and was Saxon England's foremost Benedictine nunnery. Today the massive ramparts are all that remain of the original precinct wall but the story of the community is brought to life in a state-of-the-art museum.

Also in Tisbury the 12th century parish church of St. John the Baptist sits on the northern bank of the River Nadder. Its churchyard features a remarkable 1,000-year old yew tree. Just a short distance from Tisbury are the romantic ruins of Old Wardour Castle, a beguiling French-style residence built in the 13th century. The unusual hexagonal ruins now stand in a picturesque lakeside setting. There are elaborate rock grottoes and turrets to explore.

Accommodations
27 beds in single rooms and a few double rooms. Baths are shared. All rooms have washbasins and tea/coffee making facilities. Both

men and women are welcome. The house can be requested for exclusive use of a group with a minimum of 15 paying guests.

Amenities

All meals can be supplied on request but arrangements must be made in advance. Towels and linens are supplied. A variety of meeting and sitting rooms are available for guest use. The house has its own private parking and cars can also be easily parked along the street. One room is accessible to the disabled.

Cost per person/per night

Full board £46.
B&B £26 first night, subsequent nights £24.
A deposit is required to secure the booking.

Directions

By car: From London take the M4 to M25 south. From M25 take M3 towards Southampton. At the intersection with A303 go towards Andover and follow A303 until signs to Warminster on A36. Take the exit to Warminster and continue to the top of the hill by a church on the right and then bear left onto Sambourne Road. Continue to mini-roundabout and at bottom, turn left. At obelisk, bear right, Ivy House is 30 yards on the left and a sharp turn into the car park.

By train: Take a train from London Waterloo or Paddington to Bath and from there to Warminster. The train station is a short walk from the House. Taxis are also available.

Contact

The Warden
Ivy House
St. Denys Retreat Centre
2-3 Church Street
Warminster
Wiltshire BA12 8PG
England, UK
Tel: 0044 (0) 1985 214824
E-mail: stdenys@ivyhouse.org
Website: www.ivyhouse.org

WEST MIDLANDS

Belmont Abbey
(Saint Michael and All Angels)

Benedictine Monks

The Abbey is situated about three miles southeast of historic Hereford. Founded in 1859, until 1917 it served as the Common Novitiate and House of Studies for the English Benedictine Congregation. During that same period, Bishop Brown of Newport and Menevia, a native son of Belmont, was given the church as his cathedral and organized a monastic chapter. In 1920 Belmont was elevated to the rank of Abbey.

The Abbey is a neo-Gothic complex, lavishly decorated, detailed and dominated by four elegant, steeply pointed arches that lead the eye

heavenwards. The exterior is composed of local pink sandstone, simple and unadorned, particularly the west front that evokes the classical monastic facades of the 14th century. The interior of the church reflects warm Bath Stone and reveals hundreds of angels in stained glass windows, statues and paintings. Out of the more than 150 angels, perhaps the finest stone examples can be seen in the nave. They are portrayed with harps, cymbals and pipes and comprise a heavenly orchestra to accompany the monks and worshippers.

Some of the most elegant stained glass can be viewed in the window at the east end that illuminates Michael trampling the dragon. Raphael the Angel and Gabriel are also depicted. Around them are angels representing the nine choirs of angels. Even more angels can be seen in the rose window above. Light from the aisle windows often suffuses the entire space. There is a beautiful wooden choir and an enormous library.

Belmont Abbey is recognized as the second largest Benedictine House in England. There are about 45 monks officially residing at the Abbey but because of the extensive pastoral commitments undertaken by the Abbey, only 20 monks are permanently in residence. The others are involved with chaplaincy or work as missionaries in the Monastery of the Incarnation in Tambogrande in the north of Peru.

Hedley Lodge, the modern and welcoming guesthouse of the Abbey, keeps the monks constantly occupied. Set on the inviting grounds of Belmont Abbey, it is encompassed by magnificent gardens. High yew hedges, rose beds and a fountain come together to present a magical milieu of peace and tranquility. The guesthouse hosts casual visitors desiring a few days of peace and quiet exploration in addition to those seeking a personal or organized retreat.

Nearby Hereford has a long and colorful history. Once the capital of Saxon West Mercia, by Norman times it was a defensive bastion between the Welsh and the English. Its cathedral was founded in Saxon times to house the shrine of Saint Ethelbert, murdered king of East Anglia. An unusual effect known as the Geometic style can be seen in the triforium arches that are triangular, almost straight-sided. Mainly Norman from the 12th century, the cathedral has undergone a number of additions. It claims the famous Mappa Mundi, a map of the world drawn in the 13th century. Its extraordinary Chained Library houses 1,500 books attached by chains to rods on 17th century oak bookcases. It is the largest library of its kind in the world. Sites of interest in the town include the Green Dragon, an old posting inn with wood paneling from the 1600s, a museum housing relics from the Bronze Age, a 15th century six-arched stone bridge over the River

Wye and traces of the city's medieval walls.

Northeast of Hereford is the well-known and popular Stratford-upon-Avon an ancient market town occupying an ideal stretch along the Avon, one of England's prettiest rivers. The town center reflects many architectural periods with emphasis on 16th and 17th century styles including rows of half-timbered houses, Victorian homes and quaint cottages.

Much of the town's focus is on its most famous native son, William Shakespeare. His home, work and family's residences are pre-sented in many venues. Shakespeare aficionados can finally get their fill of the Bard with a visit to this charming town. The well-preserved houses connected with the play-wright - his wife's cottage, his daughter's house - provide insight into life during Elizabethan times. The Gothic-styled parish church of Holy Trinity contains the writer's tomb and a monument to him. The Royal Shakespeare Theatre built in the early 1900s shelters a gallery of portraits of Shakespeare

William Shakespeare

and other actors as well as costumes and stage sets. The old Memorial Theatre where Shakespeare's works were performed after 1879 was destroyed in a fire.

Nearly due west of Hereford, Hay-on-Wye is England's mecca for bibliophiles with more than thirty bookshops, most selling second-hand books. For ten days at the beginning of June the towns hosts the Literary Festival and attracts 80,000 visitors who come to hear and see big literary names from the world over.

Heading in a southeasterly direction from Hereford in the beautiful River Wye valley region, Ross-on-Wye is a historic market town characterized by narrow streets, ancient buildings and a 17th century pink sandstone columned market house ca. 1670. The parish church of St. Mary is in the Decorated and Perpendicular Gothic style. Ensconced on a cliff of red sandstone above the water meadows and wooded valley of the River Wye are panoramic views over the river from the cliff-top gardens. From Hereford to Ross, the Wye Valley Walk follows more than a dozen miles of gentle countryside. Across the River Wye is the exceptional Goodrich Castle, a romantic ruin built in the 13th century to a square design, with large rounded towers at the corners. A winding staircase to the keep ends in outstanding views.

Also within the vicinity is Symonds Yat West on the Herefordshire side of the River Wye and Symonds Yat East on the Gloucester side. The only connection between the two banks and each hill-hugging village is by ancient hand-pulled ferries. For a small fee a ferryman pulls people across the river using an overhead rope. Symonds Yat Rock is a scenic viewpoint towering 394' above the river on the Gloucester side. From this viewpoint it is possible, between April and August, to witness peregrine falcons nesting on the opposite cliffs.

Another worthy destination from the Abbey is Ledbury, an atmospheric town offset by a core of crooked streets and narrow cobbled lanes lined with black and white half-timbered houses that lead to a gingerbread style market place, also in black and white. The Market House dominates the center of town. The brick and timber structure was built in 1653 by John Abel, the celebrated "King's Carpenter." Its original use was as a grain store but it is now a council meeting room. It is supported on sixteen oak pillars that remain from the original structure. The 12th century church of St. Michael sits beside a lovely 18th century spire and tower. Already established as an important church by the time of the Norman Conquest, the present building was completed in 1140, extended and modified in the 12th and 15th centuries.

Accommodations

17 twin or double rooms each with private bath, TV, telephone, complimentary tea or coffee maker. Non-smoking rooms or extra bed/cot on request.

Amenities

Towels and linens are provided. Laundry service, ironing board, hair dryer, newspapers on request. There is a large parking lot on the Abbey grounds. Sitting area and bar service (Cloister Bar), conference rooms and rooms for celebratory lunches and dinners are available.

Meals

The Cantilupe Restaurant provides meals to residents and guests. On request the Refectory can cater meals for 40 to 200 guests.

Cost per person/per night

To be determined with Mr. Edmund Hayward, Director.

Directions

By car: From London take M4 to Junction 15, then take A419/417. After the Gloucester bypass take the B4213 via Newent to M50 junction 3. Take the road to Ross on-Wye, and from there take the A49 to Hereford. Once in Hereford follow the A465 Abergavenny Road for two miles and turn right up to Ruckhall Road. Hedley Lodge is on the left-hand side.

By train: Take a train from London Paddington (via Newport or Oxford), Birmingham or Manchester and get off at Hereford Railway Station. From there take a taxi. The Abbey is about 3 1/2 miles from the station.

Contact

Anyone
Hedley Lodge
Belmont Abbey
Hereford, HR2 9RZ
England, UK
Tel: 0044 (0) 1432 374747
Fax: 0044 (0) 1432 374754
Website: www.belmontabbey.org.uk
Email: hedley@belmontabbey.org.uk

Region: West Midlands   County: West Midlands   City: Birmingham

Woodbrooke Quaker Study Centre

Religious Society of Friends (Quakers)

Region: West Midlands   County: West Midlands   City: Birmingham

Woodbrooke is the Quaker Study Centre in the United Kingdom. Located in Selly Oak, a suburb of Birmingham, the Centre is only 15 minutes from town but isolated by its own extensive grounds that form the largest organic garden of Birmingham. "You wouldn't think you are only fifteen minutes away from the city center," said Heather, in charge of Public Relations.

The grounds of Woodbrooke were part of the property of the fine Georgian house that was George Cadbury's family home until 1903. George Cadbury, himself a Quaker, was one of the owners of Cadbury Chocolate, the main UK chocolate manufacturer. When he decided to move from his house he had a vision of a place where Quakers could study and donated the house to the Religious Society of Friends. Woodbrooke first commenced as a study center but slowly developed into a retreat, spirituality and conference center. Today the Centre offers a large variety of residential options. Come as an individual, as a group, for a study course or simply for a holiday in the area.

The house preserves one of the largest Quaker libraries, second only to Friends House Library of the Friends House, London. The library contains about 10,000 texts, some of which date back to the 1500s and is open 24 hours a day for residential guests.

A team of volunteers tends the beautiful grounds. Chemicals are banned. The garden boasts a tranquil lake with an island and an authentic Victorian boating house, a labyrinth, Chinese garden, wet meadows, woodland walks, herbaceous borders and the walled kitchen

Garden labyrinth

garden that provides most of the vegetables for the house's kitchen. Tours of the garden are available on the first Sunday of each month from May to October and last about an hour. The cost is £1 per person.

Selly Park Museum is set in the leafy area of Bournville and provides visitors with a glimpse of life in simpler times and displays an assortment of old furniture and household items. A Tudor timber-framed manor house dating to the 15th century, it is one of the oldest buildings in Birmingham. Headquarters of Cadbury Brothers, Bournville started life as a garden village built by the company (Cadbury) for its workers in the late 19th century.

Within about ten miles of the Centre is a pastiche of small towns and villages. Edgbaston is a district of wide tree-lined roads fringed with elegant houses that in the past few years have become interspersed with more modern buildings yet it still retains much of its 19th and early 20th century charm. The Plough and Harrow Hotel occupies a gracious brick structure built in the Victorian era. This perfectly epitomizes the Edgbaston of yesteryear when nearly all the properties were of similar style and proportion. The town is home to the Birmingham Botanical Gardens and the massive complex of Birmingham University that is overseen by towering Big Tom, the university clock.

Nearby Dudley was once known as the Capital of the Black Country. It was here in the 17th century that coal was first used and its vast iron works prospered until almost the end of the 20th century. Dudley was granted its market charter in the 13th century. Since that time the lively outdoor market has been a focal point drawing visitors to the town. The market is held in a pedestrianized square every day except Sunday. The Black Country Museum offers insight into the history of mining. A number of interesting trips are also run on the network of canals in the type of narrow boat traditionally used for transporting coal.

The ruins of Dudley Castle have dominated the town since it was built in Norman times and the castle is one of the most important ruins in the West Midlands. Its splendid keep has sweeping views over seven counties.

A castle was recorded in Dudley at the time of the *Domesday Book of 1086* but this is believed to have been a wooden structure from an earlier date. Most of the ruins that can be seen today date from the 12th and 13th centuries. It served as a fortress until after the English Civil War and then was left to the ravages of time and a fire of 1750.

South of Birmingham, Lapworth has not changed very much over the centuries. The village offers a becoming mix of ancient properties that mingle harmoniously with barn conversions and new buildings. An age-old village visitors are drawn both to the beautiful surrounding Warwickshire countryside and to Lapworth's lovely church with its detached battlemented tower and steeple. The church also presents some Norman remains. A tall nave with a clerestory of Perpendicular square-headed windows distinguishes the architecture. The interior displays a carved monument ca. 1928 and there is an early 14th century octagonal font.

Ackwood House is another Lapworth showplace. The timber-framed Tudor is set in remarkable grounds and features a superb oak floor in the hall, a paneled gallery and magnificent timber roofed great hall added in the mid 1920s. Throughout the interior are fine collections of needlework and tapestry.

Continuing south, Lapworth is close to the Tudor delights of Henley-in-Arden. Hidden amidst the verdant lanes of Warwickshire, this pleasant town has maintained much of its original allure and character with buildings covering every period of history going back to medieval times. In the center of town stands the old Market Place and the remains of the 15th century Market Cross, one of the few still existing in Warwickshire. The one-mile High Street is classified as a Conservation Area and contains many buildings of architectural interest including oak timbered properties dating from the 15th, 16th and 17th centuries. They have been beautifully preserved, hence its singular designation. The Guild Hall is a half-timbered Elizabethan building. It has been extensively restored although many of the original timbers remain. The Guild Hall and Walled Garden can be viewed by application to the Custodian at the Guild Cottage.

The parish church of St. John the Baptist dates from 1448 and replaced an earlier structure. It is in the Perpendicular style and the square turret topped tower has a clock. The handsome interior of the church displays a splendid altar and an intricately carved oak choir backed by a stained glass window.

Throughout Henley are reminders of Shakespeare country. Mary Arden's house is close by as is Anne Hathaway's cottage. The area presents an altogether English scene and is filled with picturesque thatched cottages and mellow brick wisteria-clad farmhouses enclosed by fields grazed with cattle and lamb.

Region: West Midlands	County: West Midlands	City: Birmingham

Accommodations

There are 69 rooms, mostly singles, 45 with private baths. A few are twins and doubles and there is one family room. All have tea and coffee making facilities, desk and washbasin. Wi-fi Internet access is available in each room. Bedrooms especially adapted for the disabled (with private bath) are also available.

Amenities

All meals are supplied with the lodging, from B & B to full board. Towels and linens are provided. There is a sitting room, a cellar with audio and TV equipment, billiard table, table tennis and conference rooms. There is also a lake with a boat and a garden with volleyball and croquet courts available to guests. The house is accessible to the disabled.

Cost per person/per night

B&B £39, half board £48, full board £56.

Directions

By car: Take M40 from London to Birmingham. Take M42 west to join M5. Exit at A38 and look for signs to Woodbrooke. The house is located on this main road that connects Birmingham to M5.

By train: Take a train from London Euston to Birmingham and then a bus # 61, 62, 63, or 64 to Selly Oaks. All the buses stop in front of the Woodbrooke gate.

Contact

Anyone by phone, by email or by the enquiry link on the website
Woodbrooke
1046 Bristol Road
Selly Oak
Birmingham B29 6LJ
England, UK
Tel: 0044 (0) 1214 725171
Fax: 0044 (0) 1214 725173
Website: www.woodbrooke.org.uk
Email: enquiries@woodbrooke.org.uk

Region: West Midlands   County: Worcestershire   City: Cropthorne

Holland House

Worcester Diocese

Holland House is a striking 17th century black and white timbered Tudor structure set along the River Avon. Surrounded by a quintessential English garden that meanders down to the riverbanks, the house was once a private mansion. After peace was declared at the end of WWII it became a diocesan retreat house. Today it is still owned by the Worcester Diocese and run by a Warden, currently Reverend Ian John Spencer.

The complex comprises the original 17th century Tudor buildings with later additions. The oldest part is the Library, enhanced with beamed ceilings and leaded light windows. The Drawing Room, added in 1900, is an atmospheric, elegant room with an Adam-style fireplace, large windows and high ceilings. Bedrooms are situated in the half-timbered thatched roof building. The conference room was built at a later date to suit the needs of larger groups.

Holland House takes great pride in its four-acre garden that includes a large terrace, formal gardens, a croquet lawn, rose, herb and peace gardens in addition to a rich kitchen garden that supplies the homegrown produce used by the House throughout the year. There is also a recently restored Victorian Greenhouse. It provides a space for cultivation and a peaceful spot where guests may linger. Holland House Gardens are members of the National Gardens Scheme and they are open to visitors. The House offers hospitality for organized retreats for individuals and groups as well as hospitality for days of relaxation in this serene corner of Worcestershire.

The House is in Cropthorne, a small rural village of 600 inhabitants. Worcester is a great cathedral city dominated by its glorious Romanesque cathedral. Built of red sandstone between the 12th and 14th centuries, the arched and pillared crypt is the oldest part of the cathedral and was erected around 1084 by Bishop Wulfstan to insure a place of safety for worshipping the relics of saints. The cathedral's ancient possessions include fine carved misericords and King John's Tomb, the oldest royal effigy in England. The tomb is carved from Purbeck marble and quite probably was once painted and bejeweled. Its architectural highlights include an unusual circular chapter house, ca. 12th century and medieval cloisters. It preserves sixty-five monuments including the royal tombs of King John and Prince Arthur. Other notables are recalled in gorgeous stained glass. The cathedral buildings lie within one of the oldest parts of Worcester and are assembled around a College Green.

North of the cathedral in the city's pedestrian-only area is the Guildhall. Built in 1721 to a design by Thomas White, a

Worcester Cathedral and its misericord

pupil of Sir Christopher Wren, the fascia of the Guildhall is one of the finest examples of early Georgian architecture in the country. The interior harbors a superb staircase that leads to the beautifully decorated Queen Anne Assembly Room.

Southeast of the cathedral, the Commandery is an outstanding half-timbered structure, a warren of nearly five dozen rooms that wanders from medieval times to the Victorian era. Several other historic buildings can be seen along Friar and New Streets. Greyfriars ca. 1480 was built to provide a sanctuary for travelers. The picturesque Tudor House is a fine timber-framed building dating from the 15th century while Nash House is a four-story Elizabethan house. The oldest church in the city is St. Helen whose beginnings can be traced to 680 AD.

Since the early 1800s Worcester has been known for its connections with worcestershire sauce. Lea and Perrins was founded in 1825 and still remains in Midland Road. The town is also home to the famous porcelain works of Royal Worcester. On the factory site is the Dyson Perrins Museum where rare and very beautiful pieces of porcelain, made in the factory over the centuries, are exhibited.

Holland House is quite close Evesham and Pershore. Historic Evesham lies between the Malvern and Bredon Hills and the Cotswolds. It is particularly beautiful in the early spring when the region is highlighted by a mass of colorful flowers. Viewing the Evesham skyline from across the waters of the River Avon provides a dramatic glimpse of the spires of two churches behind the tower of Evesham's historic abbey. The abbey is a pre-Conquest foundation of the Benedictine Order. Under Norman rule it flourished and became a popular pilgrimage center. At the height of its power and fame, the abbey church had fifteen altars, symbolic of the affluence enjoyed by the resident monks. This prosperity ended with the Dissolution of the Monasteries. At that time several of the monastic buildings were demolished. What remains is well worth viewing: The abbey gateway, cloister archway, almonry and two churches built within the confines of the abbey. The finest of the relics is the bell tower dating from around 1533 and thought to have been built by Abbot Clement Lichfield who ruled the order at that time. The abbey's grounds are set out in a series of monastic gardens featuring old ponds together with a pretty 18th century garden of herbs and other delicate plants.

Pershore is an appealing market town famous for its elegant Georgian architecture and lovely abbey. The abbey church, originally a Benedictine monastery, is distinguished by a lantern-tower, a Norman south transept and a Norman crossing. The lantern tower rises on massive arches of the Romanesque period and probably dates to 1330. The interior of the church houses relics from the past including a round font displaying intricate carving. The choir is Early English with beautiful vaulting. On the north bank of the Avon, the river is spanned at Pershore by a six-arched medieval bridge.

Broadway, at the foot of the Cotswold, is memorable for its ancient main street and the well-worn stone flags of its arched Market House. Little has changed since medieval times and the appeal of the town is evident in its gracious houses. All built of honey-colored Cotswold stone, the houses and cottages ramble haphazardly along pleasant green-bordered roads. Steep gables of the larger houses rise above the roofline of the dormer windowed cottages and here and there are black and white thatched roof cottages. The center of the village is dominated by the Lygon Arms whose origins date to the 16th century. Broadway's High Street stretches for almost a mile before rising sharply at Fish Hill, reputed to be 800' above sea level. Further along is one of the best-known landmarks of the Midlands, the Broadway Tower. Standing where the ground rises to more than 1,000', the tower was built in 1800, a Gothic folly for the Earl of Coventry who wanted to view his family seat at Worcester, some 20 miles away.

Chipping Camden is among the most picturesque small towns in the northern reaches of the Cotswolds. The town bears all the hallmarks of the 14th and 15th centuries when it was an important wool town. Wealthy merchants brought their fleeces to do trade at the exquisite 14th century Woolstaplers Hall. William Grevel was a wool merchant who gave generously to the town and the church. His house displays a two-story carved bay window from the 14th century. The church of St. James is an imposing structure whose Perpendicular tower rises majestically above the town to a height of 120' and is one of the finest "wool churches" in the Cotswolds. Its architecture is mainly of the 15th century but the chancel belongs to the 14th. The church reveals many treasures including a 15th century brass lectern and several 16th century monuments.

The dwellings throughout this gem of a town reflect perfect examples of gracious mellow stone properties all blending together and appearing very much as if time had passed them by. The graceful curving main street is flanked by a wonderful array of stone cottages, ancient inns, terraced houses and historic homes. Some cover three stories and are beautifully gabled with fine stone mullion windows while others are two-story with bay windows.

Moreton-in-Marsh is one of the principal market towns in the northern Cotswolds. The long and wide High Street is a clue to its origin as a planned market town dating to the 13th century. Every Tuesday it holds the largest open-air street market in the Cotswolds with more than 200 stalls. The town possesses some fine buildings including a rare Curfew Tower with its original clock and bell dated 1633. The bell was run nightly until 1860 to remind people of the risk of fire at night. The parish church of St. David was originally a chapel rebuilt in 1858 in medieval style. Fine houses and shops of the 18th and 19th centuries line the High Street including Redesdale Market Hall, a Victorian Tudor building of some distinction.

Stow-on-the-Wold is an alluring market town and perhaps best known of the small Cotswolds towns. The vast market square testifies to the town's former importance. At one end stands the medieval cross, a reminder of the market's heyday. It was placed there to encourage traders to do business fairly under the sight of God. At the other end are the town stocks, shaded between an old elm tree. Around the square is an elegant array of Cotswold town houses all built in the local stone. The town stands exposed on a 700-foot high hill at a junction of seven major roads including the Roman Fosse Way, the ancient Jurassic Way and the Salt Way.

Accommodations
25 rooms -18 singles and 7 twins. Baths are shared and located on each floor, along with tea/coffee making facilities.

Amenities
All meals can be provided with the lodging. Towels and linens are provided. Meeting and conference rooms, gardens, croquet fields, chapel, licensed bar and dining room.

Cost per person/per night
B&B £45, lunch £12.5, dinner £15.

Special rules
Closed at Christmas and Easter. Maximum stay one month.

ENGLAND

Directions

By car: From London take M40. Exit at Oxford and take A40, bypass Oxford and take A44 to Evesham. Pass Evesham and continue on A44. After passing the village sign for Cropthorne, turn off the A44 at the signpost Village Centre / Fladbury. After the right-hand bend, take the first left into the first proper lane (Kennel Bank) that leads into the house's parking lot. Follow the signs through the garden to the House. Pay attention, due to 2007 floods, the current B4084 used to be the A44 whereas the current A44 used to be the B4084. Signposts on the actual roads are correct but some online mapping services label these roads incorrectly. If confused contact the house before starting the journey.

By train: From London Paddington to Evesham and take a taxi to the House.

Contact

The Warden
Holland House
Main Street
Cropthorne
Pershore
Worcs, WR10 3NB
England, UK
Tel: 0044 (0) 1386 860330
Fax: 0044 (0) 1386 861208
Website: www.hollandhouse.org
Email: enquiries@hollandhouse.org

Offa House

Diocese of Coventry

Set in a prominent position embraced by two acres of gardens, Offa House features beautiful views of the rural countryside of Warwickshire. The house itself is a Grade II Georgian structure situated beside the church of St. Gregory. Originally built as a vicarage for the village of Offchurch, in 1961 it was converted into a retreat house of the Diocese of Coventry.

The House offers a wide range of retreats, conferences, meetings and events. The programs are available on the their website. They also provide a venue for a relaxing holiday in a strategic but quiet location near many places of interest.

Offchurch is a small village three miles from Royal Leamington Spa but despite its size, it played a role in the history of the country. Founded at a crossroads between the Fosse Way and Welsh Road, the village held an important position in Saxon times, as authenticated by archaeological finds. Moreover tradition holds that it was home to Offa, King of Mercia who reigned from 757 to 796 and who had a palace on the site of the present Bury House. King Offa built a church (hence the name of the village) to commemorate his son's death. The original church no longer exists but St. Gregory was built by the Normans on the same ground, mostly between 1110 and 1120. The interior of the church reveals a stone coffin, believed to be Offa's, but again, no hard evidence exists. Legends holds that if you jump off the roof of the church, Offa will come out and catch you from falling (not a suggestion).

During the centuries following the Norman Conquest, Offchurch became the property of the monks of Coventry until the Dissolution of the Monasteries in 1539. At that time it was granted to one of the King's commissioners – Sir Edmund Knightely whose descendants were in possession of the Bury House and its surrounding lands until 1919.

There are many beguiling towns and villages near Offchurch and the Offa House. Quite close by is the village of Compton Verney which takes it name from the great house acquired in the 15th century by the Verney Family. John Verney was granted the estate in 1430 by King Henry VI. He was the first in a line of Verney ownership that was to last for over 500 years. From his hands the house passed to his son Richard who set about building a new and more substantial residence, an impressive neoclassical mansion made distinctive with landscaping by Capability Brown. The grounds with their great stands of limes, cedars and oaks, decorative lake and ornamental bridge accentuate the graceful lines and elegance of the house.

Compton Verney possesses a rich and varied history as acknowledged in the ancient relics found around the Verney estate. The name Compton translated into Old English means settlement in a valley and there is evidence of a Roman settlement. Flints and Iron Age pottery have been found, indicative of an earlier occupation. Remains of cottages along the lake are possibly from medieval times when a manor was established by the Murdak family in the 12th century and at that time the village was known as Compton Murdak.

Northeast of Offa House the small town of Alcester was developed as a market town in Roman times. It grew from a settlement at the meeting point of two roads and two rivers, the Arrow and the Alne. Today the town is enveloped by luxuriant rolling countryside with thatched cottages and old farmhouses. Its High Street is full of antiquity with black and white timber-framed Tudor houses standing alongside handsome Georgian red brick structures. The town hall was built in 1618 and the church, dedicated to St. Nicholas, is from the 14th century. The Heritage Centre fully explores Alcester's Roman history and exhibitions depict everyday life in and around this one-time Roman settlement. Another Alcester attraction is Kinwarton Dovecote, a charming circular building dating from the 14th century that still houses doves.

A short distance from town, Ragley Hall is a Palladian structure designed by Robert Hooke in 1680. It stands majestically in well-maintained formal

Ragley Hall

gardens within a beautiful Capability Brown parkland. As well as being architecturally stunning, the stables house an impressive collection of carriages that evoke the extravagance of times past.

The village of Coughton is dominated by Coughton Court, a place that has been central to the heart of the village and its inhabitants for centuries. Since 1409 it has been the home of the Throckmorton family and holds a unique niche in English history because of its close connections with the Gunpowder Plot of 1605. Behind the Tudor gatehouse is a courtyard and knot garden that leads to lawns and fine vistas of the Warwickshire countryside. The house is lodged in twenty-five acres of gorgeous gardens. The interior shelters interesting paintings and rare antiquities including Jacobite relics.

North of Offa House and a few miles below Stratford-Upon-Avon, the land rises to form Ilmington Down,. At 854' it is the highest point in Warwickshire. Ilmington is a sprawling village that possesses much of the quintessential charm of the Cotswolds – large mellow stone houses with beautiful mullion windows interspersed with black and white ivy clad cottages and pretty gardens. The village has two greens, known locally as Lower and Upper Green. Two attractive properties are situated at the end of Upper Green – the Manor House dates from the 16th century, the Crab Mill from 1711.

Also north of Offchurch is the pleasant town of Kenilworth with its long, illustrious history. The open countryside surrounding the town is very pastoral; old meadows are grazed by cattle and sheep and here and there are ancient timber-framed cottages and red brick farmhouses. The town reveals several buildings of note from the Georgian and Victorian periods. The essence and true glory of Kenilworth though lies in the atmospheric ruins of Kenilworth Castle where Elizabeth I was entertained by her favorite, Robert Dudley, Earl of Leicester. Originally built as a fortress in the 12th century, it wasn't until two centuries later, when elaborate domestic quarters were added, that it became a castle of grace. To wander the castle ruins is to walk hand in hand with history.

Accommodations
There are two types.

Inside the main house: 19 singles, 4 doubles and 4 twins. 15 rooms have private baths. All rooms have a washbasin with hot and cold water.

Offa House Lodge: A small cottage on the grounds with a double, twin and single room (up to 5 beds); baths are shared.

Amenities
All meals can be supplied with the lodging. Guests staying in the cottage may prepare their own meals in a kitchen at their disposal. Towels and linens are provided. There are meeting and conference rooms, a small library and a chapel. The house is accessible to the disabled and with prior notice special dietary requirements can be met.

Cost per person/per night
£60 standard rate for full board. Other costs to be determined when reservations are made.

Special rules
Guests are required to change their beds on the last morning of their stay.

Region: West Midlands | County: Warwickshire | City: Offchurch

Directions

By car: From London take M40 and leave it at junction 13. Take A452 to Leamington Spa. On entering Leamington Spa take the A425, following the Southam signs. On reaching Radford Semele (2 miles), turn left into Offchurch Lane (sign-posted, opposite the White Lion Pub). After another mile take the left fork (sign-posted) and bear right at a sharp bend at the top of the hill. The entrance to Offa House is on the left immediately before the parish church. There is a green sign outside.

By train: Take a train from London Paddington or Marylebone to Leamington, then a taxi to Offchurch. The cost for the taxi ride is about £7-8.

Contact

Anyone

Call or send an email

Offa House
The Coventry Diocesan Retreat House and Conference Centre
Village Street
Offchurch
Nr Leamington Spa
Warwickshire CV33 9AS
England, UK
Tel: 0044 (0) 1926 423309
Website: www.offahouseretreat.co.uk
Email: offahouse@btconnect.com

Region: West Midlands   County: Warwickshire   City: Princethorpe (Rugby)

Princethorpe Retreat and Conference Centre

Missionaries of the Sacred Heart

    The Centre lies in a peaceful corner of Warwickshire on the edge of the grounds of Princethorpe College, only four miles from Coventry, yet in a space away from noise and traffic. It is an ideal setting for a retreat or relaxing holiday. The rural countryside of Rugby District surrounds the house with views over open fields and bluebell-laden woods. The Centre runs its own spiritual program and offers hospitality to private individuals, groups and organizations.

Established as a Benedictine Monastery in the 1860s by a group of Benedictines coming from France, today the Centre is owned by the Missionaries of the Sacred Heart but run by a team of lay people and a priest. "It is not a listed building but it is treated as one, being on the grounds of Princethorpe College," said the woman in charge of bookings.

Princethorpe College was designed and built by the famous British architect Pugin and occupies the buildings of the former St. Mary's Priory, a French Benedictine monastery founded by a group of nuns from Montargis seeking asylum from the French Revolution.

Princethorpe is a small village located halfway between Royal Leamington Spa and Rugby and is the crossroads that form the Fosse Way, a former Rome road that linked the main cities of the time. The Roman road is the only road that has retained its Latin origin: Fosse comes from Latin "fossa."

The roots of Royal Leamington Spa stretch back to the *Domesday Book of 1086*. It was Queen Victoria who put the "Royal" into Leamington Spa when she bestowed the title in 1838. Most of the fine Regency and early Victorian houses close to the bank of the River Leam remain from this legendary period but the famous natural springs have been known since the Middle

Royal Pump Room

Ages. In 1810 the Royal Pump Room was opened and enclosed by landscaped gardens for private use only. Later in the century when the fashion for "taking the waters" began to decline, the park was opened to the general public. The famous Jephson Gardens opposite the Pump Room originated in the 1940s and are dominated by lakes peppered with fountains and lovely tree-lined promenades. A church has stood at the heart of Royal Leamington Spa for over 900 years. The present structure dates from the 19th century and represents a superb example of Victorian-Gothic architecture. It has an elaborate interior and many interesting historic treasures.

Rugby is a pleasant town delineated by narrow streets, open squares and a market. The town center offers a mix of architecture as reflected in the modern shop fronts beneath upper stories revealing buildings from the Victorian and Edwardian periods. There are also Victorian houses in tree-lined Regent Place. Rugby is the home of the Rugby Public School, the place where William Webb Ellis carried the ball instead of kicking it and thus, in 1823, the game of Rugby football was born. A plaque on a wall beside the school celebrates the exploits of Mr. Ellis.

South of Rugby is Sulgrave, home of George Washington's ancestors. Presenting a picture typical of English tranquility, the main drive into Sulgrave is lined by grass verges and trees. There is an interesting medley of cottages and houses that have stood in this place for hundreds of years. One has the date 1636 engraved on its porch. Sulgrave Manor was built in 1550 by Lawrence Washington, a wool merchant from whom George Washington was descended. Now a museum it displays many mementos of the president and his wife. The medieval church of St. James still has the 17th century pew used by the Washington family.

Warwickshire, in the heart of England, is one of the most popular counties. Warwick, its namesake town, is an appealing historic town on the River Avon that lays claim to many medieval buildings and a truly magnificent castle. Warwick experienced a great fire in 1694 that destroyed much of its central streets and buildings allowing for some fine Georgian buildings and a new church tower to arise from the ashes. Many structures of interest survived the fire including the town's medieval Guildhall as well as a group of timber-framed buildings around Oken's House, home of Thomas Oken, Warwick's 16th century bailiff and public benefactor. Oken's House now contains a doll museum with a collection of several hundred antique dolls. St. Mary's is a fine building dating to pre-Norman times and contains a splendid medieval tomb. The church also has a 174' tower that offers fantastic views of the town and countryside.

Warwick Castle was built on a hilltop first fortified by William the Conqueror in 1068. The castle was merely a timber stockade around the top and base of a large earth mound. In 1260 stone replaced the timber structure and so began the edifice that stands today. The Castle is a breathtaking sight on the banks of the River Avon. An outstanding structure set

Region: West Midlands   County: Warwickshire   City: Princethorpe (Rugby)

Warwick Castle

on sixty acres, it is distinguished by walls and turrets. Visiting the castle is like a trip back in time with its torture chamber, ghost tower and castle armory. The castle also contains handsome landscaped gardens created by Capability Brown in the mid 1700s.

Accommodations
10 beds in 4 single, 2 twin and 1 double room. Baths are shared; each room has a washbasin.

Amenities
Meals are not supplied with the lodging. A fully equipped kitchen and dining room are available to guests. Outside caterers can be used as well. The house's website has a link to local caterers. Linens are supplied; towels are not. There are two conference rooms, gardens, chapel and small orchard.

Cost per group/per night
The house is rented as a whole, either per evening, half days, full days, overnight, week-end or by the week.
Per day/night £125, per weekend £375.
Other prices are to be determined when reservations are made.

Special rules
Closed at Christmas. The house is rented as a whole to small or larger groups but not to single individuals.

Directions
Since the house is isolated, it is best accessed by car.
By car: From London take M40 to Grimbury, exit at junction 11 and follow the signs to A423. Follow A423 until the village of Princethorpe. Staying on the A423, the access road to the Centre is on the left 300 yards up the hill past the left-hand junction with the B4453.

ENGLAND

By train: Take a train from London Euston to Rugby or Coventry and then a taxi to Princethorpe.

Contact

Anyone
Princethorpe Retreat and Conference Centre
Coventry Road
Princethorpe
Rugby
Warwickshire CV23 9QF
England, UK
Tel: 0044 (0) 1926 633357
Mobile: 0044 (0) 7901 858686
Website: www.princethorperetreatcentre.org
Email: info@princethorperetreatcentre.org

Shallowford House
Property of Lichfield Diocese

Ensconced in the rolling Staffordshire countryside, Shallowford House is a 19th century red brick structure set within four acres of gardens; a haven of peace and quiet and a place to enjoy garden games such as croquet. The vegetable gardens provide much of the produce for the House kitchen. The House belonged to J.T. Webser's family until 1938 when he donated it to the Diocese of Lichfield. The House welcomes individuals and groups seeking a relaxing stay and offers spiritual retreats and conferences. There is a detailed program available on the website.

Staffordshire pottery

Staffordshire (abbreviated to Staffs, which means stone) is a landlocked county in the West Midlands region of England. It is one of the towns of the Potteries District. Many different types of pottery were produced over the years including slipware, which showcased the simplicity and liveliness that made it among the most desired objects of ceramic collectors. At the end of the 18th century, fine china (porcelain) manufacturing began. Famous Staffordshire potters include Wedgwood, Minton and Spode.

The Staffs is tucked between two urban sprawls, Birmingham and Manchester, but the area reveals an abundance of natural beauty including Cannock Chase and the Peak District known as the Roaches.

Cannock Chase was once the expansive sweep of a great medieval Royal hunting forest. Just south of Shallowford House it is a surprisingly remote region of high sandstone heather and bracken heathland with birch woodland and pine plantations. The perfect venue for outdoor enthusiasts, Cannock Chase is dissected by secluded valleys and framed by a landscape of parklands and attractive villages. Footpaths and bridleways including the Staffordshire Way, span the length and width of the county covering a terrain called "Parkland Staffordshire."

The Peak District is a region of great natural beauty with rugged, peat-covered moorlands and magnificent limestone dales interspersed with a smattering of towns. It is the locale of Britain's first national park, the Peak District National Park. Chatsworth House is in the district; a grand house and home of the Dukes of Devonshire, major landowners in the area. Also within the district is Haddon Hall, home of the Manners family. It is notable because it was left untouched for many centuries before being restored in the early 20th century and thereby provides a peek into a medieval manor house.

Chatsworth House

Southwest of the House, Litchfield retains its old-world character with pockets of historic charm. A pretty market town, it is notable for its elegant three-spired cathedral, a feature unique to England and known as the Ladies of the Vale. Built of red sandstone, the west front is particularly handsome with four galleries of niches containing over a hundred statues of saints. The cathedral is dedicated to St. Mary and St. Chad. The latter saint remained a popular figure inspiring many miracles. From the 8th century onward the saint's body was interred in a Saxon cathedral that lies beneath the present building. In the 11th century a Norman structure replaced the Saxon one. A few pieces of the Norman stonework are still visible in Consistory Court. The octagonal Chapter House was completed in the 13th century and is one of the most attractive parts of the church. It features charming stone carvings and houses an exhibition of the cathedral's greatest treasure, the *Lichfield Gospels*, an 8th century illuminated manuscript. The cathedral shelters two important art treasures as well: The stunning 16th century Flemish stained glass from the Cistercian Abbey of Herkenrode and *The Sleeping Children* sculpted by Francis Chantry at the request of Ellen Jane Robinson in memory of her deceased daughters. Lichfield is also the birthplace of Dr. Johnson, writer of the first authoritative *Dictionary of the English Language*.

Stoke-on-Trent, about an hour from Shallowford House, is considered the home of the pottery industry. It grew from six towns and several villages to become a unified city in the early 20th century. The

Region: West Midlands   County: Staffordshire   City: Stone

Gladstone Pottery Museum is a Victorian complex of workshops, kilns and galleries where visitors can see how 19th century potters worked. Ford Green Hills is a 17th century house complete with a period garden. The rooms are decorated with an outstanding collection of textiles, ceramics and furnishings. The Potteries Museum & Art Gallery presents a fine assemblage of English pottery and ceramics.

Shrewsbury makes for another interesting day excursion. An ancient Saxon and Norman stronghold, this historic market town preserves a largely unaltered medieval street plan of steep narrow streets and alleyways lined with timber-framed black and white buildings from the 15th and 16th centuries. One such structure, Rowley's House Museum, preserves

Shrewsbury Castle

a collection of prehistoric, Roman and medieval relics including a mirror from the second century. The town boasts over 600 listed edifices including Shrewsbury Castle, a red sandstone fortification that guards the entrance to the town; and the abbey church of the famous Shrewsbury Abbey, a former Benedictine monastery founded in the 11th century. The church was also built from red sandstone and dedicated to St. Peter and St. Paul. A striking early-Gothic west tower decorated with a statue of Edward III defines the structure. Forming a loop around the town center, the River Severn is laced with inviting walks. The town hosts the Shrewsbury Flower Show, one of the oldest and largest horticultural events in England.

Accommodations

27 bedrooms: 15 singles and 12 doubles, some with private bath. One en-suite room is accessible to the disabled. The House is presently under refurbishment to increase the number of en-suite bedrooms.

ENGLAND

Amenities
Towels and linens are supplied. All meals can be provided on request. There is no self-catering but there is a tea bar where guests can prepare tea and coffee.

Cost per person/per night
Full board £55.
Bed & Breakfast £28.

Directions
By car: From London take M6 and exit at junction 14 marked "Stone A34 – Eccleshall." Take A5013 towards Eccleshall. After passing through Great Bridgeford, take the right turn sign-posted "Norton Bridge – Izaak Walton's Cottage – Shallowford." Shallowford is on this road and will be reached after crossing the railway line two times on two narrow bridges. The House is about 500 yards beyond the second bridge on the left-hand side among some trees. It is set back from the road. For further information on directions, see the website.

By train: Take a train from London Euston to Stafford (Virgin Trains). Get off at Stafford and take a bus to Norton Bridge (buses run infrequently – see the timetable on the website) or take a taxi to Shallowford, about 5 miles from the train station.

Special rules
Closed at Christmas and Easter, unless there is a booking for a large group.

Contact
Shallowford House
Shallowford
Stone
Staffordshire, ST15 ONZ
England, UK
Tel: 0044 (0) 1785 760233
Fax: 0044 (0) 1785 760390
Website: www.shallowfordhouse.org
Email: info@shallowfordhouse.org

**YORKSHIRE
and the HUMBER**

Ampleforth Abbey (St. Laurence Abbey)

Monks of the English Benedictine Congregation

Ampleforth Abbey is in the north of England, approximately 25 miles north of the city of York. Established in 1802, it is home to a Benedictine community of monks and is considered one of the most important institutions of the monastic rebirth in England. The first monastic foundation was made in 604 in Westminster, near London. Edward the Confessor restored it after its destruction in the Middle Ages. In 1540 Henry VIII dissolved the monastery. It was restored by Mary Tudor only to be dissolved again by Elizabeth. By 1607 only one of the Westminster monks was left alive – Fr Sigebert Buckley, who, together with other English monks of the Cassinese Congregation went to Saint Laurence's in Lorraine, France in 1613. At Saint Laurence the English monks were trained for the English mission and secretly traveled to England to work as priests.

In 1792 the French Revolution and subsequent suppression of the monastic orders in France forced the monks to return to England where they founded new institutions. They resided in Lancashire before settling at Ampleforth in 1802. The Abbey was completed in 1857.

Ampleforth Abbey and College

Today there are 80 monks in the community, half of whom live at Ampleforth while the others are involved in the parochial apostolate. The monks run a Benedictine co-educational boarding school. Ampleforth College, which has over 600 pupils, is one of the largest and most important Catholic schools of the country. Nearby is its prep school, St. Martin's Ampleforth, where some of the monks also work. The community runs fourteen parishes and has a permanent private hall, St. Benet's at the University of Oxford.

The beauty of the abbey church lies in its simplicity; the exterior is comprised of grey stone, the interior a mixture of stone and white-washed walls. Unlike most churches that face east, the church's main entrance is from the south door. There is a triumphal arch over the main altar that symbolizes the victory of Jesus over death and sin. Our

Region: Yorkshire   County: North Yorkshire   City: Ampleforth

Lady's Chapel contains a French carved statue of Mary ca. 14th century. The heart of the church is the choir where the monks gather to pray. The oak stalls were made by the famous "Mouseman" of Kilburn, Robert Thompson. His nickname derives from his carving a mouse on all his pieces. Elegant stained glass windows also adorn the choir.

Mouseman's mouse

The seemly market town of Ampleforth lies along the southern edge of the Hambleton Hills and abuts the North York Moors National Park. The setting is one of striking contrasts and its natural beauty has provided inspiration to many. It is a tableau of gentle, rolling countryside of purple heather moorland, patchwork farmland, ancient woodland and wildflower-rich vales that stretch out to meet rugged coastal cliffs and golden sandy beaches. Charming market towns and vibrant coastal resorts sit side by side with picture postcard villages, castles, abbeys and stately homes.

Quite close to Ampleforth Abbey is the majestic, almost regal, Rievaulx Abbey. Idyllically set in a wooded dale sheltered by hills, it overlooks verdant fields and the River Rye. A former Cistercian abbey, it was founded in 1132 by twelve monks from Clairvaux Abbey as a mission center for the colonization of the north of England and Scot-

Rievaulx Abbey

land. With time it became one of the great Cistercian abbeys of York-shire, second only to Fountains Abbey.

The remote location of the abbey was ideal for the Cistercians whose doctrine was to follow a strict life of prayer with as little con-tact as possible with the outside world. Throughout the centuries it saw many changes in its position, wealth and primary intentions. By the 15th century the original Cistercian practices had been abandoned in favor of a more comfortable lifestyle. At the time of the Dissolution of the Monasteries, Henry VIII ordered the buildings rendered unin-habitable and stripped them of their valuables. Although Rievaulx is in ruins, there's no denying its stoical beauty as reflected in the stonework, towering pillars and elegant arches of its past glory.

Within the nearby vicinity are a number of noteworthy towns and villages. Malton has been the historic center of Ryedale since Roman times with a fort established on the northern bank of the River Der-went at what is now Orchard Fields. The village of Old Malton, an Anglican settlement, developed around a Gilbertine priory, fragments of which remain in the church of St. Mary. The present town of Mal-ton holds a street market on Saturdays and farmer's markets at various other times. An eclectic mix of architecture, shops, inns and tea rooms enliven the marketplace. The Malton museum maintains a collection of Roman artifacts including Roman pottery, a Roman cheese press, Roman keys, chalk figurines, sandals and more. There is also a restored Malton Roman Goddess painted wall within the exhibit and numer-ous archaeological relics. Malton offers easy access into the North Yorkshire Moors and the Yorkshire Wolds.

Just north of Ampleforth, Helmsley is one of the most popular bases for access into the North Yorkshire Moors National Park and the Cleveland Way National Trail that originates in historic Helmsley. The town's market square is graced with a Gothic monument and stone cross and is a popular place in the summer season.

Set amidst incredible banks and ditches are the dramatic medieval ruins of Helmsley Castle. Walter Espec – "Walter the Woodpecker" probably began the fortress after 1120. Renowned for his piety as well as his soldiering, this Norman baron also founded nearby Rievaulx Abbey and Kirkham Priory. The Crusader Robert de Roos and his de-scendants constructed most of Helmsley's surviving stonework de-fenses during the late 12th and 13th centuries including a pair of immensely strong barbican entrances and the high, keep-like east tower that still dominates the town. (Barbican is a fortified outpost used for defense purposes.) But Helmsley is more than just a medieval fortress. During the Elizabethan period, the Manners' family remodeled the castle's chamber block into a luxurious mansion whose fine plasterwork and paneling still partly survive. The castle's first and last military test came during the Civil War. Sir Jordan Crosland held it for King Charles, during a three-month siege by Sir Thomas Fairfax starved who Crosland's soldiers into submission in 1644. Fairfax dismantled the defenses but spared the mansion and subsequently it became the home of his daughter and her husband, the Duke of Buckingham.

Accommodations

Hospitality is one of the chief monastic works of the community with three monks working full-time in the Hospitality Department, while others assist with retreats. It is open to visitors on an individual basis and to parish groups, youth groups, university students and guests who wish to participate in advertised retreats. There are a total of 55 beds distributed in a number of buildings: The Archway has 4 single en-suite rooms; the guesthouse has 6 single rooms, 2 of which are en-suite; the Central Building has 3 twin en-suite rooms with a beautiful view from the third floor. The Grange has a number of single rooms, some en-suite as well as a chapel and library, conference rooms and a kitchen. Perfect for large groups, Alban Roe House consists of dormitory accommodations with kitchenette for drinks only, meeting rooms and a spacious garden. There are also a small number of rooms with en-suite facilities.

Amenities

Meals are provided for residents. Bed linens are provided but guests must provide their own towels. Most rooms have tea/coffee making facilities or access to a kitchenette. Conferences are held in The Grange where there is also a small library. The Sports Centre is open to visitors for swimming and squash. For information on the Sports Centre, contact them directly at: 0044 (0) 1439 766740,

Cost per person/per night

Resident full board per day £48, B&B per day £30. bed only £9, lunch £9, supper £9. Non-resident per day £17.50.

Note: A non-refundable deposit of £25 is required on booking. All prices are VAT inclusive. Check website for current rates.

ENGLAND

Special Rules

Pets are not allowed. Curfew is from 11:00 PM to 6:00 AM. Guests are asked to help the staff by stripping their bed upon departure.

Directions

By car: From London take M1 north. Leave M1 at Leeds at the junction with A64. Continue on A64 towards York. Take A1237 (bypass) north around York and after several roundabouts turn left onto Helmsley Road (B1363) which leads to Sutton-on-the-Forest, Stillington, Brandsby and Gilling East towards Oswaldkirk. At Oswaldkirk turn left. The main entrances to the abbey and college are on the left approximately two miles further and are clearly marked by green signs.

By train: Take a train from King's Cross, London to York. From there take a bus to Ampleforth. Buses do not run frequently so check the website timetable. www.stephensonsofeasingwold.co.uk.

Note: Alternatively take a taxi. Ampleforth Abbey has a preferential rate (about £30) with some taxi companies. Check their website for details.

Contact

The Hospitality and Pastoral Office
Ampleforth Abbey
York YO62 4EN
England, UK
Tel: 0044 (0) 1439 766889/766486
Fax: 0044 (0) 1439 766755
Email: pastoral@ampleforth.org.uk
Website: www.ampleforth-hpo.org.uk (hospitality);
www.ampleforth.org.uk (general)

Region: Yorkshire   County: North Yorkshire   City: Appletreewick (Skipton)

Parcevall Hall

Diocese of Bradford

Parcevall Hall is settled in an isolated but beautiful position in the spectacular Upper Wharfedale in Yorkshire Dales National Park. It lies on a steep hillside embraced by the splendid Parcevall Hall Gardens, sixteen acres of formal and woodland gardens overlooking Simon Seat and the Wharfedale.

The complex and its gardens were once the home of Sir William Milner (1893-1960), a great benefactor of Bradford Diocese and of

the Shrine of Our Lady of Walsingham. The house dates to 1584 and was originally a farmhouse. It became a Hall thanks to the enlargements and improvements made during the 19th century. Sir William Milner was a passionate gardener and embellished the gardens with many specimen trees and shrubs collected from Western China and the Himalayas. As a gardener Sir William chose his site wisely. At the top of the gardens the alkaline soil overlays the limestone rock and at the foot of the hill, the soil is acid over gritstone, an ideal environment for rhododendrons.

During the time the gardens were enhanced, the house was restored and extended as well. In 1960 after Sir William's death, the entire property was donated to the Shrine of Our Lady of Walsingham. The shrine leased the house to the Diocese of Bradford but retained management of the gardens. The diocese added a new wing dedicated to the memory of Sir William and opened the doors of this unique

retreat house in 1963. Parcevall Hall combines the charm of an old house, the scenic beauty of its gardens with tranquil, unspoiled rural surroundings. This medley contributes to the popularity of the Parcevall Hall and the reason it is booked up to three years in advance. The Hall offers hospitality to individuals and groups for holidays, retreats, workshops, conferences and celebrations. A program of retreats and events organized by the Hall is available on the website. In addition to its welcoming atmosphere, the Hall offers delicious food prepared by the Warden who won the "Cook of the Year" award in 1990 after a rigorous national competition. The late Princess of Wales presented the award.

Guests of Parcevall Hall have access to the gardens, the only English Heritage Registered Gardens open to the public in Yorkshire Dales National Park. Enclosed by a belt of woodland, the verdant landscape features various sections including an array of gardens and trails. For visuals and additional information visit Parcevall Hall Gardens at: www.parcevallhallgardens.co.uk

Appletreewick in Wharfedale is a delightful hamlet backdropped by the 1550 Simon's Seat. Known as "Aptrick" to its residents, it was once a center for lead mining but farming and tourism are the dual economies of today.

Eight miles from Appletreewick is the ancient market town of Skipton, chartered by King John in 1204. Enclosed by handsome scenery and long considered "The Gateway to the Dales," the town's other abid-

Skipton Castle

ing features are the Leeds and Liverpool Canal, the historic Holy Trinity Church, parts of which date to the 12th century and an extraordinary 900-year old castle.

Historically a community of sheep farmers settled in the town during the 7th century and in 1066 it was granted to the de Romille family. At that time Robert de Romille built the original castle of which only the gateway remains. The present castle dates to the time the Clifford family took possession in the 14th century. The last Clifford to own it was Lady Anne who died in 1676. It was Lady Anne who restored Holy Trinity Church, where several Clifford family tombs are preserved. The church displays an impressive 12th century font with a magnificent Jacobean cover in the form of a spire and an early 16th century screen.

Sitting at the top of the main street and encircled by green lawns, the layout of Skipton Castle is breathtakingly scenic. One of the most complete, well-preserved medieval castles in England, the massive twin towers to either side of the gatehouse dominate the town today just as they have for centuries. The grooves of the portcullis (a heavy timber or metal grill that protected the castle entrance and could be raised or lowered from within the castle) and the opening for the drawbar of the castle entrance door can still be seen. Also apparent are the mason's marks in the stonework of the main entrance and the conduit court. Marking stone is an ancient tradition and stone masons throughout the ages have marked any stone they dressed to insure the receipt of proper payment for their work.

Lawns and cobbles inside the walls enhance the main building and its shaded courts lend an air of serenity. Every part of Skipton Castle is open for public view, from the lowly kitchen with its adjacent outside privy to the mighty towers, superb banqueting hall and romantic bedchamber. A tour of the castle can include the daunting dungeons below ground and a climb to the top of the watchtower for outstanding views.

Within a twenty mile radius of Parcevall Hall is a potpourri of inviting towns and villages. To the northwest, Bainbridge is the epitome of a Dales village with its beguiling old stone cottages and well-quarried stream. It lies close to fells and lonely tarns and is dramatically overlooked by the 675' high Seat (stones built into the shape of a high-backed seat) found at the side of the famous Buttertubs Pass, a spectacular high mountain road that leads across the moors. The pass is so-called because near its summit the road passes by a group of fluted limestone potholes, known as the "Buttertubs."

In 1587 Queen Elizabeth granted a charter to the little village of Askrigg, just west of Bainbridge. In the 20th century the village claimed its place in history as the setting for the TV series based on James Herriot's stories of a vet's life in the Yorkshire Dales. Askrigg has remained largely untouched and looks as it would have when James Herriot and his colleagues learned their craft. In the market square stands the cross often seen in the fictional village of Darrowby in the TV series. It is opposite the church of St. Oswald, ca. 15th century. The church harbors treasures of its historic past and, interestingly, the gravestones in the churchyard proclaim the occupation as well as the name of those buried there. The town features handsome Georgian properties and the Kings Arms, once an 18th century coaching inn. In the leafy lanes around the village are attractive cottages interspersed by vast farmlands, peacefully grazed by cattle and sheep.

James Herriot

Also nearby amid the glorious scenery of the Yorkshire Dales National Park is the village of Gayle. It is on the passage of the Pennine Way and is circumscribed by stunning fell scenery. Gayle boasts traditional mellow Yorkshire stone properties and a tranquil atmosphere. One of its memorable sights is the Durley Beck as it rushes over shelving rock to course through the village where it is crossed by an ancient stone bridge. A vista of wilderness country unfolds around Gayle making it idyllic for walkers seeking solitude and a myriad of fells (hills or low mountains) and becks (brooks or streams). Gayle is part of what is considered Herriot Country and it is said that the well-known author/veterinarian visited Gayle the day before his marriage and returned the day after with his new wife Helen.

ENGLAND

East of Bainbridge and lying on the edge of the Yorkshire Dales National Park is the market town of Richmond developed on lands granted to William Rufus by William the Conqueror in 1071. Shortly afterwards Richmond Castle was built for the purpose of protecting Swaledale against border raids from the Scots. The castle survives to this day, its 100' tower and partial curtain walls dominating the town. The castle is famed for its medieval latrines and for having the oldest Norman hall in the UK.

Richmond is home to the famous Georgian Theatre Royal and the award-winning museum dedicated to the illustrious Green Howard's Regiment. The museum displays rare regimental memorabilia spanning the decades of the past three centuries including the Collins Collection of headdress and uniforms from 1768 to the present day. The museum presents a vivid portrayal of the life of the regiment in peace and war together with archive film of both world wars. The town claims a wealth of stunning architecture. Its attractive roofline is the result of great and small properties built along sloping, hilly roads, and winding lanes around what is the largest cobbled market place in England.

The remains of Richmond Castle occupy a dramatic cliff top site above the River Swale. Scollards Hall, the hall block of the castle, is situated in a corner of the courtyard and is believed to be the oldest castle hall in England. It was built with exceptionally thick curtain walls whose triangular form follows the oddly shaped site on which the castle stands. The most prominent relic of the castle is its great keep. Built as an upward extension of the original gatehouse, the fine 11th century archway is well preserved. From the top of the keep and castle walls are wonderful views of Richmond, the Swale and countryside.

Accommodations
28 beds in 17 single, double and twin rooms. Only four rooms have private baths, the rest are shared.

Amenities
All meals are supplied with the lodging. It is possible to chose full board, half board or just bed and breakfast. Towels and linens are supplied. There are two sitting rooms and a well-equipped conference room. The Hall is accessible to the disabled.

Cost per person/per night
£50 for full board. Other costs to be determined when reservations are made.

Special rules

Curfew at 10 PM.

Directions

By car: From London take M1 to Leeds and then A660 and A65 to
Skitpon. Before Skitpon take A59 and then B6160 to Bolton Abbey.
From Bolton Abbey travel north along the B6160. Turn right at
Barden, cross the River Wharfe and follow the road towards Apple-
treewick. At the T-junction turn right, and then right again down the
hillside for Skyreholme. Beyond this hamlet take the left fork to the
Hall.

By train: Public transportation is difficult. However there is a train
from London King's Cross to Skitpon and then a taxi to the Hall.
The cost is approximately is £15 – £20.

Contact

The Warden
Parcevall Hall
Appletreewick
Skipton
North Yorkshire, BD23 6DG
England, UK
Tel: 0044 (0) 1756 720213
Fax: 0044 (0) 1756 720656
Website: www.parcevall.bradford.anglican.org
Email: Messages can be sent to the Warden through the link on the
website.

Region: Yorkshire   County: North Yorkshire   City: Brompton-by Sawdon

Wydale Hall
Diocese of York

Wydale Hall is a gracious 18th century house lodged on fourteen acres of well-tended formal gardens and woodlands, just one mile off the main road from Scarborough to Pickering, on the edge of the Yorkshire Moors. The site offers stunning panoramic views over the Vale of Pickering and the distant Yorkshire Wolds. The wolds is a vast, untrodden arena of green, rolling countryside. Dotted around this lovely landscape are stately country houses such as Sewerby Hall and Gardens, Sledmere House, Burton Constable Hall and Burton Agnes Hall. This is a land steeped in history, a land of enchanting villages with pretty greens, duck ponds and old churches that seem mostly unchanged for hundreds of years.

The Hall, formerly a private manor, belongs to the Diocese of York. A team of lay personnel runs the institution that offers hospitality to families and individuals for relaxing stays exploring the area as well as organized retreats or private conferences and workshops. Wydale Hall takes pride in its extensive grounds, recently remodeled to include formal terraces, woodland, a walled garden, labyrinth, sensory prayer walk and children's play area.

Throughout the surrounding countryside are many interesting walks, for both experienced and novice walkers. The nearby wavewashed coast is just a stone's throw from the Hall. The Yorkshire coast is one of unexpected sights, a milieu of huge variety, from gently shelving sands that stretch for miles to spectacular cliffs haunted by huge flocks of seabirds and sprinkled with pretty villages, fishing harbors and historic resort towns.

A worthwhile itinerary can encompass many of the area's villages. Levisham, an isolated moorland village overlooks Newton Dale. This highly scenic spot is one of the stopping places for the North Yorkshire Moors Steam Railway that travels a riveting journey through spectacular scenery between Grosmont and Pickering.

The focal point of the small village of Lastingham is its church, built on the site of a monastery founded by St. Cedd in 654. When the

Danes invaded they destroyed the monastery and it wasn't until 1078 that restoration began. The peacefulness of the Norman church's setting belies its turbulent past. The handsome clock face tower with turrets and a crypt of mellow stone is singularly beautiful. The churchyard reveals moss-covered graves from several centuries.

In the area encompassing Lastingham is the alluring North Yorkshire National Park, a wonderland of forests and moors crisscrossed by sparkling streams and dotted with sturdy stone cottages, ruined castles, abbeys and churches. Just north, the village of Rosedale Abbey is hidden in a lush green landscape of sweeping hillsides, meadows and gorgeous scenery. The village derives its name from a former 12th century Cistercian priory, now just a romantic ruin but once home to a group of nuns, the first to establish commercial sheep farming in the area.

The charms of the Yorkshire Dales have lured visitors for centuries, their peace and solitude recognized in medieval times by holy men who established great abbeys, many now atmospheric ruins scattered across the terrain. One such place, Osmotherley, is a quaint unspoiled village on the edge of the North Yorkshire Moors circumscribed by moors and pastureland. The village possesses an ancient marketplace and has remained largely unaltered for decades, if not centuries. Osmotherley is quite close to the ruined Mount Grace Priory founded in 1398 as a Carthusian Charterhouse. The resident order took a vow of austerity and each monk lived as a virtual recluse in his own little cell. Within the ruins are fifteen identifiable cells, one of which has been reconstructed to clearly show how the monks lived and worked. They met only for church services and for the Saturday meal. The priory evokes memories of the past and the presence of the monks is almost tangible.

Accommodations
There are two types.
Main Hall: 64 beds in 32 rooms ranging from singles to family rooms with 3-4 beds. Each room has a private bath. There are 15 rooms with private baths that may pre-booked.

Amenities
All meals can be provided with combinations ranging from B&B to full board. Towels and linens are provided. There are several meeting and conference facilities, a chapel, extensive grounds and a small library. Closed from Christmas to mid-January.

Accommodations

Emmaus Centre: 36 beds in small dormitories with shared baths, plus four Hope Wing Bedrooms sleeping up to 4 guests. The rooms are completely accessible to the disabled and two are en-suite.

Amenities

Meals are not supplied with the lodging but guests can prepare their meals in the fully equipped kitchen and dining room. Linens are supplied; towels are not. Meeting room, extensive grounds with children's adventure area, a football pitch, multi sports pitch and wooded area suitable for camping. Towels, linens and parking are available to guests.

Cost per person/per night

Costs depend on the type of accommodation and number of meals included. The cost of the Main Hall is £29.00 B&B, £39.50 dinner and B&B, £55 full board. The Emmaus Centre is £11 per person per night.

Directions

By car: From London take M1 and then A1 towards Manchester/Leeds. Exit at junction 45 and take A64 to York. Proceed on A64 to Malton. Take A169 to Pickering. In Pickering take A170 towards Scarborough. Wydale Hall is sign-posted along this road. By train: From London King's Cross to Scarborough or York and then take #128 bus outside the station (buses depart every hour to Wydale Lane). The bus stop is about 1.5 miles from Wydale Hall. Contact the Hall prior to arrival to arrange transportation from the bus stop.

Contact

Anyone
Wydale Hall
Brompton-by Sawdon
Scarborough
North Yorkshire, YO13 9DG
England, UK
Tel: 0044 (0) 1723 859270
FAX 0044 (0) 1723 859702
Website: www.wydale.org
Email: retreat@wydale.org or admin@wydale.org

Whirlow Grange

Registered Charity

Whirlow Grange is a 1860s house on the outskirts of Sheffield. Its enviable situation combines the proximity to an interesting city with the stunning panoramas of the Peak District National Park only four miles away.

Whirlow Grange began as a private house and was converted into a retreat and training center in 1953 by Reverend Leslie Hunter, Bishop of Sheffield from 1939 to 1962. George Pace, a famous York architect designed the Chapel of the Holy Spirit. In 2004 after a major renovation, the bedrooms were converted into en-suite facilities. At that time the management of the house passed into the hands of a registered charity that operates in association and with the support of the Diocese of Sheffield.

Lay personnel run the house and offer hospitality to individuals, families and groups for holidays, retreats, conferences and celebrations. There is also a program of spirituality events at Whirlow Grange available on the website. The house also lays claim to an award-winning garden. "Its beauty is in its variety and large number of different plants and shrubs," said the Warden.

Sheffield is England's fourth largest city and lies on the River Don at the foot of the Derbyshire Hills. An industrial city, it is a popular base from which to explore the Peak District. Sheffield itself also has a number of parks and a beautiful greenbelt area. Dating mostly from the 15th century, the former parish church of St. Peter and St. Paul is defined by a landmark tower and spire that can be seen from every part of town. The interior is quite lovely with a nave, aisles and chancel. Light from the dramatic stained glass floods the cathedral, illuminating the beautiful floor. The historic treasures of the church include the tombs of three Earls of Shrewsbury.

The varied and seductive scenery of the nearby Peak District National Park is an enthralling pastiche of limestone peaks and crags, silver rivers, lofty wooded areas, caves, caverns, reservoirs, lonely moorland and gentle green valleys interspersed with ancient stone towns and villages showing relics of a rich industrial heritage. Amid all this are splendid churches, great houses and vast estates.

Approximately ten miles south of Sheffield is the town of Chesterfield, well known for its strange landmark, the crooked spire of its parish church. Although the spire has made St. Mary and All Saints famous, the church itself is a worthy building, showing fine 14th century architecture. Cruciform in design and beautifully proportioned, it perpetuates a splendid Anglo-Saxon font, three medieval screens and a number of monuments to local Chesterfield families.

Chesterfield has been a market town since the 12th century. Comprised of more than 200 stalls, its famous Open Market is a colorful three times a week event. The town possesses some attractive buildings including the Town Hall, a long-fronted building with an impressive pillared entrance.

A short distance from Chesterfield is Chatsworth House, one of the most celebrated historic houses in England. Built in the 17th century for the 1st Duke of Devonshire, the elaborate beauty of Chatsworth can be credited to its state apartments. The Great Chamber is the largest room of these apartments; with a ceiling painted by Verrio; the detailed mantelpiece by Samuel Watson. The room is accented with elegant tables and chairs, wonderful paintings, silver and other priceless objects. The chapel is a place of cool beauty, its altarpiece carved from alabaster. The walls and ceiling were painted by Laguerre and Ricard. Chatsworth is settled amid wondrous grounds, parkland and majestic woodland. The

Chatsworth House

fountain dates to the 19th century and was designed by Joseph Paxton who also planted many of the rare conifers that can be seen today.

Still further south is Haddon Hall, a medieval and Tudor manor house in a beguiling setting. The interior displays a fine example of a medieval kitchen and an Elizabethan long gallery. It is the home of Lord and Lady Edward Manners whose family has owned the house since 1567. Rooms on display include the dining room with heraldic paneling, heraldic painting on the ceiling and carved medallions in the alcove; the banqueting hall, complete with minstrels' gallery; and kitchens that appear as though they have not been touched for centuries. The Tudor long gallery is an elegant room with paneling and large bay windows affording wonderful views over the gardens. The ancient family chapel contains a series of remarkable medieval frescoes. The rooms preserve period furniture and fine paintings including miniature portraits of Henry VII and his Queen. The house is enveloped by gardens laid out in terraces during the 17th century. Haddon Hall has been the setting for many films and TV programs, including *Pride and Prejudice* starring Dame Judy Dench.

Hardwick Hall, approximately 15 miles due east of Haddon Hall, is one of the best surviving examples of Elizabethan architecture in England and is said to have "more glass than wall" because of its striking, honey colored frontage and extensive windows. It houses an outstanding collection of 16th century embroidery, tapestries, furniture and portraits and boasts one of the finest private art collections in the country, spanning 4,000 years from ancient Greece to modern art. The 105-acre garden contains a comprehensive herb garden, rose collection and orchards.

Accommodations
21 single, 1 double, 7 twin and 1 king size room. All rooms have private baths. Access is provided for the disabled.

Amenities
All meals are supplied, from B&B to full board. Guests may also request special dietary menus. Towels and linens are supplied. There are five conference rooms, a chapel, licensed bar and parking lot.

Cost per person/per night
Costs to be determined when reservations are made.

Region: Yorkshire	County: South Yorkshire	City: Sheffield

Directions

By car: From London take M1 and exit at junction 29. Take A617 to Chesterfield. Before entering Chesterfield take A61 towards Sheffield. Pass three roundabouts and approach the fourth round-about in the left-hand lane. Turn left - signed (A621) Bakewell and (A625) Castleton and then immediately occupy the right-hand lane to turn right in 200 yards (also signed Beauchief). Descend a hill through a housing suburb to roundabout at bottom - Abbey Lane. Turn left - signed (A621) Bakewell and (A625) Castleton and follow road to traffic lights. Go straight across at traffic lights - signed Castleton B6068 (A625), follow up through wooded areas and bear left at next junction into Whirlowdale Road (straight and tree lined). At the T junction turn right, Whirlow Grange Conference Centre is immediately on the left.

By train: Take a train from London St. Pancras or London King's Cross to Sheffield. Once in Sheffield take a taxi or a bus to Whirlow Grange. Buses that go to Whirlow Grange are #272, #214 (Doyles Coaches), #65 (TML Coaches). For timetables go to www.first-group.com.

Contact

Conference Coordinator by phone to make contact and determine availability. A deposit is necessary to secure bookings.
Whirlow Grange
Conference Centre
Ecclesall Road South
Sheffield, S11 9PZ
England, UK
Tel: 0044 (0) 1142 363173
Fax: 0044 (0) 1142 620717
Website:
www.whirlowgrange.co.uk
Email:
info@whirlowgrange.co.uk

Region: Yorkshire   County: North Yorkshire   City: Sleights (Whitby)

Saint Oswald's Pastoral Centre

Order Anglican Sisters of the Holy Paraclete

Situated in the wild outstanding beauty of North Yorkshire Moors between Sleights and Aislaby, St. Oswald's is a small complex of buildings. The Centre is run by the Anglican Sisters of the Holy Paraclete and several of the sisters live at the center. St. Hilda's Priory, in nearby Whitby, is the motherhouse.

St. Oswald's Close was built on the grounds of the Esk Valley by Lady Armatrude de Grimston, a benefactress of the Congregation of the Holy Paraclete. After her death in 1982, the property was donated to the order and developed into a pastoral and retreat center whose purpose is to offer hospitality; be it for a time of rest and relaxation or spiritual retreats. Guests are welcome individually or as a group.

The spectacular landscape provides the ideal setting for memorable walks, simple relaxation or the pursuit of creative endeavors such as painting. It is a three-mile walk to the historic port town of Whitby with its abbey ruins and winsome harbor.

ENGLAND

Yorkshire natives are known to be fiercely proud of their region and rightly so. "God's own country," as it is fondly known by its inhabitants, is a huge, stunning milieu of rolling dales, heather-clad moor, dramatic coastline and cosmopolitan cities. The Yorkshire coast is a venue of unexpected sights; from gently shelving sands that stretch for miles to soaring cliffs, haunted by huge flocks of seabirds and sprinkled with pretty villages, fishing harbors and historic resort towns.

West of the Moors are the Yorkshire Dales, sweeping green vales dotted with sheep and farmhouses. The terrain claims natural features such as the limestone pavements at Malham and Brimham Rocks in Nidderdale. Near the village of Malham are the high cliffs of Malham Cove with its extensive limestone pavements and dramatic Gordale Scar gorge whose near-vertical sides rise over 100 meters. The peculiar and idiosyncratic shapes of the eroded rocks of Brimham Moor have been given nicknames by locals such as Smartie Tube and Idol Rock. The formations were created out of millstone grit, a tough kind of sandstone carved by erosion during the last Ice Age over 80,000 years ago. The limestone was used to build the dry stone walls that imbue this part of Yorkshire with its distinctive checkerboard look.

Nearby are two World Heritage Sites –Fountains Abbey and Studley Royal Water Garden, a prime example of a Georgian landscaped garden. Created by John Aislabie, it is among England's most important Georgian water gardens with neoclassical statues and follies. It is defined by a formal, geometric design and expansive vistas. The design was inspired by the work of French landscape gardeners. Fountain Hall was built by Stephen Proctor between 1598 and 1604. Some of the stone he used was from the ruins of the abbey.

Fountains Abbey

| Region: Yorkshire | County: North Yorkshire | City: Sleights (Whitby) |

Set in the naturally beguiling Skell Valley, Fountains Abbey is one of the largest, most magnificent and best preserved of Britain's ruined abbeys. Founded in 1132 by Cistercian monks after a dispute that culminated in a riot at St. Mary's Abbey in York, the abbey buildings were constructed with stone taken from the Skell Valley and designed to reflect the Cistercian ideal of simplicity and austerity. The church's nave and transepts are in the Traditional style; the tower is Perpendicular. The finest feature is the Chapel of the Nine Altars in which the pointed arch makes its first appearance in England. The extensive monastic buildings have been largely preserved and contribute to the monastery's imposing appearance.

Quite close to Fountains Abbey is the small city of Ripon replete with winding streets and a broad, symmetrical marketplace fringed with Georgian houses. It is best known for its cathedral and the watch, which has been announced since the Middle Ages by the Wakeman. Every night at 9 o'clock he still sets the night watch in the Market Square. The cathedral is comprised of a medley of styles and was erected over a 7th century Saxon crypt, the oldest in England. It is renowned for its collection of thirty plus misericords of the choir stalls that include both pagan and Old Testament examples.

Just a few miles from Sleights, the historic fishing village of Whitby is part of the Heritage Coast of North East England. It is a locale of historical interest and was home to famous 18th century explorer and voyager Captain James Cook. Whitby also lays claim to one of the finest examples of an Anglo Saxon church in England. The coastal towns of the North Yorkshire Moors enjoyed their heyday in the 18th century and for several hundred years Whitby has been home to a highly successful fishing fleet. There is a strong maritime tradition in the town and to this day there are many reminders of its illustrious past.

Whitby's huge whaling fleet is commemorated in Pannet Park Museum. Captain Cook learned his seamanship on colliers sailing from here. Of the many historic buildings to be found in town is St. Mary's church, magnificently perched atop a flight of steps. The church contains fine examples of early 18th century craftsmanship. The ruins of St. Hilda's Abbey can be seen high above the town's East Cliff. The River Esk divides the old part of the town from the newer West Cliff that is connected to the harbor via a passage cut between the rocks.

Legends abound in this area and a short trip along the coast from the Centre leads to Robin Hood Bay where the more notorious trade of smuggling was carried on. This quaint town has cobbled streets and clusters of tiny cottages crammed into the gap between the sea and the steep cliffs. The cottages, most of stone with bright red roofs, cling precariously to the cliffs upon which the village is built.

This area represents one of the richest stretches of coastline for fossils in England. Low tide exposes a seabed full of tide and rock pools and offers wonderful examples such as the oyster-like Liostrea and coiled ammonites – known in these parts as St. Hilda's serpents. The oldest rocks are said to date from the Jurassic Period. The only access to the village is on foot down a long, narrow and precipitous road. This trip is not advised for the faint-hearted and sturdy walking shoes are recommended.

A walk across the bay to nearby Ravenscar at low tide can be rewarding. The scenery is memorable, especially when the waves are tinged bright copper by a golden, setting sun. Over the centuries the village has had a continuing battle with the sea and raging storms have claimed many buildings. The road into the village is steep and twists at sharp angles, but there are handrails to help visitors navigate their way down.

Accommodations
There are two types of accommodation, catered and self-catered.

Catered accommodations:
Inside the main house: There are 10 singles and 3 doubles. Baths are shared.
Hillside Cottage: A short distance from the main house, it has 4 singles and 1 double. Baths are shared.

Self-catering accommodations
Grimston Rooms: There are 3 self-contained mini-apartments each with a kitchen, en-suite bathroom and bed-sitting room. Hospitality in the apartments is for one person only and only for long periods of time. Linens are provided, towels are available on request, meals are not supplied.

| Region: Yorkshire | County: North Yorkshire | City: Sleights (Whitby) |

Amenities

For catered accommodations only, towels and linens are provided. All meals are provided with the lodging. Hospitality is expected on a full-board basis, but guests can opt out as long as they provide notice to the sisters. Sitting room, a well-equipped art room and chapel are available for guest use.

Cost per person/per night

Voluntary contribution. Suggested donations £30 a night or £200 for a week. A deposit of £20 is requested to secure the booking.

Special rules

Closed at Christmas and various times between July and August (check with the sisters).

Directions

By car: From London take M1 north to A1 towards York. Take A64 (York-Malton-Scarborough). On the Malton bypass take A169 towards Pickering. Sleights is 16.5 miles past Pickering. Once in Sleights turn left after the River Esk (Woodlands Drive – Private Drive). Saint Oswald's is 1/2 mile up the hill on the left.

By train: Take a train to York from London King's Cross (London-Newcastle-Edinburgh line), get off at York and take a train to Sleights. Before arriving, arrange with the sisters to be picked up at the train station.

Contact

The Sister in Charge
St. Oswald's Pastoral Centre
Woodlands Drive
Sleights, Whitby
North Yorkshire, YO21 1 RY
England, UK
Tel/Fax: 0044 (0) 1947 810496
Website: www.stoswaldspastoralcentre.co.uk
Email: ohpstos@globalnet.co.uk

Region: Yorkshire   County: Hambleton   City: Wass

Stanbrook Abbey at Crief Farm
Nuns of the English Benedictine Congregation

The community of Benedictine nuns occupying Stanbrook Abbey was founded in 1523 by seventeen-year old Helen More, St. Thomas More's great-great-granddaughter, who, with the financial means supplied by her father, started a monastery in Cambrai, Flanders. A group of nine exiled Englishwomen embraced the Benedictine Rule during the troubled reign of James I. During their exile, Dame Gertrude (Helen) More and Dame Catherine Gascoigne were the twin pillars of the community in the heroic years of its foundation. Under the influence of Father Augustine Baker, a lawyer who had joined the religious life in adulthood, the young nuns consolidated their spirituality in a "tradition of prayer, breadth of mind and freedom of spirit."

During the French Revolution the nuns were forced to leave their monastery with only a few minute's notice. Four nuns died during the hard days of their imprisonment in Compiègne, France, whereas the rest of the community managed to reach England. Their search for a new site ended when they started a monastery at Stanbrook in the Severn Valley, Worcestershire. The famous architect Edward Welby Pugin designed the abbey church in Gothic Revival style.

After 170 years at Stanbrook, the large monastery no longer suited the community's needs and the nuns decided to move to North Yorkshire where the aura of silence and the striking beauty of the environment fulfilled the spiritual needs of the community. In June 2007 the nuns began construction of the new monastery. As of this writing, they are in the course of moving from Stanbrook to Crief Farm, the site of the new monastery. Crief Farm is just north of the tiny village of Wass on the slopes of Wass Moor within the North York Moors National Park. It is smaller in size but closer to the requirements of a 21st century monastery. As the sisters put it: "which seeks to conserve the community's human and financial resources and to be sensitive to ecological and environment concerns."

The new monastery aims to be sustainable, consuming as little energy as possible; a place where the sisters will be able to live in harmony with the unique landscape of the National Park. The complex is installed on 56 acres and consists of the monastery, some agricultural buildings and nine Scandinavian lodges rented to guests for holidays or retreats.

Stanbrook is celebrated for its traditions of Gregorian chant, devotional literature and fine printing. The translations of the writings of St. Teresa of Avila are still in print a century after publication by The Stanbrook Abbey Press, the oldest private press in England.

The traditions and rich landscape of the Yorkshire Moors and Coast have inspired writers, artists and explorers throughout the ages and continue to do so today. There is an amazing wealth of archaeological remains awaiting discovery, from flint tools and camps of the first hunters, religious crosses and stone waymarkers to concrete and steel bunkers from the Cold War.

Religious communities have had a strong impact on the area's history and the dramatic remains of abbeys at Byland, Rievaulx and Whitby provide insight into life in the Middle Ages. The ruins of Byland Abbey are just a few miles from Wass. Byland was one of the three great monastic houses of the north and its stunning features include elaborate tiles and a great rose window. The beautiful ruins, set in the shadow of the Hambleton Hills, represented a superb example of early Gothic architecture and inspired

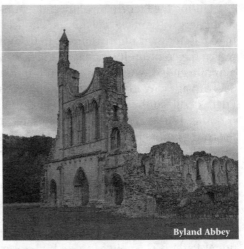

Byland Abbey

the design for the famous York Minster Rose Window. Its collection of medieval floor tiles *in situ* is the largest in Europe.

The environs of Stanbrook Abbey are marked by towns and villages possessing monuments of architectural and historic interest. Coxwold features attractive architecture and an imposing parish church that dominates the village. Its Shandy Hall, a beautiful house on the edge of the North Yorkshire Moors, was the home of Laurence

Sterne from 1760 until his death in 1768 and the place where he created his masterpiece, *Tristam Shandy*. The house conserves the world's finest collection of Sterne's works, letters, illustrations and ephemera.

The market town of Thirsk is perhaps better known as James Herriot's town. Alf Wright, author of the James Herriot novels, lived and practiced as a vet in Thirsk for 50 years; the town became his inspiration for the fictional Darrowby. At the center of Thirsk is the restored cobbled market square with a clock tower dating from 1896. A popular outdoor market is held every Monday and Saturday.

Northallerton is the largest market town in Herriot Country. Set in the rich farmland of the Vale of Mowbray, it holds a market every Wednesday and Saturday along both sides of its broad High Street. Quite close to town and set amid woodland below the North York Moors are the 14th century ruins of a Carthusian monastery. Experience the simple and austere life of a monk in the reconstructed cell and herb garden. The 17th century manor house, built on the ruins of the monastery guesthouse, is a rare structure of the Commonwealth Period.

Pickering is an inviting market town known as the Gateway to the Moors. It is reputed to be the oldest town in the District, dating back to 270 BC when it was founded by Peredurus, King of the Brigantes. It is the starting point of the North Yorkshire Moors Railway, an 18-mile steam railway running through the incredible scenery of the North York Moors. At the top of the town's sloping marketplace is the parish church of St. Peter and St. Paul. Secluded by a cluster of cottages and shops, the church preserves a magnificent spire that can be seen for miles and a remarkable collection of medieval wall paintings, among the most complete sets in Britain. Other interesting features include the font, thought to be of Saxon origin, and the pulpit made by Hepplewhite, famous 18th century cabinetmaker.

Pickering Castle is a classic 12th century motte and bailey affair. The grassy mound and curtain walls punctuated by tall towers are the most prominent features of this royal fortress. The mound was raised by William the Conqueror and the stonework added for Henry III as a defense against the Scots. Set amidst one of the largest forests in the country, Pickering Castle was used by a succession of medieval kings as a hunting lodge. By the time of the Civil War its military purpose had long been abandoned and most of the castle was left to decay. A special exhibition in the chapel explores the castle's history.

Accommodations

For up-to-date information, visit the website or call the nuns. The lodges have 4/5 beds each, in single, double or multiple rooms. They are conceived for self-catered holidays and are well equipped. There is a kitchen, central heating, TV and barbecue. Towels and linens are provided.

Directions

By car: From London take M1 and the A1. Exit at junction 49 and take A168 to A170 east. Turn into Wass Bank Road but prior to entering Wass follow the signs to Crief Farm.

By train: Take a train from London King's Cross to Thirsk and then a taxi to the monastery.

Contact (for the monastery)
Guest Sister
Stanbrook Abbey at Crief Farm
Wass
York YO61 4AY
England, UK
Tel: See the website
Fax: See the website
Website: www.stanbrookabbeyfriends.org or www.stanbrookabbey.org.uk
Email: Check the website

Contact (for the cottages)
Tony & Anne O'Brien
Crief Farm
Wass
York, YO61 4AY
England, UK
Telephone and Fax: 0044 (0) 1347 868207
http://www.cottageguide.co.uk/crieflodges
Email: crieflodges@stanbrookabbey.org.uk

Sneaton Castle Priory (St. Hilda's Priory)

Anglican Sisters of the Order of the Holy Paraclete

Saint Hilda's Priory and Sneaton Castle share the same expansive grounds and are situated within walking distance from the historic and charming seaside town of Whitby, an excellent gateway for exploring the outstanding beauty of the North Yorkshire Moors and Coast.

Saint Hilda's Priory is the motherhouse of the Order of the Holy Paraclete and the place where the order was founded by Margaret Cope in 1915. Over the years the community grew and founded new communities in West and Southern Africa. The main ministry of the order originally had been education but as the community grew, its scope extended to include chaplaincies, parish work and retreats.

Sharing the site of the Priory is Sneaton Castle, formerly St. Hilda's School. The castle was built by Colonel James Wilson in 1819 and eventually became the property of the order in 1923. The castle has recently undergone a major refurbishment and become a conference center for day and residential events. It continues to be the property of the Priory but is managed by lay personnel.

The Priory is named after Hilda, patron saint of Whitby. She was born in 614 to a noble family and was the niece of King Edwin of Northumbria. In 657 she came to Whitby to establish a new monastery. Under her influence the double monastery (comprised of monks and nuns who lived separately but shared the same church) prospered and Whitby became a center of learning, as witnessed by Caedmon, one of the first Saxon poets and a member of the monastery. In 867 the abbey was destroyed and then rebuilt in 1078. That structure lasted until the Reformation when it was destroyed by Henry VIII. The abbey fell to ruins but what remains has become a prominent landmark of Whitby.

One of the most scenic ports in England, Whitby and its harbor are set in a ravine at the mouth of the River Esk. Apart from being a major fishing town, Whitby was also the most important whaling port of Northern England and the whale-bone arch on West Cliff attests to this past activity. Spreading below ancient Whitby is a maze of cobbled alleyways and narrow streets that run down to the busy quayside. The houses date to the 13th and 14th centuries. Its harbor side houses and small shops are filled with crafts, curios, antiques and jewelry made from Whitby Jet, a dark black fossil mineral dug from its cliffs since Victorian times.

Perched on a dramatic rocky headland, Whitby Abbey has been one of England's most powerful spiritual centers since the dawn of Christendom. Dark Age Kings and Queens, saints, poets and warriors were all buried here and it was here, in Christian England's early years, that the date of Easter was decided. Viking raiders sacked it. Norman pilgrims rebuilt it. From the old town, mounting the 199 steps from the harbor to the haunting remains of the abbey is an exhilarating journey. It was the moody magnificence of the abbey ruins that gave Bram Stoker, master of Gothic horror, the inspiration to write his famous book, *Dracula*. Within the ancient walls is a memorable state-of-the-art gallery that outlines the building's centuries-long history and explains why it is one of Britain's most important heritage sites.

For many Yorkshire is where English history comes to life. Across the region walk in the footsteps of Kings, Queens, saints and warriors at any of the eighteen English Heritage Sites that evoke whispers of the past within the walls of ancient castles, medieval abbeys and grand Victorian mansions. The compelling beauty of the environs has provided the backdrop to many movies. The coastline is abundant in fossils and dinosaur footprints and provided the impetus for William Smith – father of English geology

Whitby Abbey

– to establish the internationally renowned museum of geology, the Rotunda Museum in Scarborough.

Forty miles of stunning and varied coastline frame the eastern edge of the Yorkshire Moors and Coast. Largely undeveloped, the soaring cliffs, harboring secrets from the Jurassic Age, plunge down to the sea, sheltered bays and endless sandy beaches. Watch as black cormorants whip low cross the sea and stand on rocks with wings outspread. Observe puffins and guillemots as they clumsily fly home to their clamoring chicks on the cliff face.

The North York Moors National Park has the largest expanse of heather moorland in England. Stunning at any time of year, it is especially outstanding in late summer when the heather blooms and a sea of purple stretches out as far as the eye can see. The pristine nature of the park makes it a haven for a variety of plants and wildlife. Tread gently through this remarkable landscape and travel around aboard the nostalgic North Yorkshire Moors Heritage Steam Railway or hop on Moorsbus, a network of buses linking the main towns with the attractions and countryside of the North York Moors.

Near the Priory is the small Edwardian resort of Filey. A former fishing village the immense arc of golden strands south of this quaint resort lead to Bempton and some of the finest chalk cliffs in Britain. They are home to the only mainland gannet colony in England and much of the year these incredible seabirds soar and plummet in search of fish.

Scarborough is also close to the Priory and noted for its extraordinary castle. A fortress has stood at this spot for some 3,000 years – ever since Iron Age times. Its imposing ramparts and battlements have sheltered Kings and Queens and defied Viking marauders, medieval barons and Civil War besiegers. Legend holds that the ghost of Richard III still haunts its halls. History seeps from the massive stones of Henry II's towering keep. Displayed in the Master Gunner's House is a rare Bronze Age sword that provides a link with a more distant past, before even the Romans came to this splendid natural fortress. From the castle's viewing platforms, gaze out across the North Sea and imagine the sentries who guarded the castle's ramparts for so many centuries.

Accommodations

120 beds in double rooms in two types of accommodations.
Standard rooms: About 95 guests can be accommodated in double standard rooms with easy access to a large number of bathrooms with showers and toilets. There is also a TV lounge for guests.
En-suite rooms: Saint Francis House can accommodate 26 guests in 11 twin-bedded rooms and 1 family room, all with private bath. Saint Francis House is rated by the Tourist Board as a 4-star facility. Two rooms are accessible to the disabled.
Sneaton Castle specializes in groups but families and individuals are also welcome.

Amenities

Towels and linens are provided. All meals can be provided. They are included for groups, however, individuals and families can also choose that type of boarding. There are meeting and conference rooms, refectory, bar and lounge, washers and dryers, two tennis courts, table tennis, billiards, playing fields and a playground for younger children. There is a chapel and an extensive garden with quiet areas for contemplation.

Cost per person/per night

Independent guests, B&B rates.
Adult: Standard £25; en-suite £35, children 0-2 years are free of charge, ages 3-14 years - standard £15, en-suite £35.
Full meals and buffets £7, packed lunches £5, light afternoon tea £3.25, full afternoon tea £5.

Groups (12 adults minimum) rates: £24 to £49 depending on the room and number of meals. Children 0-2 are free of charge, ages 3-16, £14.25 to £39 depending on room, number of meals and age of the child.

Directions

By car: From the north take A19 and leave it at Middlesbrough. Take A171 to Whitby. Once in Whitby follow the signs to Sandend and take B1460 to Sneaton Castle (do not go to Sneaton Village). From London take M1, exit at junction 45 and then take A64 towards York, continue on A64, pass York and then follow the directions to Malton. From there take A169 towards Whitby via Pickering. Once in Whitby follow the signs to Sandend and take B1460 to Sneaton Castle (do not go to Sneaton Village). By train: Get off at York or Scarborough and take a coach to Whitby. Once in Whitby take a bus to Castle Road (every 20 minutes) or a taxi to the Priory.

Contact

The reception
Sneaton Castle Centre
Whitby, YO21 3QN
England, UK
Tel: 0044 (0) 1947 600051
Fax: 0044 (0) 1947 603490
Website: www.sneatoncastle.co.uk or sneaton@globalnet.co.uk
Email: reception@sneatoncastle.co.uk

The Bar Convent
Congregation of Jesus Sisters

Installed in the center of York, Bar Convent is a splendid Grade 1 listed building as well as the oldest convent in England. The Convent belonged to the Congregation of Jesus Sisters, a Catholic Order founded by Mary Ward, a Yorkshire woman and pioneer of education who strongly believed in the role of religious women outside the convent walls. The order now has two branches: The Congregation of Jesus and the Institute of the Blessed Virgin Mary.

The Convent was established by Frances Bedingfield as a school for Catholic girls in 1686, a time when Catholics were still persecuted. This happened after Sir Thomas Gascoigne, a renowned local Catholic, had expressed the desire to open a school for Catholic girls. He provided the money to buy a modest 17th century house just outside Micklegate Bar and invited Frances Bedingfield along with a small group of nuns to establish a school.

Neoclassical chapel and dome

The nuns had to wear plain grey day dresses to disguise their religious identity and avoid persecution. In 1696 the school was attacked by a fanatical anti-Catholic mob. Legend holds that the residents were saved by the intervention of Saint Michael who appeared on a white horse. More persecutions led to the imprisonment of Frances Bedingfield followed by a time of great poverty and distress for the sisters. The hard times ended in 1727.

The present complex of buildings encompasses the former open courtyard converted into the Victorian tiled Entrance Hall. The Great Parlour contains the portraits of early members of the congregation. The Library boasts antique books dating from 1508 to 1850 and together with its archives, forms a Catholic Study and Research Centre. The chapel and a small tranquil garden are open to visitors.

York is an ancient city with a rich 2000-year old history. Its medieval maze of narrow streets is enclosed by a grand circuit of 13th century walls. A walk along the ramparts provides wonderful views of

Victorian tiled Entrance Hall

the city. Founded in AD 71 by the Romans, it was one of the two capitals of Roman Britain. During this period influential historical figures such as Constantine the Great became associated with the city.

A compelling city, York is filled with architectural and archaeological gems around every corner, Its winding medieval streets are now home to chic boutiques, cafes and bars. The antique city walls with their gates (known as bars) offer access to central York. At the city's heart is the stupendous, awe-inspiring Cathedral of St. Peter, commonly known as York Minster, the largest Gothic cathedral in Northern Europe. The origins of the imposing Minster (minster means monastic church) date to the year 627 when the structure was a simple wooden church. The first church was rebuilt in stone a few years later and dedicated to St. Peter. But it was Egbert, first recognized Archbishop of York, who made the cathedral school and library the envy of Europe. In 741 the Minster Church burned down but was replaced by a glorious new church containing no less than thirty altars.

Over the course of the next five centuries the church was destroyed and rebuilt many times. The present edifice dates from the Norman period. The essence of the Minster began in 1220 with the south and north transepts. The north transept is famous for its "Five Sisters" graceful lancet windows topped by five smaller gabled lancets. The chapter house was begun about 1260 and represents a superb example of the Gothic Decorated style then in vogue. The ribbed wooden roof is a masterpiece of medieval architecture as are the stained glass windows. The old Norman nave was rebuilt around 1280 and was exactly twice as wide as the old, making it the widest in Europe and the second tallest (after Westminster Abbey) in England.

York's "The Shambles" is among Europe's best-preserved medieval streets, although the name is also used to refer to the surrounding hodgepodge of narrow, twisting lanes and alleys. The street itself is mentioned in the *Domesday Book of 1086* signifying that it has been in continuous existence for over 900 years. The Shambles is a mirror of the Elizabethan period. The houses that jostle for space project out over the lane in their upper stories. In some places the street is so narrow that with arms outstretched it is possible to touch the houses on both sides. A word about York street names; many end in the suffix "gate." This does not mean that the gate in question was part of the old York city walls. In this case, the "gate" comes from the Viking "gata" meaning street. The actual city gates are called "Bars," such as Micklegate Bar, Walmgate Bar and Monk Bar, the best-preserved medieval gate. Micklegate Bar is the traditional entry point for monarchs and even now Queen Elizabeth II must enter the city at this point. Walmgate Bar was built during the reign of Edward II and is the only city gate with an in-

The Great Parlour

tact barbican, a fortified outpost used for defensive purposes.

A sophisticated, lively city, the history of nearby Leeds can be traced to the 5th century when the Kingdom of Elmet was covered by the forest of "Loidis" the origin of the name Leeds. Since that time it has evolved from a major industrial center for the production and trade of wool to a center for commerce and higher education. It is home to the University of Leeds and Leeds Metropolitan University. A shopping mecca, its bustling pedestrianized streets are lined with shops, restaurants, Victorian structures and alluring arcades. But its heritage is also evident in a number of stately homes, abbeys, museums and galleries.

The Royal Armouries is a state-of-the-art museum that travels through 3,000 years of military history. Originally built to house the armor and weaponry from the Tower of London, the museum showcases live action demonstrations, intriguing films and hands-on technology exhibits. The City Art Museum has a splendid collection of

Single room

works by British artists with particular emphasis on J.S. Cotman, one of the leading members of the Norwich School. Henry Moore is well represented as well. The adjoining Henry Moore Institute is maintained in an award-winning structure and is dedicated to discovering sculpture in all its many forms but does not include any of the namesake's work. The impressive Medieval Kirkstall may be in ruins but it is still quite lovely. Founded in 1152 by Cistercian monks from Fountains Abbey, the Norman ruins offer an evocative stroll through time. The Tudor-Jacobean Temple Newsam is one of England's great historical estates with an outstanding collection of artwork including an array of Chippendale furniture. Ensconced on over 1,500 acres of park and woodland, its famous gardens were landscaped by Capability Brown. Floral enthusiasts will delight in his Rhododendron and Azalea Walks.

Accommodations
30 beds in 18 rooms: 9 singles, 4 twins, 1 double, 1 family room with shared baths, plus 1 double, 1 triple and 1 twin room with private bath. Each room has a washbasin and hairdryer, tea and coffee making facilities. Bathrooms, toilets and showers are available on each floor.

Amenities
Breakfast is included with the lodging and is served in the cafe. It is possible to have lunch at the convent's café or purchase meals outside and re-heat them in the fully equipped kitchens located on each floor. Towels and linens are supplied. There are meeting rooms, 2 sitting rooms with TV, recreation room with snooker and board games and a chapel. The institution is accessible to the disabled. A Pay & Display Long Stay car park is located opposite the Convent. Reservations can be made in advance by calling 0044 (0) 8704 283854 (see website for details).

Cost per room/per night
Single £32-35, twin/double with shared bath £60, twin/double with private bath £75, family with private bath £95.
Saturday night only stay supplement £10.
Online booking must be made 24 hrs in advance. Other reservations can be made until the day of arrival by calling the Convent (office hrs 9AM-5PM).

ENGLAND

Directions

By car: From London take M1 to A1 north. On A1 exit at junction 45 and take A64 towards York and then A1036 towards the center of the city. Follow Tadcaster Road and then Blossom Street until the Convent. The car park is in Nunnery Lane.

By train: Take a train from London King's Cross to York. The train station is a 5-minute walk from the Convent. Turn right out of the station and walk towards the traffic lights. The Bar Convent is across the lights on the corner of Nunnery Lane and Blossom Street.

Contact

Anyone
The Bar Convent
17 Blossom Street
York
North Yorkshire, YO24 1AQ
England, UK
Tel: 0044 (0) 1904 643238
Fax: 0044 (0) 1904 631792
Website: www.bar-convent.org.uk
Email: info@bar-convent.org.uk

SCOTLAND

Country: Scotland (Inner Hebrides) | County: Argyllshire | City: Iona

Bishop's House
Diocese of Argyll and the Isles

The Bishop's House on the Isle of Iona is a retreat house of the Diocese of Argyll and the Isles. Beautifully situated in a tranquil site in the shadow of Iona Abbey, the House overlooks the clear waters of the Sound of Iona and is the ideal setting for guests wishing to visit a very popular tourist destination while sharing a sense of community and peace with the other guests of the House.

In the very heart of the House is the exquisite St. Columba's Chapel, a place that represents the Episcopal Church of the Isle. The House and Chapel were built by Bishop Chinnery Haldane in 1894 as venues of "prayer, study, contemplation and Eucharist."

"There are no works of art and I wouldn't suggest coming to look at this or that ... but the chapel is very attractive and welcoming," said the Warden.

The House is managed by the Warden, her assistant and four lay staff. It offers hospitality for those seeking spiritual retreats and quiet days and those who wish to "get away" and spend a few days in a quiet atmosphere. The House can also be booked entirely by a single group. The church is open 24 hours every day for prayer or recollection and services are held daily.

The tiny Isle of Iona (1 mile wide and 3.5 miles long) is considered one of the cradles of Western Christianity. It has a long tradition of pilgrimage and mission dating back to the year 563 AD when St. Columba and thirteen followers landed at St. Columba's Bay on the sandy white beaches at the south end of the island. At that time they established a monastery and from that monastery, the Christian faith spread throughout Scotland, Northern England and beyond.

St. Columba's mission was to convert pagan Scotland and northern England to the Christian faith. Iona's fame as a missionary center and outstanding place of learning eventually spread to Europe turning it into a pilgrimage site for several centuries to come. St. Columba was a man with some unusual idiosyncrasies including banishing women from the island. The abbey builders had to leave their wives and daughters on the nearby Eilean nam Ban (Women's Island).

Today Iona Abbey is very different from the original St. Columba's settlement, an austere site of seclusion and contemplation rather than one of grand buildings. From Adomnan, who wrote Columba's biography a century after his death, it is clear that the original settlement resembled a small village with huts for the monks to live in that surrounded a modest timber church. One of Scotland's most historic and venerated sites, the grounds of the abbey and nunnery preserve a comprehensive collection of Christian carved stones, ranging in age from 600 AD to the 1600s. In front of the abbey is the 9th century St. Martin's Cross, an excellent example of a Celtic Cross of the British Isles. Perhaps the monk's greatest work was the exquisite *Book of Kells* that dates from 800 AD and is currently on display in Trinity College, Dublin.

St. Columba died in 597 and it is believed he is buried in the stone chapel attached to the abbey. After his death the monastery became a center of culture and pilgrimage. In the beginning however, access was restricted to Royal and ecclesiastical pilgrims but over the centuries, as Iona's fame grew as a holy site, more humble visitors were allowed to visit. The preeminence of Iona reached its peak when it became a sacred isle where Kings of Scotland, Ireland and Norway were buried.

From 794 until the 10th century, Iona suffered from Viking raids and in 806 AD, 68 monks were slain by Vikings at Martyrs Bay. Due to the exposed position of the monastery, all the monks but St. Blathmac abandoned the institution. The saint suffered martyrdom for refusing to divulge the treasures and relics of Columba.

With the relinquishment of the monastery, it fell into decline. When the Vikings converted to Christianity, new buildings were begun and Iona's power was revived. In 1200, Raghnall, son of Somerled, virtual King of the Isles, brought in the Benedictine Order and erected the great abbey. He also established St. Ronan's Nunnery, named after one of Iona's monks. Over 400 Augustinian nuns lived at the nunnery. One of only two Augustinian Orders in Scotland, the nunnery earned itself the name "An Eaglais Dhubh" – the black church – after the color of the nuns' robes.

The abbey prospered until the Reformation when it was abandoned once again and slowly fell to ruins. In 1938 Rev. George MacLeod founded the Ecumenical Christian Group called the Iona Community and restored the ruined abbey to its original grandeur. Unlike the rest of the abbey buildings, the nunnery has not been restored. The pink granite walls that remain, despite being ruinous, are among the finest examples of a medieval nunnery left in Britain.

Little is known of the nuns who lived here. Like the Benedictine monks, they followed a strict life of prayer and contemplation. A few clues have been left that shed some light on various aspects of their lives – the tomb of Prioress Anna Maclean is so detailed in its carving as to give a clear depiction of her dress. Some of the nuns were thought to have fled to a cave during the Reformation. Situated on the coast at Carsaig on Mull, the "Nun's Cave" has crosses carved into its inner walls.

To reach Iona Island, there is a passenger ferry that departs from the village of Fionnphort on Mull (a five-minute crossing). For a more in-depth history of Iona and St. Columba, visit the Historic Scotland Museum before taking the ferry.

Tobermory

The Isle of Mull, often referred to simply as Mull, is the third largest of the Hebridean islands and one of Scotland's most beautiful. On Mull there has been a small settlement at Tobermory from the earliest times. Modern Tobermory is distinguished by a harbor with brightly colored buildings that presents a unique and memorable image. North Tobermory Cliff Walk is a short distance from the ferry terminal. The walk leads to views of the sea and with a little luck, sightings of porpoises, dolphins and whales along with boats and ships of every description. FYI: The walk is about 100' above sea level with steep drops to the sea.

Accommodations

23 beds in 3 single and 10 twins rooms. Baths are shared.
Groups can rent the house as a whole.
NOTE: Closed from November through March.

Amenities

All meals are supplied with the lodging. Guests can choose between half or full board. Towels and linens are provided. There is a lounge, library, dining room, garden and chapel.

Cost per person/per night

Half board £50, full board £55.
Special discount for clergy, parish groups, theological students.

Special rules

Minimum stay 3 nights. Children under nine are not allowed with individual groups, but can be allowed with a group renting the whole house. Peace and quiet are required on the premises. Guests are asked to help with keeping their own rooms during their stay and helping to lay and clear away before and after meals.

Directions

NOTE: Iona can be reached by the 10-minute ferry trip across the Sound of Iona from Fionnphort on Mull. The most common route is via Oban connected by regular ferries to Craignure on Mull. There is a bus from Craignure to Fionnphort along a scenic drive. Access by car is not allowed on Iona for non-residents. Visitors must leave their car in either Oban or Fionnphort. The island is small enough to avoid the use of the car. Bike hire is available at the pier and on Mull.

By car: From London take M1, M6 and M74 to Glasgow. Take M8 and leave it at junction with A82. Take A82 north until junction with A85. Take A85 west to Oban. Take a ferry to Craignure on Mull. It is not necessary to book unless you plan to take your vehicle to Mull. Once in Mull you can drive to Fionnphort by following the signs for a 37-mile scenic drive or take the bus that meets the ferry. The ferries between Oban and Craignure and Fionnphort and Iona are run by Caledonian Macbride (http://www.calmac.co.uk/).

Country: Scotland (Inner Hebrides)	County: Argyllshire	City: Iona

By train: Take a train from London Euston or London King's Cross to Glasgow. Then take a train or a bus to Oban. Scotrail has trains from Monday to Friday from Glasgow Queen Street Station to Oban. Traveling from England to Glasgow, you will arrive in Glasgow Central. Take the shuttle bus to Queen Street Station that links the two stations. Otherwise from Glasgow use the coach services run by Citylink to Oban from Buchanan Street Bus Station. From Oban take the ferry to Craignure and then a bus to Fionnphort. From Fionnphort take the final ferry ride to Iona.
Note: The House's website has a link to updated ferry timetables.

Contact

The Warden by email or phone
Bishop's House
Isle of Iona, PA76 6SJ
Scotland, UK
Tel: 0044 (0)1681 700800
Fax: 0044 (0) 1681 700801
Website: http://island-retreats.org
Email: iona@island-retreats.org

Country: Scotland   County: Ayshire   City: Largs

Benedictine Monastery
Nuns of the Adorers of the Sacred Heart of Jesus of Montmartre

Located in Largs with spectacular views of the Firth of Clyde, the Benedictine institution was started in Dumfries by Lady Marcia Herries in 1884. In order to make reparation for the many abbeys and monasteries suppressed during the Reformation, Lady Herries invited the nuns of the French Benedictine  Monastery of Arras to introduce the Perpetual Adoration of the Blessed Sacrament. In 1988 the Monastery moved to the present location in Largs, adapting a former hotel to its needs.

The nuns live a life of contemplation and work but open their doors to residential guests who are accommodated on the upper floor. The rooms possess magnificent views of the surroundings. During the day guests may visit the Christian Heritage Museum and Tea Room. The museum traces the story of monasticism from the Desert Fathers to modern day. It contains illuminated manuscripts, ancient embroidered vestments, sacred images and statues. The Museum and Tea Room are open from April to September. Hospitality is offered year-round.

Largs is on the beautiful Ayshire coast. Blessed by the warm currents of the Gulf Stream, in recent years, it has become increasingly popular as a yachting center. It boasts some of the best sailing in Britain and hosts regattas throughout the summer months.

The town has a long attractive promenade lined with restaurants and cafes. The beach below is a mixture of stones and pebbles. A monument known locally as "The Pencil" commemorates the stormy day when a Viking fleet led by King Haaken of Norway was driven ashore and defeated by the Scots under the direction of Alexander III. The site of the battle lies just to the south of the town. It was recorded in history as the battle that ended the Norse invasion of Scotland. The Viking Experience Museum on the seafront details the history of that battle.

Country: Scotland	County: Ayshire	City: Largs

The nearby islands are places of beautiful scenery, fascinating history, outdoor activities and as Scotland is known for, some of the finest golf courses in the world. They are places of ancient castles, stunning country parks and gardens and busy market towns.

Most of the islands can be reached by ferry. The Isle of Arran, known as "Scotland in Miniature," is one of the most southerly Scottish islands. It has mountains and lochs in the north, verdant rolling hills and meadows in the south and romantic castle ruins set in splendid gardens all encompassed by a stunning coastline. Arran's history dates back so far that it becomes tangled up in Celtic myths and legends of Scotland's past. Observe the strange standing stones on Machrie Moor and muse on the checkered history of Brodick Castle, a red sandstone structure nestled in dark trees at the foot of Goatfell Mountain. It is just a couple of miles from Brodick, main port on the Isle of Arran. The name Brodick comes from the Norse meaning "broad bay." Arran means "peaked island in Gaelic."

The site has been occupied by a stronghold since the fifth century when an ancient Irish tribe founded the kingdom of Dalriada. It was probably destroyed and rebuilt many times during its turbulent history. The castle and the Earldom of Arran were granted by James IV to his cousin in 1503. That structure was demolished in 1544. Parts of the present castle date from 1588 during the ownership of the 2nd Earl of Arran who was the guardian and regent of Queen Mary.

In later years it passed into the hands of Mary, Duchess of Montrose, who revitalized the gardens. Since her death in 1957 the castle has been owned by the National Trust for Scotland.

The castle reveals a treasure trove of paintings, porcelain and furniture and is also home to the art collection of 18th century author William Beckford of Fonthill whose daughter married the 10th Duke of Hamilton. One of the rooms is known as "Bruce's Room, " but since the castle was all but destroyed in the 15th and 16th centuries, it is unlikely that Robert the Bruce actually stayed in it. The castle grounds also beckon with walking trails, one leading up Goatfel Mountain and another to the intriguingly named "Duchesses' Bathing Pool."

The Isle of Cumbrae, along with Arran and Bute, became part of Scotland in 1263. Alexander the III defeated the Norse King Haco at the Battle of Largs. Centuries of feuding over the islands ended three years later at the Treaty of Perth. In 1539 the island was divided into a number of small baronies whose names survive to this day.

Bute is a fascinating island to explore. Mount Stuart is a stately and romantic home, a masterpiece of Victorian Gothic imagination. A haven of tranquility, the 300-acre grounds offer vistas over the Firth of Clyde. Rothesay Castle is where the Stuart Kings spent their summers, a stronghold whose circular design is unique in Scotland. Spend an hour or two exploring the castle and relive over four turbulent centuries of Scottish history. Ascog Hall Fernery & Garden is a fully restored sunken Victorian fern house built around 1870. The fernery houses 80 sub-tropical fern species including specimens found in Australia, New Zealand, Fiji, Mauritius and Mexico as well as a Todea Barbara, estimated to be 1,000 years old. As an aside: The palatial Rothesay Victorian Toilets were commissioned in 1899. Their ornate design incorporates fine ceramic tiles, marbled and enameled alcoves and glass-sided cisterns.

The island is also home to a number of alluring villages. Kerrycroy was designed by Maria North, wife of the second Marquess of Bute, who was inspired by the model of an English village. This peaceful enclave boasts a fine sandy bay and stone pier.

Port Bannatyne has a colorful history. At the turn of the 19th century it was a busy port of call for Clyde puffers and passenger ships. During WWII midget submarines exercised in the bay before setting off to engage in battle with the German warship, Tirpitz. Today it is a haven for visiting yachtsmen, golfers and water sports enthusiasts.

Kingarth is a looking glass into the past. It features: A mysterious standing stone circle from the Bronze Age, the Dunagoil vitrified fort from the Iron Age and a 12th century Romanesque chapel set within early Christian monastic remains dedicated to St. Blane, native son of the island.

Accommodations
10 single and double rooms with shared baths. Both men and women are welcome. A small independent (self-catering only) cottage that can accommodate a family of 4 is available during the summer.

Amenities
Lunch and dinner are supplied with the lodging. Guests may prepare and take their breakfast in the kitchen at their disposal. Towels

and linens are provided. Inside the main house there is a dining room, living room and library.

Cost per person/per night
Voluntary contribution. Minimum suggested donation £35.

Special rules
Curfew at 8:30 PM.

Directions
By car: From London take M40 to Birmingham, then M6 north to Carlisle. From there take A74/M74 to Glasgow. Once in Glasgow take M8 and exit at junction 29. Take A737 towards Irvine and continue about 10 miles and then take A760 by following the signs to Lochinnoch. Proceed on A760 until the sea and the junction with A78. Take A78 left towards Greenock, travel half a mile and turn left into Charles Street. The Monastery is 0.4 mile further on the right.
By train: Take a train from London Euston or King's Cross to Glasgow Central and then change trains to Largs. Get off in Largs and walk to the Monastery.

Contact
Mother Prioress
Benedictine Monastery
5 Mackerston Place
Largs
Ayrshire, KA30 8 BY
Scotland, UK
Tel: 0044 (0) 1475 687320
Website: www.tyburnconvent.org.uk, search under the icon "monasteries" and then click on Scotland.

Country: Scotland (Great Cumbrae)   County: Buteshire   City: Millport

College of the Holy Spirit
Diocese of Argyll and The Isles

The College of the Holy Spirit on the Isle of Great Cumbrae is a unique historic guesthouse annexed to Britain's smallest cathedral, the Cathedral of the Isles. The island, known simply as Cumbrae, with its 10 1/4 mile circumference, is the larger of the two islands in the spectacular Firth of Clyde. It is only a few minutes by ferry from Largs in Western Scotland.

Millport is the main town of this popular holiday destination, famous for its magnificent views of the Firth of Clyde and the coast, as well as cycling, bird watching and golf. The Cathedral and the College are both Grade A listed buildings commissioned at the same time by George Boyle who later became the 6th Earl of Glasgow. The commission resulted from Boyle's determination to invigorate the Episcopalian movement in Scotland and in particular of the family-owned island of Great Cumbrae. The College was built like a "mini-Oxford" and was meant to be a theological college to train Gaelic speaking priests and be an educational and missionary center with special regard for the Diocese of Argyll.

In the late 1880s Lord Glasgow suffered a financial crash and the College was closed. Thanks to the determination of the then Bishop of Argyll, the property was not lost and the center continued as a retreat house. In 1995 the College underwent a major refurbishment to restore its original beauty. It is now a combination of a 3-star guesthouse and a Christian Retreat House open to individuals and families for short holidays and a retreat center for spiritual purposes. It also serves as a conference and study center for professional groups.

The cathedral and college have a long tradition of music with regular performances of both sacred and classical music. During the summer there are concerts in the cathedral every afternoon. It is also a popular wedding and family gathering venue.

Surrounded by formal gardens and woodland, the cathedral was built in 1851 and is the smallest cathedral in Europe seating barely 100 people. This early work of architect William Butterfield is not just a tiny cathedral, it is also a beautifully integrated collection of ecclesiastical buildings designed by Butterfield as a Theological College. It consists of two college buildings, a chapter house, hall and cloister as well as the cathedral.

Butterfield, one of the great architects of the Gothic revival, is particularly famed for Keble College, Oxford and All Saints, Margaret Street, London. Due to its remoteness and lack of public exposure, the Cathedral of The Isles is one of the architect's least known works, yet is regarded by his admirers as particularly imaginative and accomplished. Although the nave of the cathedral is only 50' by 20', its 123' steeple and tall pointed roofs make is it seem larger and more spacious than it actually is. At the same time, the unusual pyramidal shapes of the steeple offer height to counterbalance the length of the college roofline so that, viewed from any point on the ground, the effect of the cathedral is to carry the eye directly upwards – to heaven.

The cathedral's interior is typically Butterfield. While the nave is relatively plain, the chancel and sanctuary are rich in color and detail. The brightly colored tiles and stained glass windows are hallmarks of his church interiors. The use of constructional polychrome is carried out, not only on the walls and floor but also in extensive stencil work on beams, pillars and an exquisitely painted ceiling that depicts the enormous variety of wildflowers found on the island.

Millport is the only significant settlement on the island of Great Cumbrae. A small seaside resort with sandy beaches and a slightly old world sensibility, it wraps around the attractive south-facing Millport Bay with outstanding views that envelop the mountains of Arran, the island of Little Cumbrae, the Eileans, Alisa Craig and the hills of Ayrshire.

Country: Scotland (Great Cumbrae)   County: Buteshire   City: Millport

Accommodations
Up to 32 guests can be accommodated in 16 single, twin, double and family rooms (up to 4 adults). Five rooms are en-suite and can accommodate the disabled. Closed in January and February.

Amenities
B&B, half board or full board are available. Towels and linens are provided. There is a library and two common rooms. The conference rooms are available on request..

Cost per room/per night/Bed & Breakfast
Standard single £38, en-suite double £78, standard twin £65, family room £125.

Cost per person
Half board £55, full board £65. Special prices for children and groups of 10 or more.

Directions
By car: From London take M1, then M6 and then M74 as far as Glasgow. Join the M73 until the M8. Leave the M8 at junction 28A (sign-posted Irvine A737) and merge onto the A737. Join the A760 sign-posted Largs. Once at Largs there is regular ferry service to the island of Cumbrae (10-minute trip). For timetable, prices and conditions visit www.calmac.co.uk.

By train: Take a train from London Euston or London King's Cross to Glasgow and then change to Largs. Once at Largs there is a regular 10-minute ferry service to the island of Cumbrae.
For timetable, prices and conditions visit www.calmac.co.uk.

Contact
Anyone
College of the Holy Spirit
Millport, Isle of Cumbrae, KA28 0HE
Scotland, UK
Tel: 0044 (0) 1475 530353
Fax: 0044 (0) 1475 530204
Website: http://island-retreats.org
Email:cumbrae@island-retreats.org

Country: Scotland	County: East Lothian	City: Nunraw (Garvald)

Sancta Maria Abbey (Nunraw Abbey)

Cistercian Monks of the Strict Observance

Surrounded by 1,300 acres of grounds formed by gardens, woodland, moorland and lakes, Sancta Maria Abbey, most commonly known as Nunraw Abbey, is a tranquil, beautiful site only thirty miles from Edinburgh. It was the first Cistercian monastery to be founded in Scotland after the Reformation. The community inhabiting the Abbey originated from a group of monks from Mount St. Joseph Abbey in Roscrea, County Tipperary, Ireland. The monks came to Nunraw in 1946 and occupied Nunraw House, a Scottish mansion originally the site of the Convent of the Nuns of Haddington. That order was founded around 1153 by Countess Ada, widow of Prince Henry. After several vicissitudes, the land and mansion passed into private hands and was modified over the following centuries until the monks bought the mansion.

The newly founded community grew and flourished and plans for a new abbey were soon underway. In 1969 the community moved into its new home, half a mile from the previous one. The new home was built by the monks themselves with the help of an army of volunteers. Nunraw House, also called "the old abbey," became the guesthouse. The monks have been offering hospitality for refreshing stays and spiritual retreats since that time.

Nunraw House

The community blends a life of prayer with work and study, seeking to be self-supporting through the guesthouse, shop and farming. Nunraw House remains the oldest part of the complex. The house itself underwent a mid-19th century restoration and addition but has preserved some pre- and post-Reformation features including the 16th century tower. The most interesting element of the house is the painted ceiling executed in tempera sometime between 1603 and 1617 and discovered in 1864. Originally the ceiling measured 30' by 18' and was composed of fourteen strong oaken joists supporting long panels on which the colors had been laid. Today the ceiling is somewhat smaller, 20' by 17.5' but two other sections are preserved in the National Museum of Antiquities. In each panel the prominent feature is the title and armorial bearings of monarchs who ruled in medieval days.

Garvald is a picture postcard village that lies almost hidden in a fold in the hills. The parish church was built in the 1100s although alterations continued through the early 1800s.

Nearby Edinburgh is one of Europe's most alluring capitals. It is perched on extinct volcanoes rising from the sheltered shore of the Firth of Forth. Its natural setting is spread over a range of hills, overlooked by "Arthur's Seat" a miniature-like mountain. At the heart of this vibrant city lies a mighty castle with over one thousand years of history and memorable sweeping views, akin to those of Paris as seen from the heights of the Eiffel Tower.

Edinburgh is part of what is traditionally called the "Lowlands" of Scotland. Although the Lowlands are less rugged than the Northwest Highlands, they possess softly flowing hills and a remarkable coastline. The city underwent great change during the Georgian Era at which time handsome Georgian houses appeared along Prince's Street, Queen's Street and George's Street. Easy to explore on foot, the old part of town boasts most of the historic buildings for which the city is famous.

Its main street is the famous "Royal Mile" a colorful venue that is home to a wide variety of boutiques, restaurants and inns. It is also home to the Scotch Whisky Heritage Centre, John Knox's House, Cannon Gate Kirk and St. Giles Cathedral. Built in Gothic style the cathedral's most notable external feature is the Crown Spire. It contains almost 200 memorials to distinguished Scots and Scottish soldiers. Most date from the 19th and early 20th century. The church also has a notable collection of stained glass windows displaying a range of traditional and contemporary styles.

The Palace of Holyroodhouse is situated at the end of the Royal Mile. It has a long and turbulent history despite its origins as a peaceful

| Country: Scotland | County: East Lothian | City: Nunraw (Garvald) |

monastery early in the 12th century. It is entered through a distinctive pair of 20th century wrought iron gates. Many Royal personages have resided at Holyroodhouse including James IV of Scotland and Mary, Queen of Scots.

The Palace of Holyroodhouse

The "booming" sound heard over the city each day comes from the "One O'clock Gun" at Edinburgh Castle. This impressive structure, historic seat of Scottish Kings, has dominated Edinburgh for more than a thousand years and is the best preserved and most historic castle in Scotland. Perched nearly 300' above the city streets, the view of the castle on approach is simply overwhelming. On one side there is an amazing assemblage of castle buildings behind a deep moat and on the other, the rock falls precipitously from the castle walls. The differing architectural styles reflect the castle's complex history as a daunting fortress and the home of Scottish Royalty. The small St. Margaret's Chapel, Edinburgh's oldest building, dates from the 1100s and is a rare example of Scottish Romanesque architecture.

Edinburgh Castle

The castle recalls the turbulence of Scottish history from the earliest times to the last Jacobite rebellion in 1745. It remains a strong reminder of Scottish national pride. Fine views can be enjoyed from almost every part of the castle, particularly from the ramparts where Edinburgh's dramatic skyline, wedged between sea and hills, can be seen to best advantage.

An interesting day trip can be made to Berwick-upon-Tweed southeast of Garvald. During the harsh border struggles, possession of the town alternated between the Scottish and English. The town changed hands thirteen times before being declared English territory in 1482.

SCOTLAND

The stirring history of Berwick has contributed greatly to its strength and character. The strong fortifications of this walled town date from the 14th century when the wall stood at a height of over 10' and boasted nineteen towers. To ensure complete safety for the town, Queen Elizabeth I ordered a new wall to be built on the north and east sides of the town. The wall was rebuilt in 1760 and has survived as a complete circuit around Old Berwick. It remains in excellent condition and a walk along the top provides great views of the town and the harbor. Berwick Castle was erected in 1150 but was almost completely demolished by the Victorians who needed the site for the building of a railway station. The Royal Border Bridge was built by Robert Stephenson in 1850 and is connected to Berwick Station. The superb structure has 28 arches and stands 130' above water.

The Berwick of today is a charming and interesting town. Within the walls, old grey-stone buildings hidden under pink-red roofs huddle together in ancient cobbled streets. The town hall is of classical design with four Tuscan columns, a bell tower and a steeple that soars 150' skywards.

Another interesting day excursion can include St. Abb's on the coast due east of Garvald. Its natural charm lies in the fact that it was once an old fishing village and the tradition of fishing continues to this day. The town remains bright with delightful whitewashed cottages and sturdy stone houses. This lovely coastal resort is backed by a hinterland of pretty villages set amid fertile agricultural land and picturesque waterways.

At St. Abb's Head, not far from St. Abb's, the scene takes on an altogether different perspective. Here on a high headland above fields grazed with sheep and cattle, a dramatic landscape unfolds, revealing cliffs and dark, volcanic crags inhabited by thousands of nesting sea birds who dive hundreds of feet into the turbulent ocean below. This is St. Abb's Wildlife Reserve, a milieu of 200 acres owned and operated by the National Trust.

Accommodations

30 to 40 beds in single and double rooms and 1 dormitory with 10 beds. Both men and women are welcome.

Amenities

All meals are supplied on a full-board basis. There are three common rooms, a chapel and extensive gardens. Parking is available to guests.

Country: Scotland	County: East Lothian	City: Nunraw (Garvald)

Cost per person/per night
Voluntary contribution. Minimum suggested donation £30-£35.

Special rules
Curfew at 8.30 PM.
Maximum stay 1 week.

Directions
By car: From London take M1 and then A1 towards Edinburgh. Take B6370 towards Gifford and turn left following the signs to Garvald and the Abbey. The Abbey entrance is 0.6 miles from Garvald.
By train: From London King's Cross or Euston take a train to Edinburgh. Take a bus to Haddington and then a bus from Haddington to Garvald. From there walk to the Abbey.

Contact
The Guestmaster, Dom Donald
Sancta Maria Abbey
Nunraw, Garvald
Haddington, EH41 4LW
Scotland, UK
Tel: Guesthouse: 0044 (0) 1620 830228,
Monastery: 0044 (0) 1620 830223
Fax: 0044 (0) 1620 830304
Website: www.nunraw.org.uk
Email: domdonald@yahoo.co.uk or abbot@nunraw.org.uk

WALES

Caldey Abbey
Reformed Cistercian Monks (Trappists)

Caldey Island, one of the British Holy Islands, lies 2 miles south of Tenby, along the spectacular coast of South Wales. The entire island belongs to the Abbey and was founded in the early phases of Celtic Monasticism. The shrines on the islands off the Scottish coast are other examples representing that period. Many institutions have not survived the course of history, or have been occupied by other religious orders but the splendid Caldey Abbey is an exception to the rule. It maintains the austere lifestyle of contemplation typical of the early monastic rules. The island, whose name derives from the Viking "Keld Eye" – cold island, has been inhabited since the Stone Age, however, the first monastic occupation dates to the 6th century.

From 1127 to 1536 the monastery passed to an order of Benedictines who lived there until the Dissolution of the Monasteries. It was only in 1906 that the Abbey returned to a religious community; the newly founded Benedictine community under Abbot Aelred Carlyle. The monks built the picturesque Abbey, designed by architect John Coates-Carter, in traditional Italianate style. It was completed in 1910. In 1913 the community converted to Catholicism and in 1926 the Benedictines left and moved to Prinknash Abbey (see page 391), selling Caldey Abbey to the Reformed Cistercian Monks who took up residence in 1929 and have lived there since that time.

The quiet, peaceful atmosphere of the island, combined with the long monastic heritage, beautiful wooded surroundings rich with wildlife and magnificent beaches, make Caldey Island extraordinary. The Abbey is a splendid white structure that has been declared a Grade II listed building due to its peculiar design. It overlooks the Village Green and the cottages of the islanders. Simplicity is the main feature of the Abbey church. The refectory, where the monks take their meals, is an imposing, albeit austere structure with oak paneled walls and timbered roof. The cloister is covered and built around the central garden also called the "cloister garth."

The Old Priory and St. Illtyd's Church with its leaning spire are among the oldest and most interesting buildings on Caldey and represent the residence of the Benedictine Community that lived there until 1536. An ancient stone floor distinguishes the church. Built on an elevated position, the Priory is constructed from limestone and sandstone indigenous to the island. The church is still functioning and consecrated

St. Illtyd's Church

to the Roman Catholic rite. The oldest structure of the complex is probably the tower. Originally it was built as a fortified residence for Robert Fitzmartin, a 12th century Norman knight who owned the island and donated it to his mother Giva. She in turn donated it to the

Benedictine monks of St. Dogmael's who inhabited the complex until 1536. As testified by the Caldey Stone, the Priory is also believed to occupy the site of the original 6th century Celtic monastic settlement. The stone, inscribed in Celtic and Latin, was excavated on the grounds of the Priory and is now on display in the church.

St. David's is Caldey's parish church. It is set on a small hill above the village, in the same area that has been a sacred place occupied by pre-Christian burial grounds dating back to Roman-British periods. In keeping with the Celtic belief that islands represented a bridge between earth and heaven, it was therefore the place where they buried people of the mainland. The pretty Norman chapel is decorated with stained glass windows designed and made by Dom Theodore Bailey, one of the Benedictine monks who lived at Caldey Abbey in the early 1920s. The largest windows depict St. David, patron saint of Wales, King David of Israel, Our Lady and St. Helena. Perhaps though, the most striking images are those of the Tree of Life and the fish window where the ancient Christian symbol is rendered in contemporary style.

St. David's

The Trappist monks lead an austere life in accordance with their strict rule. They attend seven services a day, starting at 3:15 AM and ending at 7:30 PM. Other activities focus on farming and the production of milk, butter, cream, yogurt, ice cream and confectionary. The best-known product of the monks is the world famous range of monastic perfumes and toiletries that have captured the fragrance of the island's flowers.

Every year visitors come to Caldey from Easter to late autumn. Exploration of the island can be made on foot. Apart from the Abbey and the medieval churches and Priory, the village has a lighthouse with wonderful views of the Pembrokeshire Coast, Presli Hills and Tenby. There is also a museum of Caldey's history, a post office and a shop that sells the products made by the monks.

Tenby is one of Wale's most attractive holiday resorts. Its name in Welsh, Dynbych-y-pysgod, means "The little fort of the fishes." Fine Georgian houses backed by a well-preserved medieval cliff-top town overlook its handsome harbor. Surrounded by a 13th century wall that includes the Five Arches Barbican Gate, this unique Victorian town is a place of narrow cobbled streets and lanes. The South and North Beaches are beautiful. The coastal path is an alluring route revealing South Pembrokeshire in all its glory and linking many of its beaches and coves. The coastline is habitat for a variety of sea birds and wildlife that is not generally found in such numbers elsewhere in the UK. With a little bit of patience, seals, porpoises and dolphins can often be seen.

The Tenby Museum and Gallery was founded in 1878 and is situated on the site of an old castle overlooking Castle Beach. The exhibits and information cover the geology and archaeology of Pembrokeshire, a history of Tenby and an art gallery.

Accommodations
There are two types.

The monastic guesthouse: There are 6 single rooms and shared bath. Open only to men, it offers hospitality mainly to religious members or men wishing to share the monastic life with the monks. All meals are taken with the monks. Towels and linens provided. Silence is required after compline (7.30 PM).

St Philomena's Guest/Retreat House: The guesthouse is open to men, women and children. There are 22 singles and 1 double room, baths are shared. Guests are invited to attend daily services.

Amenities
All meals are supplied with the lodging on a full-board basis. Towels and linens are provided. There is a dining room, lounge, sitting room, library, chapel and a small kitchen with coffee/tea making facilities. A comprehensive range of snacks and drinks is available throughout the day at the Tea Garden. The post office provides all the normal services of a sub post office in addition to postcard and special covers that receive a Caldey Island frank. The museum offers a glimpse into the history and heritage of Caldey. There is a shop selling the perfumes and toiletries made by the monks of Caldey. There is another a gift shop offering a wide range of items including products made on the island such as the famous Abbots Kitchen Chocolate and Shortbread.

Country: Wales	County: Pembrokeshire	City: Caldey Island (Tenby)

Cost per person/per night

Voluntary contribution. Suggested minimum donation: £30 full board.

Special rules

Curfew at 10 PM. Closed from the end of October to the week before Holy Week. Maximum stay 1 week.

Directions

By car: From London take M4 until its end and then take A40 to A477 and finally A478 following the signs to Tenby. Guests must leave their cars in Tenby. A Park and Ride bus is available from Tenby's North Beach Car Park to the harbor when the Tenby "pedestrianization" scheme is operating (summer holiday period). Car parking is available in Tenby at the Multi-Story Car Park, Salterns Car Park and North Beach Car Park - pay and display. All are within a 10-15 minute walk from the harbor. The monks suggest the first or last boat to the island with the cargo. They are free of charge for guests of the monastery and is usually uncrowded.

By train: From London Paddington take a train to Swansea, then change to a train to Pembroke Dock. Get off at Tenby. It is a 10 minute walk to Tenby Harbour. From there take the ferry to the island. The monks suggest the first or last boat to the island with the cargo. They are free of charge for guests of the monastery and usually uncrowded.

Note: Boats sail from Tenby's Harbor to the Caldey Island while St. Catherine's Island, just offshore, is linked to the town at low tide.

Contact

Call or send a fax to Brother Senan, the Guestmaster.
Caldey Abbey
Caldey Island
Pembrokeshire, SA70 7UJ
Wales, UK
Tel: 0044 (0) 1834 844453 or 1834 842632
Fax: 0044 (0) 1834 845942
Website: www.caldey-island.co.uk
Email: info@caldey-island.co.uk
(The monks prefer to be contacted by telephone.)

Country: Wales County: Flintshire City: Hawarden

St. Deiniol's Library
St. Deiniol's Library Charitable Trust

St. Deiniol's Library is a unique institution located on the outskirts of the historic village of Hawarden, not far from the border between Wales and England. It is the only residential library in Britain, the second most important library in Wales and one of the finest small conference venues of North Wales.

It was founded by the eminent Victorian statesman William Ewart Gladstone. After his death in 1898 it was donated to the nation and became a tribute to his 63 years of active political life during which he became prime minster four times. A statue of Gladstone stands in the village.

Gladstone's collection of books was started when he was a very young man. A voracious reader, he collected more than 32,000 books during his lifetime. As well as keeping a detailed record of searches of bookshops and book catalogs, he had the habit of annotating books. Often he did his reading in Hawarden Castle, his nearby residence, in the study he called "Temple of Peace." In his later years he began to plan how he could make his collection accessible to other readers and scholars and started to amass books on divinity and humanity with the thought that these type of texts would be important to members of all Christian denominations as well as people of other faiths.

In 1898, right before his death, he built a structure where his beloved books were to be transferred. Gladstone himself, helped by his daughter and valet, made the move. Once the move was completed, he appointed the trustees to care for his collection and then made a large donation that allowed the building of the present structure designed by John Douglas. It was inaugurated in 1902 by Earl Spencer. A residential wing was completed in 1906 when the first resident was welcomed.

During the ensuing century, the library accumulated over 250,000 books, mainly focusing on the subjects that most interested Gladstone including theology, philosophy, classics, art and literature. Other important collections housed by the library are Gladstone's own correspondence and the Bishop Moorman Franciscan Collection dedicated to the founder of the Franciscan Order. The Gladstone family remains one of the most important members of the Charitable Trust that operates the institution. A large percentage of the permanent staff is composed of clergy members.

St. Deiniol offers hospitality to visitors interested in a restful holiday in North Wales and to scholars, clergy and students. It is also an ideal residence during a sabbatical. The library has a varied program of in-house courses and seminars throughout the year in addition to scholarship and graduate traineeship. A haven for writers, St. Deiniol has seen more than 150 books written here, thanks to its inspiring atmosphere.

Nearby Chester (in England) was founded by the Romans almost 2,000 years ago and is the only city in England to have preserved its medieval walls in their entirety; they form part of the original Roman defenses. Chester was an important military station and trading town until the Romans withdrew from Britain. The site became deserted and remained so for five centuries. The medieval town flourished as a port until the silting of the River Dee during the 15th century. Chester continued as a commercial center and its fortunes revived during the rich 18th and 19th centuries. A galleried tier of shops known as "The Rows" characterizes the town.

The town of today preserves grand buildings representing every period of Chester's long, illustrious history. The handsome, sandstone cathedral dates from the 14th century and is noted for its intricate and lavishly carved woodwork, its Lady Chapel and the Cloisters. Of the black and white buildings, the most outstanding are God's Providence House, Bishop Lloyd's House and Old Leche House and a number of ancient timbered inns. The ornate clock above Eastgate was erected to commemorate Queen Victoria's Diamond Jubilee.

Due south of Hawarden is the last of the great Welsh castles built by Edward I that survive to this day. Begun in the latter half of the 12th century by Roger Mortimer, one of Edward I's generals, Chirk Castle was completed in 1310. At the end of the 16th century the castle was bought by the merchant adventurer Sir Thomas Myddelton who converted it into a fine country house. Today it displays superb examples of decoration from the 16th to 19th centuries and is still inhabited by Myddelton's descendents.

The exterior of the castle has changed little; the dungeon, portcullis gate and stone steps leading to the watchtower remain as originally built. The interior shows the remodeling carried out in the 19th century under the direction of renowned architect

Chirk Castle

A.W.N. Pugin. Joseph Turner designed the staircase in 1777 and the first floor staterooms are from the same period. They are adorned with lavish Adam-style decorations. The long gallery with its carved paneling and mullion windows was built during the 17th century. The salon and drawing room have elaborate ceilings and all the rooms contain fine furniture, portraits and tapestries.

The castle is embraced by gardens and parkland. There is a delightful shrub garden, lime tree avenue and the thatched Hawk-House as well as a woodland in what was once a medieval hunting park. Entered through ornate wrought-iron gates, the park commands wonderful views over nine counties.

Due west of Hawarden in the beautiful Vale of Clwyd, in a setting overlooked by the hills of the Clwydian Range and the Hiraethog Moors, is the ancient market town of Ruthin. One of the most picturesque towns in northeast Wales, Ruthin began as a Welsh settlement. Its name means "the red fortress" as it was built on a red sandstone hill as a strategic lookout over the River Clwyd. Its 700-year heritage is mirrored in splendid half-timbered medieval buildings including the National Westminster and Barclays banks in St. Peter's Square. National Westminster was formerly a 15th century courthouse and prison. According to legend, Maen Huail, a boulder outside Barclays, is where King Arthur beheaded Huail, his rival in a love affair.

The town has a rich architectural history making it an outstanding Conservation Area. St. Peter's Church was founded in the early 14th century and displays a lovely Tudor oak roof with hundreds of carved panels. The 17th century Myddleton Arms is a pub whose unusual Dutch-style dormer windows are known as the "Seven Eyes of Ruthin."

Accommodations

There are 33 recently refurbished rooms. Rooms are single, double or twin. Some have private bath, all have phones, ISDN connections and tea/coffee making facilities.

Amenities

Dinner, bed and breakfast are always supplied. There is a restaurant and coffee shop that can supply lunch and other refreshments. Towels and linens are provided. There are conference and meeting facilities and a chapel. Guided tours of the library are available on the 2nd Saturday and 4th Tuesday of each month at 11.00 AM. Tickets are limited; booking is recommended. Cost: £2.00 per person.

Country: Wales	County: Flintshire	City: Hawarden

Cost per person/per night

Standard rate £44 dinner, bed and breakfast.

Clergy rate £33 dinner, bed and breakfast.

Student rate £28 dinner, bed and breakfast (available for full-time students only).

Residential group rate £33 dinner, bed and breakfast.

Supplement for en-suite rooms £12.

Check the website for special offers.

Directions

By car: From London take M6 north to M56 west until it ends and merges into A5117. Then take A550 and follow the signs to Hawarden, then to St Deiniol's on A550.

By train: Take a train from London Euston to Chester, then a bus or taxi to Hawarden (6 miles).

Contact

Anyone
St. Deiniol's Library
Church Lane
Hawarden
Flintshire, CH5 3DF
Wales, UK
Tel: 0044 (0)1244 532350
Fax: 0044 (0)1244 520643
Website: www.st-deiniols.com
Email: enquiries@st-deiniols.org

Country: Wales   County: Flintshire   City: Holywell

St. Winefride's Guest House

Bridgettine Sisters

St. Winefride's Guest House is the newly renovated accommodation for the pilgrims visiting St. Winefride's Well – the oldest shrine of unbroken pilgrimage in all of Great Britain. The Well and Guest House are situated in Holywell, a place that clearly owes its name to the presence of the well whose history began almost 1400 years ago.

Legend holds that in 660 AD, St. Winefride was beheaded on this site by Caradog, a local chieftain who was enraged by her rejection of his advances. Seeking safety, the girl had fled to her uncle St. Beuno – one of the most important Welsh saints –but was reached instead by Prince Caradog's sword. A spring arose from the spot where her head had fallen. Tradition holds that St. Beuno replaced the head on Winefride's shoulders and restored her life; Caradog was swallowed by the ground whereas Winefride lived as a nun for the remaining years of her life.

In any case, Winefride was an extraordinary character, venerated since her death around the end of the 7th century. Records of the miraculous healing powers of the spring started in the 12th century when the first shrine was built and continue to this day. The shrine was the property of the prosperous Basingwerk Abbey until its dissolution in 1537. Innumerable pilgrims have traveled to the spring to pray for healing, to bath in the cold, clear water before walking down, kneeling and kissing a stone cross.

The uninterrupted flow of pilgrims that included eminent personalities and royalty was partially slowed during the Reformation but never stopped. This occurrence has contributed to Holywell's unofficial title of "Lourdes of Wales."

The shrine is a singular building, considered one of the Seven Wonders of Wales as noted in an old anonymous rhyme. It is said to

St. Winefride's Well

be the finest example of a medieval holy well in Britain. First erected around the beginning of the 12th century, the present building is a Grade I Scheduled Ancient Building dating back to the early 16th century. This remarkable, richly ornamented structure was probably built by Margaret Beaufort to replace the earlier building in thanksgiving for the victory of her son Henry Tudor (Henry VII) over Richard III at Bosworth Field. Set on a steep hillside under Holywell, it consists of two floors. The well chamber is an open structure on the downhill side whereas a chapel forms the floor above.

The clear waters occupy a basin shaped like an eight-pointed star. The waters then flow into a more recent pool. The vault is lavishly adorned by the intricate designs that match those of the columns and the pool. The chapel has a three bays aisle that mirrors the vaults of the well chamber below. Five hundred years of graffiti on the walls of the crypt attest to the unbroken faith in the well's healing powers. It is a place of pilgrimage where candles of hope still shine. The shrine is open most days of the year.

An official pilgrimage is held every year with the date dependent on the year although the actual St. Winefride's Feast Day is on June 22nd. As it has happened for over 1,000 years, bathing at St. Winefride's is still possible. A detailed timetable of all official events, bathing times and pilgrimages is available on the shrine's website.

In 2005 the former Victorian Custodian's House was restored and converted into a library and museum housing a collection of artifacts and documents illustrating the worship of the saint throughout the centuries. The library contains a touching collection of letters related to the healing claimed through the intercession of the saint. But perhaps the most impressive assemblage is that of the hundreds of wooden crutches discarded by the healed.

Almost due south of St. Winefride's is the pretty town of Llangollen on the River Dee. Spanned by a 14th century bridge, the town also boasts the ruins of the 13th century Castell Dinas Bran. Towering high on an isolated hill above the Dee Valley, the ruins occupy one of Britain's most spectacular sites. A rugged, foreboding pinnacle, the hillock was the ideal spot to erect a castle. It seemed completely impenetrable, commanded views for miles around and offered quick recognition of an approaching visitor. Yet the native Welsh Princes of Powys occupied the hilltop for only a few decades. Among others, the castle is also reputed to be the legendary hiding place of the *Holy Grail*.

During the summer months there are boats on the Llangollen Canal that sail from Wharf Hill and across the outstanding 1,007' long Pontcysyllte Aqueduct built by Thomas Telford, a Scottish engineer responsible for many of Britain's roads, bridges and canals. This masterpiece of canal engineering took ten years to complete. The town is also renowned for the International Musical Eisteddfod held every July. Amateur singers perform alongside famous soloists and choirs from throughout the world.

Heading west from Llangollen is the gray stone-built town of Bala, a Welsh-speaking community. Bala is a small mountain-ringed town set beside the largest natural lake in Wales. There is a narrow gauge railway that follows the lakeshore for four miles and reveals alluring scenery.

From Bala an interesting excursion can be made to Dolwyddelan Castle in the Lledr Valley in Snowdonia. The castle is just west of the village of the same name. It stands impressively on a rocky ridge commanding the Lledr Valley, one of the principal passes through Snowdonia. Believed to have been built between 1210 and 1240 under the command of Prince Llywelyn the Great, its purpose was to guard the road into the core of his kingdom and watch over his vital upland cattle pastures. Defended by rock-cut ditches and a steep drop, the castle is dominated by a rectangular keep tower. The strategically sited castle became a prime target for English attack during Edward's conquest of Wales. The fall of Dolwyddelan was a turning point of the campaign allowing the English army into the heartlands of Gwynedd. The Welsh built fortress then became a link in Edward's famous chain of strongholds. After many centuries the castle fell into decay but with the stunning backdrop of the wild Snowdonia Mountains, the picturesque ruins later proved a magnet for romantic landscape painters and tourists. Victorian reconstruction restored the keep to something of its former grandeur and today the castle remains a lasting memorial to Llywelyn's strategic achievements and to the skills of the men who actually built it.

Accommodations

31 beds in en-suite rooms equipped with bath or shower, central heating, telephone and TV. There are single, double and family rooms plus a disabled room and a lift for the disabled. In addition to the reception lounge there is a resident's lounge on the first floor.

Amenities

All meals can be supplied with the lodging on a B&B or full-board basis. Towels and linens are supplied. Adjacent to the Guest House is the Bridgettine Convent whose lovely chapel is open to pilgrims and visitors who are invited to attend the liturgical worship.

Cost per person/per night

To be determined when reservations are made.

Directions

By car: From London take M1 until the intersection with M6, then take M6 until the intersection with M56. Take M56 west until the intersection with M53. Continue on M53 until it merges into A55. Take A55 Expressway westbound and leave it at junction 32 sign-posted Holywell and follow brown Heritage signs to St Winefride's Well. Eastbound, leave A55 at junction 31 and follow A5026 into Holywell and then brown Heritage signs to St Winefride's Well.

By train: Take a train from London Euston to Flint and then a taxi to St.Winefride's Shrine or St.Winefride's Guest House.

Contact

Mother Superior
St. Winefride`s Guest House
20, New Road
Holywell, Flintshire CH8 7LS
North Wales, UK
Tel: 0044 (0) 1352 714073
Fax: 0044 (0) 1352 712925
Website: www.saintwinefrideswell.com
Email: stwinefrides@bridgettine.org

Country: Wales   County: Breconshire   City: Llangasty (Brecon)

Llangasty Retreat House
Dioceses of Swansea and Brecon and Llandaff

Llangasty Retreat House nestles among the Welsh hills between Abergavenny and Brecon on the shores of Llangors Lake in the Brecon Beacons National Park. The House enjoys spectacular views across Llangors Lake towards the western fringe of the Black Mountains. It is a peaceful venue and a haven for wildlife lovers who can admire the rare beauty of the surroundings. Llangors Lake is a Site of Special Scientific Interest and claims vast numbers of visiting birds as well as a large variety of wildflowers (including orchids) that color the meadows during the summer months.

Llangasty was originally built in the 1870s as a Victorian Rectory and Vicarage for the local church. In 1947 Miss Dorothy Raikes, who lived nearby and believed that the site should continue to serve its religious purposes, acquired the property and converted it into a retreat center in 1954. Miss Raikes, in keeping with her family's long tradition of active work in the local parish, personally managed the house for 18 years until she donated it to the Sisters of Charity. The sisters successfully continued her work until 1996 when they decided to donate it to the Dioceses of Swansea and Brecon. Today a charitable trust runs the institution.

The House offers hospitality to individuals and groups, either self-organized or run by the House (a program is available on the website). They also welcome guests wishing to get away and enjoy the beauty and tranquility of this ideal site. Depending upon availability, priority may be given to groups and individuals with spiritual purposes.

St. Gastyn is only a five-minute walk from the Retreat House. The church was rebuilt in 1848 by Robert Raikes of Treberfydd – Miss

Country: Wales   County: Breconshire   City: Llangasty (Brecon)

St. Gastyn

Dorothy's grandfather, on the site of an ancient church founded by St. Gastyn, a 5th century hermit venerated nowhere else but here. The church is a Grade II listed building with a Victorian interior.

The Brecon Beacons are among the most beautiful parks of Wales. Most of the park's mountains are formed from red sandstone and appear like beacons, hence the name. The landscape combines native trees, conifers and broad areas of moorland. Much of the region is high, open country, with smooth, grassy slopes on a bedrock of red sandstone. Within the park are numerous waterfalls, the most famous of which is the Henryd Falls at Coelbren. There are several caves including Dan-yr-Ogog, a labyrinth of chambers where guided tours are offered.

The Central Beacons dominate the skyline south of the town of Brecon and rise to almost 900 meters at Pen y Fan, the highest point in southern Britain. Further west is the sandstone massif of Fforest Fawr comprising a series of hills known as "Fans," with Fan Fawr being the highest. Water rushing southwards from this has formed steep river valleys with incredible waterfalls. The most westerly block of sandstone is Y Mynydd Du, The Black Mountain, culminating in the summit of Fan Brycheiniog at 800 meters. It contains two enchanting glacial lakes, Llyn y Fan Fach and Llyn y Fan Fawr.

Brecon/Aberhonddu lends its name to the mountains and the national park and lies in an alluring milieu in the valley of the Usk. It presents many fine Georgian houses on narrow, compact streets, remains of the medieval town walls and a 12th century castle. The typically Welsh fortess-like church of St. John is built of local red sandstone.

The Monmouthshire and Brecon Canal is considered Britain's most scenic canal and much of its length lies within the park's boundaries. A landlocked waterway, it runs for 35 miles from the old market town of Brecon to Five Locks, Cwmbran. It follows the scenic Usk Valley and offers glorious views of the Brecon Beacons. Unlike many other canals, the Brecon Canal has trees along much of its

Monmouthshire and Brecon Canal

route, an array of wildflowers on its banks and is home to mallards, moorhens and a variety of fish and butterflies.

A dozen or so miles east of Llangasty is Longtown Castle with an unusual cylindrical keep at the top of an enormous earthen motte. Longtown Castle was built around 1200 with 15' thick walls and offers vistas of the Black Mountains.

Wales is often called the Land of Castles and is home to some of Europe's finest surviving examples of medieval castle construction. The Normans, having practiced their techniques in England and elsewhere, understood that the first rule of successful occupation was to make sure new territories were overrun. To this end the Normans developed the castle. Castles did not exist anywhere in Wales before the Norman Conquest but over the following two centuries, many hundreds were built. First and by far the largest group of castles were those built by the Anglo-Norman lords of the March (from the French word marche meaning frontier).

There are few castles in Wales that can boast a more incredible location than Carrer Cennen, a haunting, atmospheric place, a castle that appears to spring out of legend and fairytale. Its stout, weather-beaten ruins crown a sheer limestone crag overlooking the remote Black Mountain. The castle, although damaged over the centuries by warring forces and the elements, presents a dramatic picture and is charged with a sense of the past. The first construction was probably built by the Welsh Prince Rhys Ap Gryffydd in the 12th and 13th centuries although there is some evidence of prehistoric and Roman occupation on the site. One legend suggests that the original fortress dates back to the Dark Ages and the Welsh Knight Urien Rheged and his son Owain, knights during the reign of King Arthur.

Interesting excursions from Llangasty can include Llangadog, Capel Gwynfe and Bethlehem, three villages set in the beautiful Carmarthenshire countryside in the west of the national park. Llangadog is in the heart of the Towy Valley halfway between Llandeilo and Llandovery and is surrounded by lovely rolling hills and pastures. Capel Gwynfe is a small village with a picturesque church dating from 1898. It was voted Village of the Year for Carmarthenshire in 2004.

Bethlehem is perched on the hillside overlooking the Towy flood plain. The Bethlehem Post Office is renowned for franking cards at Christmas. Each year thousands of people send their cards to be stamped with the Bethlehem postmark. Behind the village is Garn Goch, site of an impressive Iron Age hill fort.

Accommodations

Inside the main house there are 6 twins and 11 singles. Two rooms on the ground floor are en-suite and suitable for the disabled. The rest of the bathrooms are shared. In the adjoining cottage there are 2 twins and 1 single with a shared bath.

Amenities

All meals are provided. It is possible to have B&B, half board and full board. Towels and bed linens are provided. Inside the main house there is a large comfortable lounge with views across Llangors Lake to the Black Mountain, a library, newly refurbished dining room with windows overlooking the lake, prayer crypt and chapel. Inside the cottage there is a lounge that can also serve as meeting room.

Note: Closed from December 20th to January 3rd.

Cost per person/per night

Tariff varies from weekdays to weekends £46-50 full board, £35-37 half board, £25-27 B&B. Updated price list is on the website.

| Country: Wales | County: Breconshire | City: Llangasty (Brecon) |

Directions

By car: From London take M4 to Newport and follow the signs to Abergavenny on A449 and A40. Leave Abergavenny on the A40 and pass through a village called Crickhowell. Keep on the A40 until the village of Bwlch. Follow the road through the village until the War Memorial and turn right at sign-posted Llangors. After the turn the road narrows for about 200 yds. Turn left at sign-posted Pennorth. Follow the lane for about a mile until a sign saying Llangasty and Llangasty Church. Turn right and the Retreat House is about 400 yds down this lane on the left.

By train: Public transport is difficult to Llangasty. However there is a train from London-Paddington to Newport/Gwent (destination Swansea/Cardiff). Change at Newport for Abergavenny. Arrange with the House to be picked up there.

Contact

Send an email to The Warden
Llangasty Retreat House
Llangasty
Brecon, Powys, LD3 7PX
Wales, UK
Tel: 0044 (0) 1874 658250
Website: www.llangasty.com
Email: enquiries@llangasty.com (or use the link on the website)

Country: Wales   County: Bridgend   City: Newton (Porthcawl)

St. Clares' Prayer Centre
Sisters of St. Clare

St. Clares' Centre is ideally located on Clevis Hill in the charming village of Newton, just a few minutes from the busy and popular seaside resort of Porthcawl in the county of Bridgend, South Wales, half an hour from Cardiff. The Centre's pretty grounds overlook the sea, the village green and the 12th century church of St. John. A ten-minute stroll from the Centre ends at Newton Beach and a Glamorgan Heritage Coast path. This walk allows exploration of some of Southern Wales' most spectacular coastline and countryside including the splendid sand dunes of Merthry Mawr that backdrop the beach. This area is popular with walkers, horseback riders and windsurfers.

The Centre was donated to the sisters of St. Clare by a local woman as a thanksgiving gift in the 1930s. The sisters converted it into a boarding school and in more recent years, into a prayer center. The sisters offer hospitality for guided retreats to individuals and groups as well as a venue of relaxation in their tranquil, peaceful home.

The quaint village of Newton lies in an area designated as a Site of Special Scientific Interest. Founded in the 12th century as "New Town" it was a thriving port and its main attractions are Candleston Castle, a 14th century fortified manor house inhabited until the 19th century and the church of St. John near the Centre. About 800 years ago the church was erected as a fortress by the Knights of the Order of St. John of Jerusalem. The massive tower was extended in the 15th century and is 54' high with 4'6" thick walls. The shape of the construction is due to its foundation on sand. It features a handsome west door added during the 15th century restoration.

Near the church is St. John's Well, believed to possess curative waters. Newton Burrows is an archeological area where 3000-year old burials were found. The relics indicate that there were settlements of the Iron Age as well as Celt and Roman populations.

Porthcawl boasts some of the finest beaches in Southern Wales and includes Rest Bay and Trecco Bay, both of which have been awarded the coveted International Blue Flag. There's a historic harbor

Country: Wales	County: Bridgend	City: Newton (Porthcawl)

quarter with an old lighthouse, watchtower and lifeboat station as well as the Jennings Warehouse, one of the oldest dockside buildings in Wales.

North of Porthcawl is Kenfig National Nature Reserve, an impressive conservation site. South of the town is the thatched cottage village of Merthry Mawr, dramatized by the Merthry Mawr Sand Dunes. A short walk from Merthry Mawr and standing proudly on the banks of the River Ewenny, are the remains of 11th century Ogmore Castle. Although it is one of the smallest castles in Southern Wales, Ogmore is also one of the most beguiling. The castle is a short walk from Merthyr Mawr and can be reached by crossing the Swing Bridge and a set of stepping stones. Check the tide tables though, the tide changes very quickly and unexpectedly in this area.

Just a couple of miles from Ogmore is Coity Castle. The castle retains several Norman features. Its foundation can be traced to the 11th century with additional sections, including the great hall and the middle gate, added in the 14th century.

Caerphilly Castle

Not far from Porthcawl is Caerphilly Castle. Covering 30 acres the castle is one of the largest in Europe. Its imposing towers and defensive moat presented a formidable obstacle to advancing armies in the 13th century. The castle's leaning tower leans more than its famous counterpart in Pisa.

WALES

Heading due east, an easy day trip can include Cardiff, capital of Wales, and one of Europe's youngest capitals. A century ago it was the busiest coal port in the world. Today the docks have been transformed into a dazzling waterfront complex with museums, theaters, shops and over 330 parks and gardens. The city center is a mix of new and old. The roots of the part Roman, part Norman, part Victorian Cardiff Castle can be traced to the first century. But the castle's most indelible mark was left by the Marquess of Bute, once the owner of Cardiff Docks and at the time, the richest man in the world. A man of extravagance, the lavish decoration and architecture in the castle are reminders of his wealth. The town's modern High Street shops are interlaced with old Victorian and Edwardian arcades while Millennium Stadium, a sports and music venue, towers over the Cardiff skyline.

A short walk from the center of the city leads to the National Museum in Cathays Park. Exhibitions on art, archaeology, natural history and geology offer insight into the history of Wales. The museum boasts work by Monet and Van Gogh and has the largest collection of Impressionist paintings outside of Paris.

Welsh history can be explored in depth at the pretty village of St. Fagans and the National History Museum, located a short distance from the city center. The spectacular open-air museum is set in 100 acres within the grounds of St. Fagans Castle. Ancient structures from throughout Wales have been brought from their original site and re-created brick by brick. They visually relate the story of rural and industrial Wales. Events and craftspeople demonstrating traditional skills, such as potters, blacksmiths and wood carvers, add to the experience.

Northwest of Porthcawl sits Swansea, a city perfectly situated on the edge of a five-mile bay. Birthplace and long-standing inspiration of poet Dylan Thomas, Swansea is distinguished by award-winning parks and gardens in addition to world-class cultural and sporting facilities including the Dylan Thomas Centre, the Wales National Pool, the Liberty Stadium and Wale's largest indoor market. The National Waterfront Museum in the Maritime Quarter offers an interactive interpretation of Wales' industry and innovation in science, manufacturing and medicine. Swansea is defined by charming streetscapes and its proximity to the gorgeous Welsh coast. Further along the bay is the beautiful Victorian seaside resort of Mumbles, known for its local pottery, hard-carved lovespoons and whimsical candy-colored cottages lining its narrow streets.

Famous for its castles, almost every town in Wales has fortified remains in one form or another. Southern Wales boasts some of the most remarkable in the country. In the vicinity of Swansea are three castles. Oxwich is a Tudor Mansion created by Sir Rice Mansel and his son in the 16th century. In its heyday, the castle was known for its grandeur and the lavish lifestyle of the Mansels reflected in the remaining design elements.

Dinefwr Castle is set within the Dinefwr Park and very close to the village of Llandeilo. The castle offers commanding views of the Tywi Valley. Most likely built in timber around 1155, stone replaced the wooden structures in the 13th century. The castle can be explored via the wall walk.

Llawhaden Castle is a short distance from Dinefwr. A three-story edifice, the earth and timber ringwork fortress was built by Bishop Bernard in the 12th century. Impressive additions were added in the 14th century, some of which can be seen today.

A county town, rich in heritage and history, nearby Bridgend is at the heart of the Glamorgan Heritage Coast. Pilgrims on their way to St. David's in West Wales would wade through the flowing river and for this reason a little humped back bridge was built in 1425. Part of the bridge was washed away in a flood in 1775 and rebuilt in its present design. Gazing down over the town and the little bridge is Newcastle, the oldest part of Bridgend Town. Now a conservation area comprised of a cluster of tiny cottages and houses, in medieval times pilgrims would stop in this place for shelter.

Accommodations
10 beds in 6 single rooms, a few of which can be turned into doubles. Both men and women are welcome. Baths are not in the rooms, but are located right outside the rooms and can be turned into private baths.

Amenities
Breakfast is always provided. Other meals are provided only to those participating in an organized retreat. Guests have to purchase the rest of their meals in town. Towels and linens are supplied. There are conference and meeting rooms, a chapel and large parking lot.

Cost per person/per night
About £30 B&B.

WALES

Special rules
Maximum stay 1 week.
Closed in August, Christmas and Easter.

Directions
By car: From London take M4 and exit at junction 37. Proceed south following the signs to Porthcawl. At the roundabout take the second exit and follow the road until the next roundabout and take the third exit, A4229. Follow this road to the next roundabout (Newton) and take the third exit sign-posted Trecco Bay. Take the second street on the left – Clevis Crescent and then the second left with a "dead-end" sign and follow the signs to the Prayer Centre, the first house on the left after the Prep School.

By train: From London Paddington take a train to Bridgend and then a bus to Newton.

Contact
Sister Bronach Meehan
St. Clares' Prayer Centre
Clevis Lane
Newton, Porthcawl CF26 5 NR
South Wales, UK
Tel/Fax: 0044 (0) 1656 783701
Website: www.stclares-prayercentre.co.uk
Email:srbronach@talktalkbusiness.net

Country: Wales   County: Conwy   City: Penmaenmawr

Institute of the Sacred Heart of Mary Sisters

Sisters of the Sacred Heart

Noddfa, the local name for the Institute, is owned and managed by the Sisters of the Sacred Heart, an order founded in Beziers (France) in 1849. The aim of the order is to improve the quality of life both locally and globally. The sisters acquired the house in 1937 and converted it into a convent and in the 1970s, into a retreat center. The house was built in 1861 for the cousin of the then prime minister. It is a charming ancient building that has preserved its original atmosphere. In addition, it is well situated and only a ten-minute walk from the center of Penmaenmawr. It possesses views of the hills and the sea that encompass the glorious coast of North Wales. The bright and breezy seaside resort of Penmaenmawr is a Blue Flag award-winning beach. The Institute provides an ideal location for both nature and history lovers; it is just a short distance from spectacular Snowdonia National Park, the historic town of Conwy and its castle, the quaint seaside town of Llandudno and many other places of interest.

Country: Wales	County: Conwy	City: Penmaenmawr

Noddfa is a Welsh word for "haven" or "refuge" and the surrounding acreage is a treasure of nature graced by various gardens. Near the Institute are more formal gardens with flowerbeds, shaded paths and two labyrinths. Behind the complex are shrubberies and wooded areas. There is also a walled vegetable garden that supplies much of the food for the Institute. The sisters offer hospitality for restful holidays, to individuals and groups for spiritual retreats and holiday breaks for caregivers and parish groups. It is also a great venue for family celebrations.

North Wales is among the most poplar tourist areas in the British Isles and boasts many vibrant coastal resorts. The region of Snowdonia has long been popular with walkers and climbers. The mountains of Snowdonia are so challenging that world-class climbers practice in the region before going on expeditions elsewhere. There are more than 90 peaks over 2,000'. At 3,560', Mount Snowdon is the highest in England and Wales. Much of the central inland area of the country is a mountainous arena of breathtaking scenery.

Within the scenically varied Snowdonia National Park, the largest in Wales, there are mountains, moors and seas, rocky peaks and green hills, wooded valleys and sublimely beautiful estuaries. Snowdonia's slopes, a volcanic jumble of screes and cliffs rising to razor-edged summits, have attracted walkers and climbers for centuries. It was amidst the boulder-strewn Glyderau, a neighbor of Snowdon, that the team that first conquered Everest trained in the early 1950s. Snowdonia has its gentler side too. Around Ffestiniog and Betws y Coed are sheltered vales clothed in ancient oak woodlands, rivers and waterfalls and the hauntingly beautiful heather moorlands of the pristine Migneint.

The Institute is quite close to Conwy, a classic walled town with a circuit of walls over three quarters of a mile long guarded by no less than 22 towers. The 13th century walls exist almost intact around most of the old town and Conwy appears much as it has throughout the ages. The castle and the walls were built by King Edward I between

Conwy towers

1283 and 1289 as one of the key fortresses in his "iron ring" of castles erected to contain the Welsh. Conwy Castle remained an English enclave in North Wales for 200 years. The castle is a gritty, dark stoned fortress that evokes an authentic medieval atmosphere. It towers above the Conwy Estuary and is backdropped by the dramatic Snowdonia skyline.

The castle has no concentric "walls within walls" because they were not needed. Conwy's massive military strength springs from the rock on which it stands. Soaring curtain walls and eight huge round towers imbue the castle with an intimidating presence undimmed by the passage of time. The views from the battlements are nothing short of spectacular looking out across the mountains and sea and down to the roofless shell of the castle's 125' Great Hall. It is from these battlements that visitors can best view Conwy's ring of town walls.

Conwy also contains the smallest house in Britain. It lies tucked into the town wall next to the medieval gate leading from High Street to the quay, a potpourri of centuries-old fishermen's cottages. The house is in the *Guinness Book of Records* with dimensions of 3.05 meters x 1.8 meters. It had been lived in since the 1500s and inhabited until 1900 when the owner, Robert Jones, a 6' tall fisherman, was forced to vacate on the grounds of hygiene. The rooms were too small for him to fully stand up. The house is still owned by his descendants. Aberconwy House is the town's only surviving 14th century merchant's house. It is in the care of the National Trust. Another fine house is Plas Mawr (great mansion) built in 1576 by the Wynn family.

Thomas Telford built the Conwy Suspension Bridge that spans the River Conwy next to the castle. Completed in 1826 it replaced the ferry at the same point. Telford matched the bridge's supporting towers with the castle's turrets. The bridge, now open to pedestrians only, together with the toll keeper's house, is part of the National Trust.

Nearly due north of the Institute is the small mountain-ringed town of Bala. It lies at the head of Llyn Tegid. The lake is home to a unique fish called the Gwyniad, considered a form of herring and apparently a relic of the ice age. The lake's name comes from "Tegid Foel" a character in the *Mabinogi*, a series of Welsh stories and legends from King Arthur's time.

Bala is a historic market town within the boundaries of Snowdonia National Park. The street layout, set up by Roger de Mortimer from

Country: Wales	County: Conwy	City: Penmaenmawr

Chirk Castle in the 14th century, is marked out in square courts. Stryt Fawr, the main street, is wide and has shops along its length and is where the original markets were held. Two side lanes, Arenig and Plase were attached to the old Tomen, a typical large Norman castle mound or motte located at one end of the town (now a garden).

Halfway between Penmaenmawr and Bala is the popular inland resort of Betws-y-Coed. Much of the town was built in Victorian times and is the principal village of the Snowdonia National Park. Set in a splendid valley of woodland and mountains, it is ideal for outdoor pursuits. The grandeur of the area is enhanced by cascading waterfalls, hilltop lakes, river pools and ancient bridges. Since Victorian times artists have flocked to the region drawn by its beauty. Of exceptional interest are the many bridges in the area. Pont-y-Pair was built in 1468 and is buffeted by foaming water after heavy rain. Nearby Miner's Bridge is where miners crossed the river on a steep ladder to their work.

Thomas Teldord's iron Waterloo Bridge was built in 1815 and bears the cast iron inscription, "This arch was constructed in the same year as the battle of Waterloo was fought." Not far away are Conwy Falls and the beautiful Fairy Glen where the River Conwy flows through a narrow gorge.

At Capel Garmon, just east of Betws-y-Coed, is a celebrated cromlech, a 5,000-year old Neolithic burial chamber. Capel Garmon offers views of the mountains of Snowdonia and entry to Swallow Falls where the Llugwy River hurls itself into a chasm and the river rushes down from the mountains. This milieu of crags, jagged rocks and foaming cascades is considered one of the loveliest of North Wales.

Accommodations

There are 16 single, 3 double and 6 twin rooms in the main house and 6 rooms in a self-catering cottage on the grounds. Baths are shared in both types of accommodations except for two rooms in the main house.

Amenities

On request all meals are provided with the lodging in the main house. Guests staying in the cottage have to prepare their own meals in the kitchen at their disposal. Towels and linens are provided in both types of accommodations. In the main house there are several meeting and conference rooms, a reading room and gardens.

Cost per person/per night
To be determined when reservations are made. (Up-to-date prices might be available on the website.)

Special rules
The Institute is open all year except at Christmas. Curfew upon arrangement.

Directions
By car: From London take M1 until the junction with M6. Take M6 and proceed north until junction with M56. Take M56 west until junction with A550 following the signs to A55. Proceed on A55 west. Get off the A55 at the roundabout signed for Penmaenmawr (Exit 16). Follow the road as far as the Mountain View Hotel. Take a sharp left into Conwy Old Road. Continue for half a mile. The entrance to Noddfa is on the right opposite Tan-y-Foel cemetery.

By train: From London Euston take a train to Holy Head and stop in Llandudno. From there take a taxi to Noddfa. Taxis are available from outside Llandudno Junction Station. Some trains stop (by request) at Penmaenmawr Station (Chester to Pen weekdays: 11:29, 12:28, 14:28, 15:26, 16:28, 17:26, 18:25). Check times with train company beforehand. It is possible for the sisters to meet you at Pen station.

Contact
Anyone
Noddfa
Conwy Old Road
Penmaenmawr, LL34 6YF
North Wales, UK
Tel: 0044 (0) 1492 623473
Website: www.noddfa.org.uk
Email: noddfapen @aol.com or info@noddfa.org.uk

Country: Wales   County: Pembrokeshire   City: Pontfaen (Fishguard)

Ffald-y-Brenin

Ffald-y-Brenin Charitable Trust

Nestled in an isolated spot in the heart of the spectacular beauty of Pembrokeshire Coast National Park, the center is surrounded by wildlife, birds, flowers, woods, moorlands and waterfalls. The community inhabiting the center is a Christian Community Member of the Evangelical Alliance that began 23 years ago with the aim of creating a motherhouse for the scattered community. "We are like a 21st century monastic community," said Mrs. Godwin, the woman in charge of bookings. The entire community gathers at Ffald-y-Brenin various times during the year, whereas the Godwins are the two permanent inhabitants.

The center is a complex formed by various stone buildings that appear old but are not. They were built 22 years ago to reflect a sense of antiquity and then modernized in 2006. The center is very active and provides hospitality to individuals, families and groups for spiritual retreats, quiet days and restful holidays. It offers a program of events and conferences but groups may bring their own facilitators and organize individual programs. "The maximum stay would be two weeks but we are so well booked that it is almost impossible to find two weeks in a row," affirmed Roy, the gentleman in charge.

Ffald-y-Brenin is settled in the hills of Cwm Gwaun Valley two miles from the little settlement of Pontfaen/Cwm Gwaun between Newport and Fishguard. The latter was the site of the last invasion of Britain when a small French force, intent on attacking Bristol, were driven north by the weather and landed at Fishguard in 1791. The town was undefended but the French thought the red-cloaked women were British Guardsmen and surrendered without a fight.

Fishguard is comprised of the old harbor of Lower Town and is a particularly picturesque milieu with a cluster of quayside cottages. It is the place where Dylan Thomas' most famous play, *Under Milk Wood*, starring Richard Burton was filmed. Above Lower Town is Fishguard Fort, a superb viewpoint complete with cannons. The small town is a pleasant medley of narrow winding streets. Its Old Town Hall is an ancient building imaginatively redesigned in 2007 and now home to the library and indoor market as well as the *Last Invasion*, a Bayeux-style tapestry that relates the humorous story of the last invasion of mainland Britain.

Most of the Pembrokeshire coastline is a designated National Park. There are dramatic cliffs, sheltered coves and small seaside resorts in addition to offshore islands inhabited by thousands of breeding seabirds. English settlers put down roots here after the Norman conquest which explains why "little England beyond Wales" has so many English rather than Welsh place names. The Pembrokeshire Coast Path is a classic walking trail that stretches 186 miles. Inland the historic Preseli Hills hide ancient trade routes, hill forts and burial chambers.

About 40 minutes from the center is St. David's where the superb, secreted cathedral marks the holiest place in Wales. The smallest cathedral city in Britain, St. David's was granted city status by Queen Elizabeth II because of the presence of the cathedral of St. David's. The small attractive village lies within the Pembrokeshire Coast National Park and is surrounded by spectacular coastal scenery. Whitesands Bay, one of the many beautiful beaches in the area, carries the prestigious European Blue Flag Award.

| Country: Wales | County: Pembrokeshire | City: Pontfaen (Fishguard) |

12th century cathedral of St. David's

The 12th century cathedral of St. David's was built in a hollow to hide it from the gaze of marauding Vikings sailing by. The cathedral has been a site of pilgrimage and worship for centuries. Its nave is the oldest surviving part of the cathedral. The font may date back to the pre-Norman bishops while the base is believed to be from the 13th century. Bishop Gower undertook extensive works in and around the cathedral during the 14th century and the building of the Bishop's Palace is attributed to him. The magnificent ruins of the medieval palace are adjacent to the cathedral.

In 1275 a new shrine was constructed on the north side of the presbytery adjacent to the high altar. The ruined base of this shrine remains to this day and was originally surmounted by an ornamental wooden canopy with murals of St. David, St. Patrick and St. Denis of France. The relics of St. David and St. Justinian were kept in a portable casket on the stone base of the shrine. It was at this shrine that Edward I came to pray in 1284.

During the Reformation, Bishop Barlow, a staunch Protestant, stripped the shrine of its jewels and confiscated the relics of David and Justinian in order to counteract what he saw as superstition. In the south transept is a beautiful 17th century Cretan icon from the Eastern Orthodox tradition depicting Elijah being fed by ravens.

Between the center and St. David's are a myriad of villages, fishing ports and appealing beaches. Abereiddi Beach nestles in a sheltered bay and is famous for its black sand full of tiny fossils. It is one of Pembrokeshire's pebble backed storm beaches created by a huge storm in 1859. Nearby is the Blue Lagoon, a flooded slate quarry regarded as an important geological feature. The walk from Abereiddi to Porthgain is one of the best stretches along the entire coast path. Porthgain is a small coastal hamlet that was once a commercial harbor for exporting stone from the nearby quarry. It is now a popular resort center and was designated as a Conservation Area by the Pembrokeshire Coast National Park in 1997. Porthgain means "Chisel Port" in English representing the quarrying that once took place. At one time the town's cottages were occupied by the quarry workers and are good examples of "Crog lofts." The loft was a partial upper floor where the residents slept, quite similar to modern loft apartments.

Roch is a small inland village. Its most distinguishing feature is its castle, is a prominent D-shaped tower on an isolated rocky outcrop. It is believed to have been built by Adam de Rupe in the 13th century. Although it is not open to the public, the legendary castle can be seen for miles around.

The village of Dinas Cross is a long linear settlement mid-way between Fishguard and Newport. It is enhanced by a number of stone cottages set back from the road. At the Newport end of the village, a lane leads to a wonderful little cove with a sandy beach and rockpools at Cwm yr Eglwys. The Coast Path around Dinas Island presents the Pembrokeshire Coast National Park at its best.

North of Fishguard and tucked away in a steep-sided valley, is the tiny village of Moylgrove. The Coast Path around nearby Cemaes and Ceibwr is truly glorious. The remote beaches below Cemaes are where dozens of grey seals choose to give birth to their pups in autumn.

The city of Cardigan makes for a wonderful day trip. Now a thriving market town famous for its many festivals, Cardigan is an ancient Welsh cultural and commercial center on the Teifi Estuary. Its rich heritage is reflected in Georgian and Victorian buildings, traditional shops and inns and creates an altogether nostalgic picture. The town is centrally located near the fabulous Heritage Coastline of Cardigan Bay, a terrain of tranquil coastline with secluded sandy coves, award-winning beaches and towering cliffs. In the early summer months the cliffs are garlanded with flowers. The islands of the bay are set like jewels in the clear waters where dolphins, porpoises and seals abound. Inland is Cardigan Castle, now undergoing a complete restoration program. The ruins that are visible today were built during the 1240s and represent two towers, a keep and the town wall.

Accommodations

There are two types.

Main house: About 36 beds in single, double and twin rooms, some with private baths.

Amenities

Meals are supplied only to groups of 8 or more. Individuals and small groups must cater for themselves in the fully equipped kitchen at their disposal. Towels and linens are supplied on request. There is a common room that serves as kitchen and dining room. It has a fireplace and windows with views across the valley. The center includes a large and small meeting room. The smaller one can be used as a kitchen/dining area and offers a view of the surrounding area. Barbecue equipment is available on request. There is a chapel and extensive grounds to tour.

Morvil Cottage: The cottage is located about a 10-minute drive from the main house in an isolated spot with views of the sea. It has 1 double, 1 twin and 1 single/study room. There is also a fully equipped kitchen/dining room, bathroom, vaulted living room with small woodburner, CD player and radio equipment. Available from 1 week to 3 months, it is an ideal site for sabbaticals and walking holidays.

Cost per person/per night

In both types of accommodations, a voluntary contribution is requested. Up-to-date suggested donations are given when reservations are made.

Special rules

Maximum stay 2 weeks in the main house and 3 months in Morvil Cottage. The center is closed for a week at Christmas.

Directions

By car: From London take M4 to its end and then take the A40 west from Carmarthen past St. Clears and Whitland through Llandewi Velfrey to a major roundabout. At the roundabout, turn right towards

Cardigan and drive one mile to a minor crossroads and go left to Maenchlochog. At Maenclochog go right at T-junction and continue past Rosebush to major crossroads. Continue exactly 3 miles and go right to Cwm Gwaun. After 1/4 mile take the hidden left, continue down into the valley. At T-junction go right for 2 miles. The Institute's drive rises on the left adjacent to Sychbant picnic site.

By train: There is no public transportation to or near the institution.

Contact

Bookings Secretary
Ffald-y-Brenin
Pontfaen, Fishguard
Pembrokeshire. SA65 9UA
Wales, UK
Tel: 0044 (0)1348 881382
Website: www.ffald-y-brenin.co.uk
Email: info@ffald-y-brenin.org or fy.b@virgin.net

Section Two

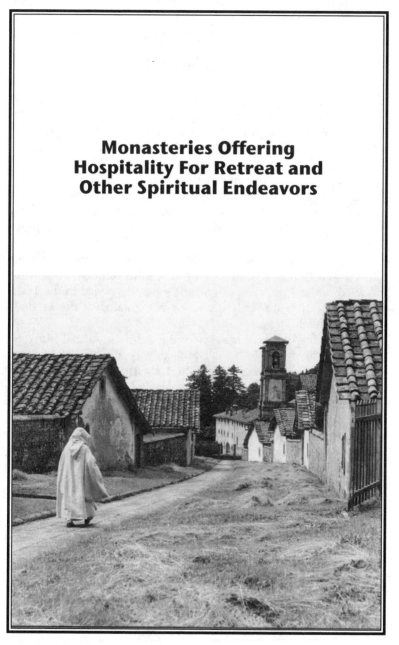

**Monasteries Offering
Hospitality For Retreat and
Other Spiritual Endeavors**

Clare Priory
Augustinian Friars

Clare Priory is one of the oldest religious institutions in England. Set in rural Suffolk on picturesque grounds along the River Stour, the Priory was established in 1248 on the invitation of Richard De Clare, whose castle ruins are situated nearby. It became the first house of the Augustinian (known also as Austin) Friars in England.

The religious occupation ended with Henry VIII's suppressions in 1538. The house passed into the hands of private families until 1953 when the friars bought it back. The Priory now serves as home for a mixed community of Augustinian Friars and lay people living under St Augustine's Rule, as well as a parish and retreat center.

The original 13th century building does not exist anymore. After a fire, a new building was erected in the 14th century and was remodeled in the 15th. New extensions were also added in the 16th, 17th and 18th centuries. Only one wall remains of the original monastic church.

Nevertheless the house has preserved some of the original 14th century features, like the Little Cloister, vaulted Porch, the stone and stained glass decorations and the Shrine of Our Lady. The shrine occupies one of the oldest parts of the Priory and contains a modern relief of Our Lady of Good Counsel based on a original fresco at Gennazzano, near Rome. The shrine attracts many local devotees and in 2008 the first official pilgrimage was held at Clare Priory the second Sunday of May.

The beautiful gardens of the Priory are adjacent to the grounds of Clare Castle Country Park and the ruins of Clare Castle. Set in a lush 25-acre wooded park, it boasts the remains of the Norman Castle with earthworks, motte and moats. The visitor's center is the former Clare's railway station. Medieval Clare is only a short walk from the Priory via the footbridge over the River Stour.

Accommodations
Hospitality at Clare Priory must not be conceived as hotel accommodations. Guests are free to visit the surroundings, but the friars wish them to take part in the daily liturgy, or in an organized retreat.
There are 11 rooms, 4 of which can become doubles. 7 rooms have private baths, 4 have shared baths.

ENGLAND

Amenities

Towels and linens are supplied. All meals are supplied with the lodging and hospitality is only on a full-board basis. There is a large meeting room and a library with video/TV.

Cost per person/per night

Suggested donation £40 per person for full board.

Special rules

Maximum length of stay Monday-Sunday afternoon. Curfew at 9 PM. No pets allowed. Guests are required to remain as quiet as possible inside the Priory.

Directions

Contact the Priory.

Contact

Kathy Reddick
Clare Priory
Ashen Road
Clare
Suffolk, C010 8NX
England, UK
Tel: 0044 (0) 1787 277326
Fax: 0044 (0) 1787 278688
Website: www.clarepriory.org.uk
Email: clare.priory@virgin.net

Region: East of England   County: Leicestershire   City: Coalville

Mount Saint Bernard Abbey

Cistercian Monks

Mount Saint Bernard Abbey lies in the quiet and secluded countryside of Charnwood Forest, a site of remarkable beauty in the heart of England, three miles from the center of Coalville, a former coal mining town dating to medieval times.

The Abbey was founded in 1835 by a group of Cistercian monks as a continuation of Garendon Abbey (1133-1538). They came to occupy the land donated by Ambrose de Lisle who wished to reintroduce monastic life in his country. The monks, as befitting the Cistercian tradition, started to cultivate and work the land and property until it was officially opened in 1837.

The original Abbey was very simple, not more than a cottage, but shortly after its founding, the Earl of Shrewsbury gave a large donation for a permanent Abbey to be erected. Augustus Welby Pugin, a famous neo-Gothic architect offered his expertise and designed the complex for free. Its Abbot, Dom Bernard Palmer was the first abbot since the Reformation. In 1963 the Abbey founded a new monastery in Cameroon and another in Nigeria.

The neo-Gothic church is one of solemn and simple beauty, perfectly in keeping with the austerity of the Cistercian Order. Its stone blends with the surroundings and the adjacent buildings and additions are in keeping with the original style.

Accommodations
There are 23 single rooms with shared baths. Men and women have separate accommodations; 13 for men, 10 for women.

Amenities
Towels and linens are provided. All meals can be provided with the lodging. There is a sitting room and a reading room that guests may use (common to both men and women).

Cost per person/per night
Voluntary contribution.

Directions
Contact the Abbey.

Contact
Guestmaster via email
Mount Saint Bernard Abbey
Oaks Road
Coalville
Leicester, LE67 5UL
England, UK
Tel: 0044 (0) 1530 839162 (Guestmaster) 832298 (Abbey)
Fax: 0044 (0) 1530 814608
Website: www.mountsaintbernard.org
Email: msbgh@btconnect

Region: East of England   County: Bedfordshire   City: Turvey

Priory of Our Lady of Peace
Nuns of the Olivetan Congregation

Turvey Priory is occupied by a group of Benedictine nuns of the Congregation of Monte Oliveto, Siena, Italy. The historic building, was once the residential home of one of the most important local citizens, Charles Longuet Higgins. In 1936 a community coming from Eccleshal went to Cockfosters Abbey (North London) to establish a branch of the Vita & Pax Foundation, a monastic community begun by Dom Constantine Bosschaerts. He worked in innovative areas of liturgy and ecumenism, fostering interreligious activities that would allow people of all denominations to feel at home in his monasteries.

The nuns continue these ecumenical activities through retreats, quiet days and open days. The nuns also produce embroidery and icons. One of the sisters is an expert iconographer and workshops are organized throughout the year.

Turvey is a small village at the border between Bedfordshire and Buckinghamshire. As with most English villages its origins date back to Roman times. All the houses are still in stone and offer a quaint sight that enhances the beauty of the countryside surrounding Turvey.

ENGLAND

Accommodations

Hospitality is offered in two cottages separate from the main house. There are 12 beds in 6 single and 3 double rooms, 2 of which are en-suite.

Note: Hospitality at Turvey is intended primarily as a spiritual experience. The guesthouses are closed between December 24 and January 15 inclusive and July 1-15. Maximum stay is one week.

Cost per person/per night

Voluntary contribution. Suggested minimum contribution is £30.

Amenities

Towels and linens are provided. All meals can be supplied on request; inside the cottage there are self-catering facilities. There is a library and extensive gardens.

Special Rules

After the last service at 7:45 PM and until 9 AM, the nuns observe "great silence." During this time they avoid speaking and invite guests to join in this practice.

Directions

Contact the Priory.

Contact

The Guest Sister via voice mail or letter (a letter and a deposit are necessary to secure the booking)
Priory of Our Lady of Peace
Turvey Abbey
Turvey
Bedfordshire, MK43 8DE
England, UK
Tel: 0044 (0) 1234 881432
Website: www.turveyabbey.org.uk
Email: info@turveyabbey.org.uk

Region: East Midlands   County: Nottinghamshire   City: Southwell

Sacrista Prebend Retreat House
Southwell Cathedral Chapter

The House offers hospitality for both private and guided retreats year round.

Directions
Contact the House.

Contact
The Warden, preferably by email
Sacrista Prebend Retreat House
4 Westgate
Southwell, NG25 0JH
England, UK
Tel: 0044 (0) 1636 816833
Website: www.sacrista-prebend.co.uk
Email: mail@sacrista-prebend.co.uk

Ealing Abbey
Benedictine Monks

Composed of an abbey and monastery, the complex is in Ealing, West London. The beautifully restored structures were built in neo-Gothic style. Golden in color and encompassed by a peaceful garden, the façade is composed of bricks with flight of stairs and a large portal. Flanked by two octagonal towers, it is adorned by beautiful stained glass windows. The resident Benedictine order lives in the tradition of medieval monks going back over 1500 years to the time of their founder, St. Benedict.

Established in 1897 as a parish of Downside Abbey at the invitation of Cardinal Vaughan, then Archbishop of Westminster, it was canonically erected as a dependent priory in 1916 with Dom Wulstan Pearson as its first prior. He later became the first Bishop of Lancaster.

The church is comprised of Ham Hill, Bere and Guiting stone with flint dressing in plinth and parapet, executed in Perpendicular Gothic style. Its multi-colored, hammer-beam roof is supported by stone arches. The west window is enhanced with stained glass depicting the Coronation of the Virgin Mary.

Accommodations
There are 5 single, 1 double and 2 triple rooms. Baths are shared. Closed at Christmas and Easter. The Guesthouse is open to men, women and families. All guests are welcome but as Father Andrew said: "We'd like our guests to have a spiritual purpose ... because we're more than a bed & breakfast."

Amenities

Meals are not supplied but there is a kitchen that guests may use. Shops are very near to the Abbey. Towels and linens are supplied. There is a dining room, lounge, sitting room with a small library, parking and a small garden.

Cost per person/per night

Suggested donation is £22.50 per person.

Directions

Contact the Abbey.

Contact

Send an email to the Guestmaster specifying the dates of arrival and departure and the purpose of your stay.

St. Benedict's Ealing Abbey
Charlbury Grove
Ealing
London, W5 2DY
England, UK
Tel: 0044 (0) 2088 622100
Fax: 0044 (0) 2088 622206
Website: www.ealingabbey.org.uk
Email: DandrewW@aol.com or parishoffice@ealingabbey.org.uk

St. Edward's House

Order Society of St. John the Evangelist

The institution is in the center of London and offers hospitality exclusively for spiritual retreats. The program of retreats is available on the website.

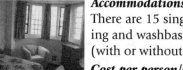

Accommodations
There are 15 single bedrooms with central heating and washbasins available for overnight stays (with or without dinner).

Cost per person/per night
Voluntary contribution.

Directions
Contact the House.

Contact
Anyone
St. Edward's House
22 Great College St.
London, SW1P 3QA
England, UK
Tel: 0044 (0) 2072 229234
Website: www.ssje.org.uk
Email: guestmaster@ssje.org.uk

Tyburn Convent

Nuns of the Adorers of the Sacred Heart of Jesus of Montmartre

Tyburn Convent is in the very heart of London, only 75 yards from Marble Arch. It is the motherhouse of a contemplative congregation founded in 1898 at Montmartre, Paris. The young community of nuns left Paris in 1901 due to the laws against religious orders. They came to London and settled at Tyburn, a well-known historical site that owes its fame to the martyrdom of more than 100 Catholic Reformation Martyrs. FYI: This was the site of the "King's Gallows" from 1196 to 1783.

The nuns lead a secluded life completely dedicated to the Perpetual Adoration of the Eucharist and manual labor. The Convent is also the motherhouse of the congregation with monasteries in England, Scotland, Ireland, Italy, Australia, New Zealand, Peru, Ecuador and Colombia.

Accommodations
There are 8 single rooms with shared baths. These are open exclusively to women. Men are not allowed in the Convent. Women are also invited to take part in the daily liturgy with the community. Priority is given to women coming for spiritual retreats or quiet days. No spiritual direction is given by the nuns.

Amenities
All meals are supplied with the lodging. Towels and linens are provided. A common room and kitchen facility are available to guests.

Cost per person/per night
Minimum contribution: £30 full board. Donations are welcome.

Special rules
Curfew at 8:30 PM.
Maximum stay is one week.

Directions
Contact the convent.

Region: London and vicinity   City: London

Contact
Guestmistress or The Mother General
Tyburn Convent
8, Hyde Park Place
London W2 2LJ
England, UK
Tel: 0044 (0) 2077 237262
Fax: 0044 (0) 2077 064507
Website: www.tyburnconvent.org.uk
Email: info@tyburnconvent.org.uk

Region: London and vicinity   County: Middlesex   City: London(Edgware)

Edgware Abbey
Anglican Benedictine Nuns

Saint Mary at the Cross, known as Edgware Abbey, is a red brick complex about 40 minutes from the center of London. It was founded in Shoreditch by Mother Monica Skinner and Fr Henry Nihill as a prayer, reading and work center. The nuns are actively involved in the care of the sick, needy and elderly in addition to offering hospitality. Edgware is a town in Barnet, a borough of Greater London in the historic county of Middlesex.

Accommodations
There are 15 single rooms with shared baths. Both men and women are welcome. Maximum length of stay is 5-7 days.

Amenities
All meals can be supplied with the lodging. Towels and linens are provided. There is a large conference room and library.

Cost per person/per night
Voluntary contribution.

Directions
Contact the Abbey.

Contact
Mother Abbess
Convent of St Mary at the Cross
Priory Field Drive
Edgware, Middlesex HA8 9PZ
England, UK
Tel: 0044 (0) 2089 587868
Website: http://edgwareabbey.org.uk
Email: info@edgwareabbey.org.uk

Region: London and vicinity   County: Kent   City: London (West Wickham)

The Emmaus Centre
Daughters of Mary and Joseph Sisters

The center is on the outskirts of Bromley, about 1 hour from London. Surrounded by an extensive greenscape, it offers hospitality to guests coming to participate in the conferences organized by the sisters, as well as to individuals coming for private retreats or quiet days.

Accommodations
42 beds in single and twin rooms with shared baths. Both men and women are welcome.

Amenities
All meals are supplied with the lodging. Towels and linens are provided. There are two large meeting rooms and a series of smaller meeting rooms.

Cost per person/per night
To be determined when reservations are made.

Directions
Contact the Centre.

Contact
The Emmaus Centre (preferably via email or phone)
Layhams Road
West Wickham, Kent BR4 9HH
England, UK
Tel: 0044 (0) 2087 772000
Fax: 0044 (0) 2087 762022
Website: www.emmauscentre.org.uk
Email: enquiries@emmauscentre.org.uk.

Curzon Park Abbey
Nuns of the Benedictine English Congregation

Curzon Park Abbey is in Curzon Park, an attractive residential suburb of Chester, the county town of Cheshire on the River Dee. It is within easy walking distance to the ancient Roman and medieval city walls, just across the famous Grosvenor Bridge. Part of the Curzon and Westminster Ward, the area is well known for having some of the city's largest and most prestigious residences.

Curzon Park Abbey is one of three monasteries of nuns in the English Benedictine Congregation. The community was started in Feltham, Middlesex in 1868 as an Anglican Benedictine foundation. In 1920 it moved to North Wales and in 1921 was accepted by the English Benedictine Congregation. In June 1988 the community moved from North Wales to its present location, which at one time was the property of an Anglican community.

Accommodations
5 beds in 2 double and 1 single room with 2 shared baths. Men, women and families are welcome.

Amenities
The retreat house is self-catering. There is a kitchen, laundry room and chapel. Towels and linens are provided. The nuns live in enclosure but it is possible to share a meal day with them on request.

Cost per person/per night
Minimum contribution is £15 per day per person.

Directions
Contact the Abbey.

Contact
The Guestmistress by email or phone
(9:00 AM to noon, 2:00 – 4:30 PM).
Curzon Park Abbey
10, Curzon Park South
Chester, CH4 8AB
England, UK
Tel: 0044 (0) 1244 671323
Website: www.curzonpark.org.uk
Email: curzonpark@benedictines.org.uk

Region: North West   County: Lancashire   City: Preston

Tabor Carmelite Retreat House
Carmelite Friars

The Retreat House is lodged in a converted farmhouse on the outskirts of Preston. It offers hospitality only for spiritual retreats. Guests have to participate in the prayers and retreat program.

Accommodations

Four single bedrooms with shared baths.

Amenities

The friars provide breakfast. The rest of the meals are self-catering. All bed linens and towels are provided.

Cost per person/per night

B&B £25.

Directions

Contact the Retreat House.

Contact

Call or send an email to the Secretary
Tabor Carmelite Retreat House
169 Sharoe Green Lane
Fulwood
Preston, PR2 8HE
England, UK
Tel: 0044 (0) 1772 717122 (Inquiries and bookings:
Monday to Friday 10:00 AM – 4:00 PM)
Fax: 0044 (0)1772 787674
Website: http://www.tabor-preston.org
Email: tabor@carmelite.net

Loyola Hall
Jesuit Fathers and Sisters

The Hall is a 19th century house encompassed by magnificent grounds formed by gardens and secular trees. It is in Rainhill, near Liverpool, and offers hospitality to individual or groups for organized or self-organized retreats.

Accommodations
43 beds in single and twin rooms, each with a private bath.

Amenities
All meals are provided. Towels and linens are supplied. Conference and meeting rooms.

Cost per person/per night
£44 per day, £352 for an eight-day retreat.

Special rules
Closed at Christmas. Guests coming for holidays, or groups organizing events other than religious retreats will not be accepted.

Directions
Contact the Hall.

Contact
Loyola Hall
Warrington Road
Rainhill, Prescot, L35 6NZ
England UK
Tel: 0044 (0) 1514 264137
Website: www.loyolahall.co.uk
Email: mail@loyolahall.co.uk

Region: North West   County: Cheshire   City: Wistaston

Wistaston Hall
Missionary Oblates of Mary Immaculate

The Hall is a newly refurbished retreat center managed by the Missionary Oblates of Mary Immaculate. It offers hospitality for individuals and groups, both for organized or private retreats.

Directions
Contact the Hall.

Contact
The Director, Rev Oliver Barry O.M.I. either by phone or email
Oblate Retreat Center
Wistaston Hall
Wistaston
Cheshire, CW2 8JS
England, UK
Tel: 0044 (0) 1270 568653
Fax: 0044 (0) 1270 650776
Website: www.oblateretreatcentre.org.uk
Email: director@oblateretreatcentre.org.uk

Worth Abbey

Monks of the English Benedictine Congregation

Worth Abbey is an active center for spiritual retreats. Hospitality is offered mainly to groups, whether organized by the Abbey or self organized by a group. A detailed calendar is available on the website.

Accommodations

Groups up to 35 can be hosted throughout the year except at Christmas and Easter. Individual guests can be hosted as well, but priority will be given to groups, therefore reservations cannot be made earlier than 2 to 3 weeks in advance.

Cost per person/per night

To be determined when reservations are made.

Directions

Contact the Abbey.

Contact

The Bookings Secretary
The Open Cloister
Worth Abbey
Paddockhurst Road
Turners Hill
Crawley
West Sussex, RH10 4SB
England, UK
Tel: 0044 (0) 1342 710318
Fax: 0044 (0) 1342 710311
Website: www.worthabbey.net
Email: TOC@worthabbey.net

Saint Augustine's Abbey

Benedictine Monks

Consisting of the abbey church, the monastery and guesthouse, the large complex is located on the top of a cliff overlooking Pegwell Bay on the Isle of Thanet in Kent. It is dedicated to Saint Augustine of Canterbury who arrived in 596 from Italy after being sent by Pope Gregory to convert the Anglo Saxon tribes.

The Abbey was founded in 1856 by Father Wilfred Alcock a member of the Cassinese Congregation from the monastery of Subiaco, Italy. He was joined by a group of young Englishmen who had been trained in Italy for an Australian mission, but instead were sent to Ramsgate at the invitation of the Bishop of Southwark.

The Abbey is considered one of the most beautiful churches of the 19th century. There are stained glass windows, representing Christ in Glory surrounded by the Angels and the Mission of St Augustine.

Region: South East   County: Kent   City: Ramsgate

Accommodations
8 beds in single rooms with shared baths. At the moment hospitality at Ramsgate is offered only to men, but the community is hoping to be able to offer it to women by 2010. Visit the website for up-to-date information on the subject.

Amenities
Towels and linens are provided and all meals can be supplied with the lodging. Guests can dine outside if they choose with prior notice to the monks. There is a small kitchen where guests can cook meals, heat food and prepare tea and coffee. There is a sitting room and a library and guests are also welcome to use the Abbey's library.

Special rules
Guests are asked to attend mass and vespers but they are free to visit the surroundings during the day. Curfew at 9 PM.

Cost per person/per night
Voluntary donation. Suggested contribution £15 per day.

Directions
Contact the Abbey.

Contact
The Guestmaster
St. Augustine's Abbey
Ramsgate, Kent CT 11 9 PA
England, UK
Tel: 0044 (0) 1843 593045
Fax: 0044 (0) 1843 582732
Website: www.ramsgatebenedictines.com
Email: StAugAbbey@aol.com

Quarr Abbey

Benedictine Monks of the Solesmes Congregation

Quarr Abbey is in Ryde on the northern coast of the Isle of Wight, a few miles off the south coast of England. The first foundation of the institution was in 1132 by Balwin who appealed to Geoffrey of Savigny (Normandy) to send a few of his monks to found a monastery. The original name of the Abbey was Our Lady of the Quarry due to the presence of an important stone quarry nearby.

In 1907 exiled monks from Solesmes (France) who had taken shelter on the Isle of Wight came to Quarr to build a new abbey. The new building was erected between 1907 and 1914 and designed by the French Benedictine Monk Dom Paul Bellot. The complex was quickly constructed by 300 local men who worked under the direction of the monk/architect. In 1922 the monks of Solesmes left the abbey, leaving behind a small group of French monks.

The Abbey is built entirely of Belgian brick, mostly red with some that are polychromatic. It is a fine example of early 20th century architecture. Some ruins of the old abbey are still visible. The tomb of Balwin, founder of the Abbey, together with that of his wife Cicely, were found in the north wall of the old abbey.

Life at Quarr Abbey revolves around daily prayers although the monks are also involved in monastic work, art and music.

Accommodations

Hospitality is offered only to men and mainly for spiritual aims.
There are eight singles, bathrooms are shared except in 3 rooms, 2 of which are equipped for the disabled.

Amenities

All meals can be offered with the lodging. Breakfast is taken privately, but guests can share lunch and dinner with the community.
Towels and linens are supplied. There is a common room and library.

Cost per person/per night

Voluntary donation, suggested contribution is £30 per day but "no one is stopped from coming for lack of finance," specified the Guestmaster.

Directions

Contact the Abbey.

Contact

Send an email to the Guestmaster
Quarr Abbey
Ryde
Isle of Wight, PO33 4 ES
England, UK
Tel and Fax: 0044 (0) 1983 884850
Website: www.quarrabbey.co.uk
Email: guestmaster@quarrabbey.co.uk

Region: South West   County: Gloucestershire   City: Clifton (Bristol)

Emmaus House
La Retraite Sisters

Emmaus House is a restful retreat and conference center located in the heart of Clifton Village, one of the thirty-five council wards of the city of Bristol and connected to the busy center of the city by the impressive Clifton Suspension Bridge over the Avon Gorge. From its favored position, the House offers spectacular views of the Cumberland Basin and the hills of Dundry.

The House is run by the congregation of La Retraite Sisters, founded in 1674 to offer retreats to women. In the course of the ensuing years, the sisters gradually focused on education, opening a school for girls in the early 19th century. The present center is comprised of two adjoining houses that were once family homes. In 1984 the complex became a conference and retreat center. The sisters are actively involved in assisting guests coming for spiritual retreats and offer a number of spiritual and professional courses.

Emmaus House is very proud of its award-winning gardens that cover one and half acres. The gardens are set in various separate areas, including a walled kitchen, herb and courtyard gardens with original Victorian cobblestones, Zen garden and small woodland walk.

Accommodations

Approximately 34 beds in 23 single and twin rooms, seven of which have private baths. Both men and women are welcome, but priority is given to those participating in the retreats run by the house.

Amenities

All meals can be supplied with the lodging. Towels and linens are supplied. There are four meeting rooms. Limited parking is available on site; priority is given to the disabled or people participating in spiritual retreats. Parking is also available on the street by the House. The House has a catering facility that supplies lunch for residents and is a fully licensed restaurant open to non-residents.

Cost per person/per night

Bed and Breakfast:
Single room standard £40, en-suite £45.
Twin room standard £60, en-suite £70.
B&B and light supper (6:30 PM):
Single room standard £48, en-suite £53.
Twin room standard £76, en-suite £86.
Lunch £6.50-£12 (light to full lunch).

Special rules

The House closes at 10:30 PM. A deposit is required on booking.

Directions

Contact the monastery.

Contact

Anyone
Emmaus House
Clifton Hill
Clifton, Bristol BS8 1BN
England, UK
Tel: 0044 (0)1179 079950 (Monday - Friday 9:00 AM – 3:30 PM)
Website: www.emmaushouse.org.uk
Email: administration@emmaushouse.org.uk

Region: South West   County: Gloucestershire   City: Cranham

Prinknash Abbey
Benedictine Monks of the Subiaco Congregation

Prinknash Abbey is near Cranham, a small town in the Cotswolds. The Cotswolds were designated as an Area of Outstanding Natural Beauty in 1966. Today it represents the largest of such areas in England and Wales. The Cotswolds Way is a long-distance footpath running mainly on the edge of the Cotswolds escarpment. Inaugurated a National Trail in 2007, it runs near Cranham and the Abbey.

The community was initially formed by Anglican monks who gradually converted to the Benedictine lifestyle eventually becoming Catholic in 1913. In 1928 the monks moved to Prinknash, blending their contemplative spirituality with active social involvement and manual work.

Over the years the Abbey has developed a 400-acre bird and deer preserve within its property that also includes a large collection of peacocks, pheasants and exotic birds. This is not however managed by the monks.

Accommodations
The monks are presently moving to their former home, and should be able to offer hospitality by the beginning of 2009. Their website has a section dedicated to hospitality that will contain up-to-date information.

Region: South West   County: Gloucestershire   City: Cranham

Directions
Contact the Abbey.

Contact
Anyone
Prinknash Abbey (at St. Peter's Grange)
Cranham
Gloucester, GL4 8EX
England, UK
Tel: 0044 (0) 1452 812455
Fax: 0044 (0) 1452 814420
Website: www.prinknashabbey.org
Email: paxprinknash@waitrose.com

Region: West Midlands   County: Shropshire   City: Marchamley (Shrewsbury)

Hawkstone Hall
Redemptorists Fathers

Hawkstone Hall is a splendid 18th century mansion set in a vast parkland in North Shropshire. The Hall, run by the Redemptorists Fathers since 1926, is an international retreat center for both religious representatives and lay people.

Until 1975 the Redemptorists Fathers used Hawkstone Hall as their priesthood house and the place where students were educated to become priests. When the students were moved to Canterbury, the Hall became a pastoral and renewal center that has hosted hundreds of priests, missionaries, religious and lay people from all over the world.

Hawkstone Hall, also known as "the secret jewel of Shropshire," still attracts many visitors. The Redemptorists Fathers, in association with English Heritage, have restored and returned the manor to its original splendor. Since 2007 the House is open to public visitors the last two weeks in August.

Accommodations
Apart from its 6 and 12 week programs, Hawkstone Hall offers hospitality for private retreats or breaks but it should not be considered a hotel. There are 52 single rooms, some with private bath. Both men and women are welcome.

Amenities
All meals, towels and linens are supplied, full board only.

Cost per person/per night
Single room per day is £58 (full board).
En-suite per day, when available, is £70 (full board).

Directions
Contact the Hall.

ENGLAND

Contact
The Guest Mistress
Hawkstone Hall
Marchamley
Shrewsbury, SY4 5LG
England, UK
Tel: 0044 (0) 1630 685242
Fax: 0044 (0) 1630 685565
Website: http://www.hawkstone-hall.com
Email: hawkhall@aol.com

Region: Scotland   County: Morayshire   City: Elgin

Pluscarden Abbey
Benedictine Monks

Pluscarden Abbey is a unique destination as it is the only medieval monastery still inhabited by monks and still used for its original purpose. Founded in 1230 the Abbey is an attractive construction in a verdant and peaceful atmosphere in a wooded corner of Scotland. The Abbey attracts numerous visitors every year but offers hospitality for spiritual retreats only.

Accommodations
Men and women are welcome but housed separately. Retreats are intended for those who wish to come on a spiritual (private) retreat (not directed) and not for vacation/holiday purposes. Saint Benedict is the Men's Retreat House and Santa Scholastica is the Women's Retreat House.

Amenities
All meals are provided along with towels and linens. There are extensive grounds that guests may use.

Cost per person/per night
Voluntary contribution.

Directions
Contact the Abbey.

Contact
IMPORTANT NOTE: Inquiries and reservations are to be made by fax or preferably by email (no telephone). For the email address use the link contained in the website.
The Guestmaster
Pluscarden Abbey
St. Benedict's or St. Scholastica's Retreat
Elgin, Morayshire IV30 8UA
Scotland, UK
Tel: 0044 (0) 1343 890 257
Fax: 0044 (0) 1343 890258
Website: www.pluscardenabbey.org

The Abbey and MacLeod Center
Iona Community

The Iona Community is an ecumenical Christian community based in the Abbey and the MacLeod Center on the island of Iona and in Camas, an outdoor center on the neighboring island of Mull. The Iona Community was founded in Glasgow and Iona in 1938 by George MacLeod. The Community took up residence and restored the12th century Benedictine Abbey and Monastery of Iona that had been abandoned since the Reformation.

Today Iona remains a center for pilgrimage and tourism. The Abbey is managed by Historic Scotland whereas the Iona Community remains as a living, worshipping presence. They do not offer retreats but rather an experience of living in the community, where guests share dormitory accommodations, eat with the staff, help with chores such as chopping vegetables, washing up, etc, for half an hour or so each day. The theme of the week is discussed and explored during the morning sessions. Guests of all denominations are welcome but only if interested in taking part in the experience that is offered. Visits are for 6 nights, arriving Saturday and leaving Friday, except for one or two exceptions such as Easter's nine-night program.

The Community runs also a center on Camas Tuath on the Ross of Mull that offers the same kind of living community experience together with an outdoor experience for young people. Closed from October to mid-end March depending each year on when Easter falls.

Accommodations
The Abbey: It has one dorm sleeping 6, one sleeping 4, two sleeping 3, several bunk bedded rooms for 2, some twin rooms and one room with a double bed. There are 3 single rooms for people with medical/disability issues. The Abbey is not disabled-friendly.
The MacLeod Center: It has 4 dormitories sleeping 5 people of the same gender (or a family of 5 in one room) and 4 dormitories sleeping 7. Each dorm has one top bunk bed. No rooms in either facility are en-suite. There are baths and showers in MacLeod Center, showers in the Abbey.

Region: Scotland   County: Inner Hebrides   City: Iona

Amenities

All meals are provided. The food is mostly vegetarian. Bed linens are provided, towels are not. In the Abbey there is a common room with a coal fire where people can make tea/coffee, read, relax and play piano. There is also a library. The Chapter House is used for the morning and evening meet-ings as well as for singing. In the MacLeod Center there is a small library and a quiet room. The community room is used for eating and for most meetings. There is a Peace Garden in front of the Abbey and seating outside the MacLeod Center.

Cost per person/per six-day program

£220-£238 depending on the accommodations.

Special rules

Six-night stays only. Guests don't have to be Christian but willing to share the lifestyle.

Directions

Contact the Abbey.

Contact

Carol for bookings at The Abbey or Camas
Paul for bookings at MacLeod Center
Iona Community
Abbey & MacLeod Centres
Isle of Iona, Argyll PA76 6SN
Scotland, UK
Tel: 0044 (0)1681 700404
Fax: 0044 (0)1681 700460
Website: www.iona.org.uk
Email: abbey.bookings@iona.org.uk or mac.bookings@iona.org.uk
(depending on facility)

Loreto Centre

Loreto Sisters

The Centre was founded in 1919 as a novitiate and school for the Loreto Order. Since 1989 it has been a retreat center for groups and individuals. Groups (20-35) are welcome in the center, whereas individuals and small groups are  accommodated in self-catering apartments.

Accommodations
Both men and women are welcome in single rooms and a few doubles. Meals are catered only for large groups.

Directions
Contact the Centre.

Contact
Anyone
Loreto Center
Abbey Road
Llandudno, LL30 2EL
Wales, UK
Tel: Center/Group Bookings 0044 (0) 1492 878031
or 0044 (0) 1492 878542
Website: www.loretollno.org.uk
Email: llandudno@loretocentre.wanadoo
or loretocentre@yahoo.co.uk

Region: Wales | County: Powys | City: Llandefaelog Fach (Brecon)

Llannerchwen

Society of the Sacred Heart

Llannerchwen is a small community of Roman Catholic sisters offering hospitality exclusively for individual guided retreats and silence retreats. Dates and program are available on the website.

Accommodations

8 bed area available for men and women but only individually and only for spiritual retreats.

Directions

Contact the Monastery.

Contact

Retreat Secretary
Society of the Sacred Heart
Llannerchwen
Llandefaelog Fach
Brecon
Powys, LD3 9PP
Wales, UK
Tel: 0044 (0) 1874 622902
Website: www.llannerchwen.org.uk
Email: llannerchwen@aol.com

Region: Wales   County: Denbighshire   City: St. Asaph

St. Beuno's Spirituality Centre
Jesuit Fathers

The Centre is a historical building beautifully installed near the coast of North Wales. It offers hospitality for individual guided retreats. Groups with their own program are welcome only if there is room available. A detailed schedule of events is available on the website. Closed at Christmas.

Accommodations
Single rooms in the main house or on the grounds of the institution.

Amenities
Meals, towels and linens are provided.

Directions
Contact the Centre.

Contact
The Retreat Secretary
St. Beuno's
St. Asaph
Denbighshire, LL17 0AS
Wales, UK
Tel: 0044 (0) 1745 583444
Fax: 0044 (0) 1745 584151
Website: www.beunos.com
Email: secretary@beunos.com

Region: Wales   County: Pembrokeshire   City: St. David

St. Non's Retreat Centre
Mercy/Passionist Sisters

St. Non was the mother of St. David. St. Non's Retreat Center is on the site of the house where she moved and where St. David was born around the year 500 AD. St. Non's is a spiritual and pilgrimage center. Twice a year the sisters run guided retreats, the rest of the year the house welcomes groups for self-organized retreats. Closed at Christmas and Easter.

Accommodations
Single and doubles rooms. Men and women are welcome. Meals are supplied.

Directions
Contact the Centre.

Contact
Anyone
St. Non's Retreat Centre
St. David's, Pembrokeshire SA62 6BN
West Wales, UK
Tel: 0044 (0) 1437 720224
Fax: 0044 (0) 1437 720161
Website: www.stnonsretreat.org.uk
Email: stnonsretreat@aol.com

Monastery Lodging Guides. Your gateway to an exceptional travel adventure.

Eileen Barish

Eileen Barish is a multiple award-winning author who has written more than a dozen books on unique travel experiences. She has been a contributing writer to *National Geographic Traveler, Guest Informant, Newsweek* and other publications. Her books have been reviewed by more than 500 major publications including *The New York Times, Wall Street Journal, Men's Health, Gourmet Magazine, Library Journal, Travel & Leisure, USA Today, Los Angeles Times* and the *San Francisco Chronicle*. Her previous books include *Lodging in Italy's Monasteries, Lodging in France's Monasteries, Lodging in Spain's Monasteries, Best Spas USA* and *Vacationing with Your Pet*. She lives in Santa Barbara, California.

NOTES